Wild Romance

Theresa Yelverton   *William C. Yelverton*

Wild Romance

*A Victorian Story of a Marriage, a Trial,
and a Self-Made Woman*

Chloë Schama

WALKER

Walker & Company
NEW YORK

Published by Walker Publishing Company, Inc., New York

All papers used by Walker & Company are natural, recyclable products made
from wood grown in well-managed forests. The manufacturing processes conform to
the environmental regulations of the country of origin.

LIBRARY OF CONGRESS CATALOGING-IN-PUBLICATION DATA

Schama, Chloe.
Wild Romance / Chloe Schama. —1st U.S. ed.
p. cm.
Includes bibliographical references.
ISBN 978-0-8027-1736-8 4341 6790 5/10
1. Yelverton, Thérèse, Vicountess Avonmore, 1832?–1881. 2. Aristocracy (Social
class)—England—Biography. 3. Upper class women—England—Biography. 4.
Yelverton, Thérèse, Vicountess Avonmore, 1832?–1881—Marriage. 5. Avonmore,
William Charles Yelverton, Viscount, 1824–1883—Trials, litigation, etc. 6. Trials
(Bigamy)—Ireland—Dublin. 7. Bigamy—England—History—19th century. 8.
England—Social life and customs—19th century. 9. Yelverton, Thérèse, Vicountess
Avonmore, 1832?–1881—Travel. 10. Voyages around the world. I. Title.
DA565.Y45S336   2009
942.08109—dc22
[B]
2009044758

Visit Walker & Company's Web site at www.walkerbooks.com

First U.S. edition 2010

1 3 5 7 9 10 8 6 4 2

Typeset by Westchester Book Group
Printed in the United States of America by Worldcolor Fairfield

For my father, who taught me how to tell a story

CONTENTS

In the summer of 2004 I lived a quiet life. I had been awarded a grant to travel and conduct research for my undergraduate senior thesis. I was spending long days in the British Library; most of my interactions took place in hushed reading rooms where voices seldom rose above a whisper and emotions surfaced only if you stole someone's desk during the lunch hour. I had come to London to research "sensation novels," a late Victorian literary genre. The problem, I discovered once I arrived, was that the novels were terrible—at least those forgotten novels that I had claimed were so critical to my research. The stories were absurd, the characters flat; superficiality reigned. I changed tactics and turned to scholarly articles, hoping that these would point me toward some minute matter of esoteric interest from which I could spin a thesis.

I found such a matter in a footnote. A real-life trial, said the note, had allegedly inspired Wilkie Collins's sensational novel *Man and Wife*. In this trial, a woman, Maria Theresa Yelverton née Longworth, accused her supposed husband, an Irish aristocrat named William Charles Yelverton, of abandoning her and marrying another woman. The two had carried on a clandestine relationship for years. She claimed it had culminated in marriage; he denied it. The 1861 trial was referred to as the "Yelverton Bigamy Trial," and it attracted national, front-page attention for weeks. Subsequent trials appealing the decision would take place over the course of the next six years,

going all the way to the House of Lords. As far as I could tell, interest
had waned as the controversy dragged out in the late nineteenth century and had all but vanished in the twentieth. This sensation had
slipped into obscurity.

After reading through the trial transcripts (eyewitness reports published by journalists), I read the letters that the couple had exchanged,
which had been bound and used as evidence. Theresa—she went by
her middle name—was particularly captivating; she wrote with abandon, pouring her flamboyant personality into her letters. Yelverton,
her ostensible husband, was more restrained and less prolific. Their
contrasting styles showcased a disparity of sentiment that heightened
the heartbreaking dynamic between them: her plaintive cries for affection were repeatedly answered with laconic restraint.

These forgotten figures became my companions that summer.
"How are you?" my parents would ask. "Guess what I discovered to-
day," I would answer and steer the conversation to antique events or
bemoan Yelverton's insensitivity. Theresa and Yelverton began to in-
vade various corners of my physical world as well as my mental con-
sciousness as I stalked the parts of London that they had occupied.
About halfway through my research that summer, I discovered that
Theresa had lived with an aunt in north London between the trials, in
a house that was only a block from where I was spending the summer.
She had led me to her story with a spellbinding finger; now she seemed
to be drawing the strings of our connection tighter.

Theresa's temporary home, 12 Randolph Road (I was staying at
nearby 39 Randolph Avenue), was covered in scaffolding when I visited it for the first time. The house was clearly in a state of overhaul:
dust covered the windows, and paint flaked from its walls. There were
paint cans and brushes clustered on the stoop and a ladder leaning
against the front of the house. Weeds flourished in the garden. One of
the construction workers eyed me with understandable curiosity as I
stood looking at the house. There was no English Heritage blue circle,
signifying historical landmark status, posted above the door; no one
else was snapping photos. But I was certain that I had discovered a
treasure.

When I stumbled upon this story in the library, I was immediately convinced that I had found the type of history that the hallowed halls of legendary landmarks tend to silence—the type that lingers in letters and haunts street corners, the type that is too often forgotten, but provides the most intimate, personal portrait of the past. As Walter Benjamin said, "To articulate the past historically, does not mean to recognize it 'the way it was' . . . It means to seize hold of a memory as it flashes up at a moment of danger."[1] There is always a danger that those who are less obviously and traditionally important, prominent, or powerful will be left out of the history of human experience. In this inadequate surveillance of the past, the human affections that bridge history are lost.

At the end of the summer I traveled to Edinburgh. I had intended to take a break from my research, but in that Scottish city, with the castle looming over me, the past seemed inescapable. I resumed the hunt and found Theresa's Scottish apartment—a place she described as "a little room, five storeys high, where we have been so happy"—where she received Yelverton during the most intimate and regular phase of their courtship."[2] The apartment was on the top floor of a narrow townhouse that had been converted into the office of a law firm, and her small window looked out over the shingled rooftops and red chimneys of the city. Theresa's life had been so entwined in legal proceedings that this seemed more than a coincidence; it was additional evidence that this story would unfold of its own volition, with graceful echoes between the past and the present resonating of their own accord. Later, I would learn that Theresa had met and befriended Horace Greeley, the *New York Tribune* editor and one-time presidential candidate, when she came to America. I had grown up in Greeley's hometown, where his statue, raised on a pedestal several feet above the ground, watched over the traffic commuting to and from New York City on the Saw Mill Parkway. My high school diploma bore his name.

When I returned to London a month later, I walked past 12 Randolph Road. Although construction was ongoing inside, the exterior gleamed with a fresh coat of paint and the ladder had been put away. From the outside it was an elegant, stately structure, a home that would soon be filled with light and life. Until now, Theresa's story, like the dusty prerenovation Number 12, has languished, even though the foundations for its restoration were already in place. Any novelist would be fortunate to invent the narrative arc that made up Theresa's life. In Theresa's words, "Life, indeed, is a wild romance, if truly written."[3] In this book, I've tried to write that truly wild romance.

Note on Theresa's Name

When historians wrote about the woman born with the name Maria Theresa Longworth in the 1960s, they referred to her as "Theresa." In later decades, she was generally called "Longworth" so that she would be referred to in the same way as her male contemporaries. In my opinion, this ostensible egalitarianism does her a disservice, discounting the possibility that her marriage to William Charles Yelverton was valid by using only her maiden name. Because I would like to preserve that possibility, I will refer to her throughout this book as "Theresa."

TIMELINE OF EVENTS

1852	August	Theresa and Yelverton meet.
1853	March	Theresa and Yelverton begin a correspondence.
1854		Yelverton is stationed in the Crimea.
1855	May	Theresa leaves Boulogne and takes a position with the Soeurs de Charité in the Crimea.
	September	Theresa and Yelverton meet in Istanbul.
1856	March	Theresa arrives in Balaclava to stay with the Straubenzees.
	June	Yelverton leaves the Crimea; Theresa travels, goes to Malta.
1857	January	Theresa returns to England and heads to Edinburgh.
	April	Yelverton supposedly marries Theresa in an irregular marriage ceremony in Edinburgh; Theresa leaves Edinburgh for Hull.
	August	Theresa and Yelverton undergo a Catholic wedding ceremony in Ireland.
	December	Theresa goes to Hull; Yelverton returns to Edinburgh.
1858	February	Theresa and Yelverton travel through the Continent together.
	April	Yelverton returns to Edinburgh; Theresa remains in France.
	June	Theresa returns to Edinburgh; Yelverton marries Emily Forbes; Theresa discovers the marriage and accuses Yelverton of bigamy.

1859	December	Theresa appeals to the Court for Divorce and Matrimonial Causes; a judge decides that the court does not have jurisdiction.
1860	July	A Scottish court combines Theresa's complaint of bigamy and Yelverton's attempt to stop her from saying they are married into a single case.
1861	March	The case of *Thelwall v. Yelverton* is decided in favor of Thelwall (and Theresa) in the Four Courts in Dublin.
	April	The first volume of *Martyrs to Circumstance* is published.
	June	The second volume of *Martyrs to Circumstance* is published.
1862	July	The case of *Longworth or Yelverton v. Yelverton* and *Yelverton v. Longworth* is decided against Theresa in the Scottish Court of Sessions in Edinburgh.
	December	The appeal of the case of *Longworth or Yelverton v. Yelverton* and *Yelverton v. Longworth* is decided in favor of Theresa in Edinburgh.
1863		Theresa publishes her correspondence with Yelverton.
1864	July	The case of *Yelverton v. Yelverton* is decided against Theresa by the House of Lords.
1867		Theresa's second appeal to the House of Lords is dismissed; Theresa leaves Britain for America.
1869		Theresa arrives in the American West.
1870		Yelverton becomes the fourth Viscount of Avonmore; Theresa assumes the title Viscountess Avonmore.
1871		Theresa moves to Missouri.
1872		*Zanita, a Tale of the Yo-semite* is published; Theresa travels through Asia.
1874		*Teresina Peregrina or Fifty Thousand Miles of Travel Round the World* is published.
1875		*Teresina in America* is published.
1880		Theresa goes to South Africa.
1881	August	Theresa begins writing for the South African newspaper *The Natal Witness*.
	September	Theresa dies in South Africa.
1883	April	Yelverton dies in France.

Wild Romance

CHAPTER ONE

Sunrise

Love, which is but an episode in a man's life,
is the entirety of a woman's.

—Madame de Staël

Somewhere, across the silver plane of dimpled water, a ship sounded its horn, and another answered. Theresa Longworth, the teenage daughter of a Manchester silk manufacturer, stood on the deck of the steamer that was to take her from Boulogne to Dover and heard the echoing calls of distant vessels. Her sister Ellen, who had escorted her to the port, stood on the shore waiting for the ship to depart. Theresa was sad to go, reluctant to leave her sister and her husband, but it was time for her to return home to England.

Although it was August, the air was damp, and Ellen perhaps began to think that her sister had underdressed. According to published reports, she wound a shawl into a ball and tossed the wadded cloth toward Theresa. As the fabric sailed through the air, it began to unfurl, spreading like a wisp of smoke. Theresa grasped at the cloth, but it slipped through her fingers and landed on the deck. The man who had been standing near Theresa reached down and picked it up. He had been watching the sisters, and now he introduced himself.

His name was William Charles Yelverton, of the Royal Artillery. He came from an aristocratic Irish family, and he was twenty-eight years old.[1] Yelverton would later claim that Theresa's foot had been stuck in the gangway, and that this was why her shawl had fallen, but he never denied restoring it to her shoulders.[2]

As the steamer moved away from the shore, the passengers who had crowded outside to wave goodbye went inside or wandered along the deck. Theresa and Yelverton remained where they were, talking through the night. The possibly indirect journey took a long time; according to Yelverton's later testimony, they left around seven in the evening and did not arrive until eight or nine the next morning.[3] When rays of light finally pierced the mist and the chalky cliffs of Dover appeared, Theresa and Yelverton had crossed more than just the water separating England from the Continent; they had taken the first tentative steps down the path that turns two strangers into lovers.

For Theresa Longworth and William Charles Yelverton, the 1850s would be consumed by their romance, the 1860s by its unraveling. The public disintegration of their relationship before the courts of Ireland, Scotland, and England would bring to the forefront several of the Victorian era's most disconcerting matters: the inadequacies of female education and upbringing, the struggles of and prejudice against single women, the inequalities of marriage and marital law. When their story became known, Theresa and Yelverton became unwitting emblems of the turmoil of their era at the same time that they evoked timeless fears and fascinations: the fantasy of infatuation, the grip of obsession, the plight of unrequited love, the despair of abandonment. They were ordinary people caught up in an extraordinary affair, forced to deal with the consequences of fame and notoriety, and forcing contemporary society to confront some of its most unsettling preoccupations.

Little is known about Theresa's early life. She was born in 1833 in Chetwood, Lancashire, the youngest of six children born to the manufacturer Thomas Longworth and his wife, Anne, née Fox. Her mother died when Theresa was four, and Theresa was soon sent to an Ursuline convent in France where she was raised as a Roman Catholic. Thomas Longworth, her atheist, nominally Protestant, father, did not give much thought to his children's spiritual well-being or education, and he was more than happy for someone else to raise Theresa. Her maternal aunt had urged him to send Theresa to France, and he did not object.

When Theresa was whisked away from Manchester in the late 1830s, she left a city that had been radically transformed in the decades just before her birth. The shift had been catalyzed—in large part—by textile manufacturers like her father. Small-scale cloth production, which had always been a central component of the North's economy, was overtaken by industrial factories where steam-powered looms turned out lengths of fabric at rapid rates. The population of Manchester boomed, increasing by 45 percent between 1821 and 1831, and the city expanded to accommodate the masses.[4] Working-class housing sprang up around the factories, while the middle classes stuck to the fringes. The grimy urban center was bisected by shop-lined thoroughfares, so that well-heeled Mancunians could pass through without confronting the lurking misery. Behind the shop fronts, some cottages barely remained standing. Resting on rotting beams, their facades were muddied by sooty stains and broken windows patched with oilcloth. Rooms were dark and damp as candles were too expensive to be carelessly used. Typhoid and cholera were rampant, and food was scarce.

If the haphazard expansion of industrial cities masked the true conditions of the working classes from their more affluent neighbors, literature made their plight visible. Elizabeth Gaskell's *Mary Barton: A Tale of Manchester Life* was written, she said in her preface, to explain the lower classes to the middle. "The more I reflected on this unhappy state of things between . . . the employer and the employed," Gaskell wrote, "the more anxious I became to give some utterance to the agony."[5] Gaskell knew her stories of suffering would anger members of her husband's Manchester-based Unitarian congregation, but she cared little about preserving their complacency. Mere "hands"—as workers were called—became full-fledged people at the pen of writers like Gaskell. Her writing extended sympathy into the dark homes of hidden neighbors and ushered shabby characters into more luminous parlors.

Not only did industrial novels march penurious wretchedness to the fore of literary works; they dramatized the effect of industrialization on women's lives. Unsupervised and in the company of their peers rather than male figures of authority, young women—who made up about half of all mill workers—gained a reputation for independence and relative sexual liberty. At the other end of the social spectrum, a few upper-class women benefited from the changing economic dynamics by assuming the responsibilities that men had, for the most part, previously held. "Business!" exclaims Shirley, the title character of Charlotte's Brontë's novel, "really the word makes me conscious I am indeed no longer a girl, but quite a woman, and something more . . . I hold a man's position: it is enough to inspire me with a touch of manhood."[6]

Though Theresa came of age removed from this particular evolving sphere of England, she probably read the bestselling novels that emerged from Manchester and took some of the lessons of this literature with her. Workers and—more important for Theresa—women were not just mute specters in society; they had something useful to contribute. Their faculties were often untapped, but they ran deep. Her father's success had proved that hard work, dedication, and an independent will could bring great reward in this burgeoning society; Theresa knew that she possessed the same qualities.

But what would achievement mean for a woman of Theresa's background? For most young women, the goal was marriage. Midcentury English girls' boarding schools did not promote many alternatives, equipping their students with competitive claws for the cutthroat marriage market, but little else. "Concealment and deception prevail at girls' school to a degree which the uninitiated would be slow to credit," wrote a critic in *Fraser's Magazine*.[7] Girls at such schools, said one reform-minded individual, "are not educated to be wives, but to get husbands."[8] When a young girl—in literature, for example, Elizabeth Barrett Browning's Aurora Leigh or George Eliot's Maggie Tulliver from *The Mill on the Floss*—did succeed in obtaining a bookish education, it was often through her own devices. Whether it was the substance or the expense (some schools cost one thousand pounds a year, double a nineteenth-century doctor's salary) that caused Mr. Longworth to reject a typical English boarding school for his youngest daughter, Theresa's education provided her with a different upbringing.

Compared to their English counterparts, at least some of the French convents where young girls were educated encouraged intelligence. The convent schools were highly regulated and formalized places, but they were run by women who took their educational duties seriously. Their goal was to produce dutiful and pious young women, and intellect was seen as a natural complement to those attributes.[9] Some convents even gave young girls rooms of their own, the treasure that Virginia Woolf yearned for decades later. "The pleasantest thing that happened to me about this time," wrote George Sand in her account of her convent education, "was having a cell to myself . . . Every thoughtful person needs times of solitude and reflection."[10] Never mind that the room was deathly hot in the summer and bitterly cold in the winter (icicles formed on her ceiling); it was her own.

Solitude was tempered by companionship that seemed less petty than relations in English boarding schools. Girls gathered daily for piano and dancing lessons, as well as more academic and practical pursuits such as history and housekeeping. The students ran through the flagstone-lined alleys, whispered in the somber cloisters, skipped in the courtyards, and made up stories about the deep, dank cellars that honeycombed the ground beneath their feet. The nuns marched two-by-two through passages that vibrated with their chanting, and bolted the heavy doors behind them, sealing the girls in their sepulchral world. Isolation did not prevent small-scale social distinctions: "There was an aristocracy and a democracy in the convent, as in the world," wrote Sand. Nor did it eliminate lessons on the social gradations of attire. The choir sisters—those who chanted the Latin prayers—"lived like patricians; their robes were white, and they wore fine linen." The generally less well-educated lay sisters were more likely to recite prayer in the vernacular and interact with the outside world. They "worked hard, and their dark clothing was of a much coarser kind."[11]

When Theresa left the convent, she had not been fine-tuned to lure a man like her English-educated peers. Her education had been mixed in its content and character, but she did have a sense of her imagination, intellect, and independence. These qualities would prove essential as the ties of family—the central building block of Victorian culture and social life—were flimsy in the Longworth clan. Her five older siblings had scattered: her two older brothers (William and Jack) to Australia and New Zealand, her sister Sara to Wales, her other sister, Ellen, to France. Her brother Thomas seems to have severed his connection to the family by the time Theresa reached adulthood. Theresa stayed in touch with her sisters, but the family as a whole was held together by tenuous threads.

Though the teenage Theresa could count on some financial support from her father, she was not able to ignore economic concerns. By the mid-1850s when Theresa returned to England, her father had amassed a considerable fortune, but she and the other children hardly benefited from his success. He kept his funds close and his affections closer. "There were disagreements between my father and his children during his lifetime," she later said; "they were of a serious character."[12] Emotional and, to some extent, financial independence was not so much a choice as a necessity for Thomas Longworth's children.

Despite her unique upbringing, Theresa now faced a common predicament: she had finished with formal education, did not want to live with her father, but was perhaps a shade too young and inexperienced to start a new family. There was a sense that Victorian girls, when they reached this posteducation, premarriage stage, would grasp at something larger than themselves to give them purpose. George Sand felt "a great yearning for love, and a void in [her] heart" when her education neared its end. She had read about devotion and felt ready to experience its transcending powers. "I needed to love some one or something that was not myself," she wrote.[13] In order to punctuate the ambiguity of their transition to adulthood, many young women turned, unsurprisingly, to the idea of "matrimony in the abstract, not *the* man but any man," said the Scottish magazine *Chambers's Journal of Popular Literature*.[14]

Schooled in romance and steeped in a sense of their limited destiny, girls latched onto potential prospects. "Any person who will snatch her out of the dullness of her life and give her something to live for—in short, something to do," was an acceptable recipient for the attentions of an idle young woman, wrote *Chambers's*.[15] Harriet Beecher Stowe, writing to her friend George Eliot about the dubious match made by *Middlemarch*'s heroine, expressed her sympathy for the recurring predicament: "I understand that girls often make a false marriage and plight their faith to an unreal shadow who they suppose inhabits a certain body."[16] Though Theresa did not quite fit the *Chambers's* or *Middlemarch* model, she fell prey to this fascination with a man and with marriage. When she met Yelverton on the steamer, she was adrift, purposeless. He gave her direction.

The start of Yelverton and Theresa's relationship depended upon two improbable events: their initial meeting and Theresa's boldness in writing—almost a year after their introduction—to a man she hardly knew. In the spring of 1853, Theresa wanted to send a letter to her cousin John Augustus Longworth—known to her as "Alcide"—who worked as a government official in Montenegro. She knew that Yelverton, the man she had met on the steamer some months before, was stationed in the same area, and she thought he might provide a willing conduit for her letters to her cousin. Alcide—a nickname he had obtained while fighting in Caucasia—had been raised by her father and was, throughout Theresa's life, more like an older brother than a cousin. When she left the convent, at age seventeen, she even lived with him in London for a time rather than return to her father's home.[17] Relations with her father had never been easy; Alcide often stepped in to provide advice and guidance when her father was absent or disinterested. Theresa may have contacted Yelverton out of genuine affection for her cousin, or she might have harbored fantasies of a reunion with the man in the military uniform. (The single woman, a contemporary wrote, was "always ready to succumb to the 'scarlet' fever"—the soldier in his redcoat.)[18] Whatever her motivation, she gained two correspondents from the request. Yelverton graciously delivered the letter and began his own exchange with Theresa.

In these early days of her correspondence with Yelverton, Theresa was cavalier, but she studded her letters with portentous insinuations of the intensity of her feelings. "We may see another sunrise," she wrote that spring of 1853, referring to the first time they had witnessed the sun shining through the Channel mists.[19] She made no promises, as her own movements were uncertain. She sailed between Naples, Tunis, Malta, Corfu, and Bosnia—a strange grand tour for a young woman, but Theresa embraced it. "I have made up my mind to turn savage; I am weary of civilization," she wrote.[20] Perhaps she sensed a fellow roamer in Yelverton.

Despite his current nomadic occupation, Yelverton descended from solid stock. He was the great-grandson of Barry Yelverton, an ambitious Irish liberal lawyer and politician who had made a name for himself by criticizing the British government's war with the American colonies, the penal laws that restricted Catholic participation in the Irish government, and the mercantilist restrictions upon Ireland. As Barry Yelverton's politics became more moderate, he was appointed to prominent positions: attorney general in 1782, then chief baron of the Irish court of the exchequer a year later. In 1785 he was elevated to the peerage, and made first Viscount of Avonmore of Derry Island, county Tipperary, in 1800.[21]

In the last years of his life, Barry Yelverton's prestige diminished. After the Act of Union of 1801, Irish peers no longer sat in the House of Lords, and when he died in 1805, he left little to his family but his title.[22] His son became principal registrar of the high court of Chancery, but his grandson (Yelverton's father, Barry John Yelverton, the third Viscount Avonmore) did not have a particularly illustrious career. One of twelve children, William Charles Yelverton did not inherit much of a financial legacy, and so the military was a sensible career choice.[23] He would be among the peers of his class (about a third of the army's soldiers came from titled or landed families) without having to exhaust his limited funds on the financially consuming competitions of society.[24] Unlike most branches of the military, soldiers in the Royal Artillery could not move through the ranks by purchasing promotions, a restriction that allowed Yelverton to further mask his relative penury.

Theresa's devotion to Yelverton began to creep into her letters. When a few of her missives went unanswered, she responded first with irritation, then with a curiosity that belied her captivation: "I set you down as one of the three standing mysteries which time alone can fathom, and laid you carefully by on the shelf as something precious in which I might still be interested."[25] When a mountain climb and a hefty dose of black coffee made her especially perceptive one night, she decided that she had determined the reason behind his inconsistency in writing to her: "You have been pitying yourself until you have persuaded someone to do it for you."[26] Yelverton responded— eventually—with solicitous affection: "Really must strongly recommend you to avoid *café nera*, ascending mountains, and becoming so terribly wide awake. If you don't take my advice I warn you your lucidity will become frightful, and your brain illuminated past the hope of recovery."[27] This was to be the pattern of their exchange: Yelverton failed to write or responded with a flip note; Theresa complained, then turned his apathy into a sign of his commitment.

Throughout the spring and summer of 1853, Theresa and Yelverton wrote to each other with increasing frequency. Yelverton wrote from Malta, Turkey—wherever his regiment happened to be. Theresa wrote from Naples, where she had settled for a time. Naples had been the summer residence of the ancient Roman elite, and over the centuries, it had retained its free-spirited character. Ever since the late eighteenth century, when the British envoy Sir William Hamilton had glamorized the expatriate social scene with long soirees and excursions to the surrounding ruins of Pompeii, the city had been a seductive spot for European travelers. By 1837, seven thousand foreigners had made it their home, many moving into the disused wings of palaces rented out by cash-strapped nobles.[28] Theresa joined the expanding ranks of the émigré population, living with a British banker and his wife.

Poised between the volcano and the sea, the city was a place of contradictions and extremes. Naples was lush but impoverished; beautiful but dangerous; surrounded by the hushed remnants of Roman architecture yet teeming with noisy barefoot beggars. The fragrance of lemons and orange blossoms floated through the streets on a clear day; dirty mineral vapors clouded them the next. When it was dry, dust hung in the air; when it rained, the streets were rivers of mud. "It results, that the higher your apartment is, the better," advised one traveler, James Whiteside—also the man who would represent Theresa in the Dublin trial twenty years later.[29]

A daily crush of people filled piazzas and goats and cows trotted through the city streets, but along the shore, where villas built on promontories glittered in the sun and violets grew on garden walls, the air was clear. Puppet shows and opera provided diversions, and fireflies pierced the pitch-black night sky like sparks. But splendor and entertainment only distracted up to a point. As the novelist Madame de Staël wrote, "There is no country where we feel more clearly the difference between amusement and happiness."[30] It was hard to understand where one stood in Naples; hidden forces moved the ashy earth beneath one's feet. "Poets naturally seized on this wonderful country as the appropriate scene for their lofty imaginations and fancies," wrote Whiteside, "for here was combined the awful with the beautiful."[31]

The relationship between Theresa and Yelverton was also shifting, becoming increasingly intimate but also increasingly unclear. When Yelverton addressed Theresa as "Miss Longworth" in one of his later letters, she indignantly replied: "By what mischance or misdeed have I become Miss Longworth again? I never grumbled at being addressed by my own name, and only thought, that having known me for one year, you had exalted me from a mere acquaintance to a certain degree of friendship. I do not know what I have done to be turned out again,—to be treated *en grande cérémonie*."[32] Yelverton replied coyly that he only called her Miss Longworth to "see if she liked it" and chastised her in return for calling him Mr. Yelverton.[33] Theresa, for her part, tried out "Carrissimo Carlo mio" (their attempts at Italian were generally bungled) for, as she explained, "William is out of the question. I abound with brother Williams, and could never recognize you under that title." Charles, the other alternative, was to her "*un peux mieux.*"[34]

While they squabbled good-naturedly, Yelverton hedged his flirtations with proclaimed indifference. "L'amore," he wrote, "is not, never was, and never can be, my insanity, temporary or otherwise."[35] Theresa did not let his supposed nonchalance dissuade her. When he told her that he took his comforts solely from material things— "I am fiancé to an armchair at the United Service Club," he wrote— Theresa saw only a shared proclivity for inanimate objects. "I fully sympathize with you in your grand passion," she flirted, "for I am almost similarly situated toward an easy chair, saving that I am not so constant as you to one object. My affections are often divided between a crazy old fiddle, with which I divert myself by driving my neighbors (when I had any) wild, and a very disreputable coffee-pot."[36]

When the situation in the Crimea escalated, Yelverton wrote to tell Theresa that he anticipated being dispatched to the East. Theresa, writing from Rome, had been feeling anxious to make her next move. Alcide was contemplating taking a military position, and if that happened, Theresa thought she might devote herself "to humanity, in the shape of a *Soeur de Charité*—I think it is a sort of vagabond life that would just suit me."[37] The Soeurs de Charité (the Sisters, or Daughters, of Charity) was a congregation founded in 1633 and purportedly instructed to say little and do much. They did not advocate on a specific side of the "female" issues of the day (temperance or women's rights, for example), but they participated in the hustle of the everyday world like few other organized groups of women—nursing, founding hospitals, building institutions, and teaching.

If not a nun, Theresa declared that she would become a *vivandière*, a civilian nurse, an occupation that she thought "might be a little more

A *vivandière*.

exciting."[38] Theresa and Yelverton continued in this vein—professing distance from conventional civilization while tightening the bohemian bond between them—through 1853 and into 1854. Theresa, like Yelverton, claimed allegiance "to the rolling-stone tribe in every particular, especially about the moss."[39] She did not need the baggage and associations that people carried through life. Her time in Naples had given her a taste for the rough edges of society, while her upbringing in the Ursuline convent had initiated her into a life—distinct from conventional civilization—where women controlled their own fates.

Her adventure would have to wait. In July of 1854, Theresa was summoned home from Italy to attend to her dying father. Theresa's sister Sara had warned her since September of the previous year that he was gravely ill. Theresa dismissed the warning; the main reason her father wanted his children to come home, she complained to Yelverton, was so that someone could keep an eye on the servants and prevent them from stealing from him in his enfeebled state. Theresa had never been close to her father, and his illness did not bring about a belated communion. Her return home only heightened the extent to which she had grown apart from Mr. Longworth, of whose atheism she despaired and whose parsimony she detested. His decease, when it finally took place, "was an awful affair," she wrote to Yelverton, "he died as he had lived, an atheist, unrelenting; with but one passion prevailing, truly as you said, to the last with diabolical earnestness." Theresa claimed immunity from that "one passion"—greed— although her disdain was almost certainly exaggerated for the sake of Yelverton's professed distaste. It was curious, Yelverton had writ- ten, "how absorbing it must be when, unlike other passions, it grows without age and increases by possession—an ever progressive and grand passion—equally present in health or sickness, until the mortal coil shuffled off."[40] The grip of avarice was, they agreed, a terrible thing. Whatever Theresa's siblings felt about their father's stinginess, they did not defend his overall character. "There was a great gather- ing of the wandering clan from all parts of the world, but there was not a word of kindness," Theresa wrote.[41]

Theresa eagerly anticipated a return to her roaming life, where she could escape the solemn shadow that had recently settled over her. But she and her brother Jack, or "Jock," as Theresa called him, remained to settle affairs (some fifty thousand pounds were left unaccounted for) once the others had departed.[42] Theresa was ill-suited to such practical tasks and complained bitterly of having been handed this burden: "I have a new language to learn, which I never dreamt of in my philoso- phy, which always begins 'whereas,' and ends 'heretofore'; or 'the aforesaid,' and the principal words are leasehold, mortgage, freehold, testator's funds, Chancery estates, *diables*, and swearing to be done ev- erywhere." Yelverton advised her to take her duties lightly. "Leave parchment to those that understand them," he wrote, assuming that she would only obtain a limited mastery of legalese, "sign nothing that you do not understand."[43]

It was not just the legal responsibilities that depressed her. Altrin- cham, the village outside Manchester where her father had made his home, was no home to her. "The people are all barbarians, speak an unknown tongue, and call us *foryneers*," she wrote to Yelverton. Smokestacks and factory bells were no substitute for the cactus plants and church chimes she had become accustomed to in Naples. Her father's cottage provided no refuge or warmth; "the house is sepulchral, and the furniture looks mysterious, and as if it knew more than it likes to say." Unwelcome pests were her constant companions; the house was "infested with rats and mice, and the ghosts of nine cats which spring out from behind any object one may have a fancy to inspect." Outside, the trees all nodded as if in agreement about some matter from which she was excluded. Ivy smothered the face of the house. There was "grass in the chinks of the walls; all the windows shake, and no door can be made fast."[44]

Considered a foreigner in what was ostensibly her hometown, confined to a house that seemed about to fall apart, Theresa did not find suitable ground on which to lay the foundations for a new life; nor did anyone tell her that her presence was required once official business had concluded. However limited her interactions with her father had been, he had maintained an ultimate authority over her actions. Now, he was no longer present to assert a distant but irrefutable power. This lack of guidance was both a blessing and a curse; the death of her father left Theresa somewhat more liberated, but with fewer defenses, and with her future stretched out before her like a great, blank canvas. She went to her sister's house in Wales to contemplate the possibilities it might hold. Her thoughts and her heart went elsewhere.

There had been some talk of Yelverton visiting Theresa in Malta in 1853; now the possibility was raised of her coming to him. "Shall, or will, or can you leave all those shadowy undefinables, and wander sunwards this winter?" Yelverton asked Theresa in September of 1854.[45] Theresa probably did long to join him, but—as Yelverton must have known—it was not easy for a young woman to travel to a war zone by herself to meet a man that her family did not know. The relationship had become a source of both comfort and pain to Theresa; Yelverton would propose the impossible, but the fantasy sustained Theresa's affection and fed her imagination.

Fateful circumstance had characterized their relationship from its unlikely beginnings, and now, as the memory of their meeting faded and their bond stretched thinner, Theresa clung to the idea that destiny would guide them toward each other once again. It was fate, or kismet, as Theresa (using a Turkish term) called it, that had arranged their introduction.[46] "I consider that the fact of my writing to you this day does not originate, as might be supposed, from the accidental cause of you once having been on board a steamer with me . . . We might have walked the ship all night and have remained strangers." A stronger force brought them together: "Your belt must have had a touch, and small cause was sufficient to produce this long effect."[47]

The "long effect"—their attachment to each other—however, was increasingly a product of Theresa's imagination, and she knew it. She began to call him "a sort of pet phantom," and often told him that only her faith ensured his existence. She was aware that her "tête à tête" was at times "a singular one" and that it might not last: "Some day my idol will come down with a smash, to my grief and horror, should anything happen to you."[48] She knew that she had put herself in this precarious position by idealizing a man she scarcely knew, but this knowledge of her vulnerability did not make her increase her defenses: "Pray don't destroy my illusions just yet—they won't last long . . . you are unkind to want to hasten my fall—to shake my crumbling tower."[49] In January of 1855—more than two years since she had last laid eyes on him—she wrote that she simply could not live without him: "I am sincerely grieved. I cannot bear to lose you—I would just as soon lose my own shadow . . . This is absurd I know you will think, because you don't care in the least about having an ideal; but I do, and you have been that to me for a long time."[50]

Theresa never lost sight of the fact that their relationship was a "strange mythic incidence" that might end before it had ever really begun, but that did not dampen the intensity of her feelings.[51] "Long before you return I shall be extinct—gone—'past like the baseless fabric of a vision, leaving not a wrack behind'; and you will never know me but as a dream . . . it has been a curious little episode in our lives, and will never occur twice to either."[52] Yelverton responded a few weeks later, weakly explaining his relative lack of zeal: "Cara Theresa mia—Incidents of the same or similar nature constantly recurring, no matter how exciting they may have seemed at first, become monotony, and, under the influence of monotony, the mind forms no new ideas." Therefore, he concluded, "I have nothing to write." He implied that a similar effect—the dulling of the perceptions through the tedium of repetition—occurred in marriage.

If, like Shakespeare's Prospero, Theresa knew that her life was filled with illusions—the baseless fabric of a vision—she was not eager to relinquish them. Though her education had been broader than the average English schoolgirl's, she was not immune to the immense pressures of the era, nor to the constant iteration that her one role in life was to be a wife and a mother. "Women dream till they have no longer the strength to dream," wrote Florence Nightingale in *Cassandra*, her jeremiad bemoaning the limited sphere of women's lives. It was only when women were left "without the food of reality or hope" of an alternative that they succumbed to their proscribed futures.[53] Bereft of affection as she was, Theresa had not yet reached the point where she would settle into a loveless marriage and an idle existence. Across the Continent, a conflict was building that would give her an outlet for her energies.

The Crimean War was fought to settle the "Eastern Question": with the expansion of the Russian Empire and the potential disintegration of the buffer of the Ottoman Empire, western European nations found themselves facing a fragile balance of power. The ostensible catalyst for the war—the competition between the Greek Orthodox and the Roman Catholic Church for predominance in Bethlehem and Jerusalem—was a symptom of the deeper malady. By May 1855, when Theresa arrived in the Crimea, the siege of Sevastopol—a port on the east coast of the Crimean Peninsula where Russia's Black Sea fleet was stationed—was in full swing.

The number of wounded British and French soldiers overwhelmed medical resources at Sevastopol, so many of the injured were sent on the four-day trip from the Crimean Peninsula across the Black Sea to Istanbul. Medical treatment in the Crimea was at best primitive and at worst cruel. One British doctor, John Hall, who commanded the army's medical staff on the Crimean front, advised against the use of

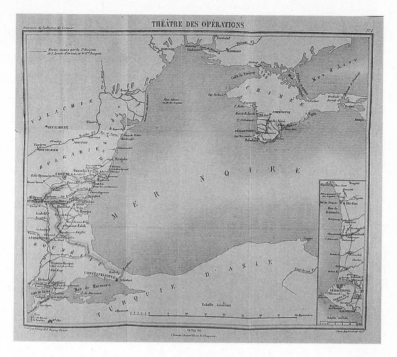

The Black Sea region.

anesthetics because "the smart of the knife is a powerful stimulant; and it is better to hear a man bawl lustily, than to see him sink silently into the grave."[54] When Florence Nightingale arrived in Istanbul late in 1855, she found long rooms filled with men who possessed "not an average of three limbs" and "four miles of beds—and not eighteen inches apart."[55] The French had set up more effective medical facilities, and the Soeurs de Charité played a large role in the daily operations of these comparably efficient French hospitals.

Theresa joined the Soeurs, possibly attracted to their relative competence, or possibly because she still felt herself a "*foryneer*" among her countrywomen and sought more like-minded companions. Although Theresa arrived before Nightingale, the strict standards of the "lady with the lamp" might have inadvertently encouraged her to stick with the supposedly lax Soeurs. The Soeurs, in Nightingale's opinion, made "no kind of attempt to introduce cleanliness, fresh air, comfort, or sanitary precaution into the dens of the poor . . . I have scarcely seen such want of personal cleanliness . . . One must live with them . . . to know these things."[56] None of the girls who lived with the Soeurs, she chastised, were "capable of keeping her own virtue."[57]

Whether Theresa's choice of the Soeurs over the British nurses derived from practical or temperamental considerations, fate, once again, seemed to encourage her decision to become a nurse. As she sailed to the Crimea, she discovered that Yelverton had traveled on the same ship, the *Great Britain*, a few months earlier while on leave. When she learned of this coincidence, Theresa was delighted. Although it meant he would not meet her in the Crimea as soon as she had hoped, it proved that their fates were entwined by "a real fact of magnetic influence"—just the affirmation that her waning confidence craved. She imagined that she had seen him walking about the ship while she was on board, as though he was "just in the next cabin."[58]

The Soeurs, Theresa realized soon after her arrival, did not lead the life of adventure she had envisioned. But she was thankful that they had welcomed her into their fold, and she carried out her duties, meeting ships as they neared the harbor in order to treat the worst of the wounded before they were brought to shore. She even earned a nickname—"sailor sister"—from the injured soldiers.[59] She maintained her distance, however, from the proscriptions of the Soeurs' lifestyle: "no short petticoats . . . a frightful costume," and of course, no men. They wanted to make her a nun after she finished her stint as a nurse, she wrote to Yelverton—"if you could only see the prison bars at my window." But, she wrote, "there are two to that bargain." Yelverton would "have as much to go through as had Orpheus in search of Eurydice," but she did not doubt that he would accept the challenge and liberate her from her self-imposed prison.[60]

Although the French hospital functioned more effectively than the British, conditions at the St. Benoit facility in Galata were not pleasant. A visiting English nurse described the increasingly dire situa-

Galata Tower, which stands at the center of Galata, the area
of Istanbul in which Theresa's convent was located.

tion as the hospital dealt with the flood of wounded soldiers: they
were low on supplies, understaffed, and plagued by indefatigable ver-
min. It was not just the soldiers who were in danger. According to
this nurse, "the toil the *Soeurs* undergo shortens their lives; many
have died of fatigue during the present war—four at the convent in
Galata within a few weeks of each other."[61]

This blood-soaked experience stayed with Theresa for years. In
her novel *Martyrs to Circumstance*, written much later, she described
the gruesome scene on board the ships returning from the front. "Between decks the air was putrid with animal decomposition and stench
of undried gore . . . the decks were wet, thick and sloppy," she wrote.
"There was a dull, heavy, indistinct sound of suppressed groans and
shrieks wrung from tortured minds and bodies."[62] A "lurid, gloomy,
sulpherous and lowering" sky loomed overhead, while "the boats on
the Bosphorus lay as still as though they had been frozen in its dull
waves." The wounded sailors were barely more alert than the flies that

Istanbul, as seen from Galata.

"lay on their backs in cataleptic trances."[63] At one point, she claimed, delirious with exhaustion and needing somewhere to rest, she sat on a pile of covered-up corpses. Her mind was so numbed by the gore that the ghastliness of her makeshift seat only later occurred to her.

If her position was not as romantic as she had anticipated and conditions were much more horrific, they at least provided new fodder for her fantasies. Not only was she a woman rescued from the chill of the Channel breezes; she was a Eurydice waiting for Orpheus. "When they are all asleep," Theresa wrote, "I steal out to the terrace, and my towers of hope rise far higher than the tall minarets."[64] For all the hellish conditions that the war created, Istanbul was still an exotic and exciting place to pass the time. In the narrow and steep streets of Galata, the shrill call to prayer and the thwack of the vendors' knives against the skins of melons reverberated. Piles of shoes lay outside the mosques, their owners fervently praying inside. In ancient cemeteries stray kittens wove between the headstones, as though drunk from the sun-warmed milk left out in saucers. The sultan had recently moved his residence from the sprawling, ancient Topkapi Palace to more modern quarters farther north, but it was easy to imagine the ghosts of veiled women still wandering the tiled corridors and ornate courtyards of the harem.

When she had longer stretches of time to herself, Theresa would travel north to Bebek, the ritzy neighborhood, where pastel-painted houses sat perched upon the shore of the Bosphorus. At night, moored ships loomed like mountains studded with pinpricks of light. In the morning, they came slowly to life like prehistoric creatures emerging from sleep and slid through the glassy water to Asia and Africa and beyond. Even surrounded by all this, she grew weary of the wait: "You are a ghost, a phantom, a coinage of my brain—that is all," she wrote to Yelverton, "a bright loveable one at first, now becoming painful and torturing."[65]

Yelverton finally did visit Theresa in September of 1855. Now in her twenties, Theresa was not quite the wide-eyed ingenue that he had met three years earlier. She had experienced the death of family and strangers, lived amid cosmopolitan bustle and war-torn towns. The creature who had written to him so plaintively now sat before him, and Yelverton, according to his later testimony during the trials, remembered the attraction he had felt at their first encounter. Whatever irritation or irreverence had surfaced in his correspondence now dissolved into desire. He slid closer on the divan, kissed her, and put his arms around her.[66] Theresa later claimed that Yelverton told her that they could be married immediately, with a bishop in the Greek Orthodox Church conducting the ceremony, but that she refused. She was a Catholic and knew the danger of a hasty marriage, and besides, she did not want to leave the hospital until the war was over.[67] Yelverton eventually had to leave, and they resumed their epistolary relationship.

Up to this point, Yelverton's inconstancy was Theresa's main worry. Their relationship had escaped the condemnation of family members or solicitous acquaintances. But when the mother superior at the convent hospital learned of Yelverton's visit, public scrutiny reined in Theresa's private fantasy. "Scandalous tongues have coupled our names together, and made the very worst of it," Theresa wrote to Yelverton after he had left. Although she had not taken the full vow of chastity (initiates were only required to take an annual vow until they made a lifelong commitment), she felt stung by the attack; "I am nearly crazy;

it takes so little to dash one's fair fame, and yet what harm have I done?" She knew she was becoming hysterical, but the accusations could have serious consequences. "A woman is so totally at the mercy of any wretch who chooses to be base enough to calumniate her."[68]

Yelverton responded bluntly. The affection he felt at the time of their meeting had dissipated with distance: "I am so sorry you are in a dilemma, if you dislike it, but I've been in one ever since I can recollect." Such inconveniences, he wrote, were part of life, and "it would be quite an impossibility" to correct misperceptions by defining "our indefinable relative position." He did not "profess to be a good guide as to right and wrong" in matters of behavior, but he would uphold that they had committed no crime. His moral rubric, he warned, was better suited to "the Rocky Mountains" or some less rigid enclave of civilization than the old society they inhabited. "Don't trust me," he wrote, "more than . . . a chivalrous savage."[69]

This was the very quality that Theresa adored, but it wasn't much use in her current predicament. Theresa took matters into her own hands. She told the mother superior that she and Yelverton were engaged. "To have spoken to her of congeniality of mind, similitude of thought, sympathy of idea, natural communion of spirit," Theresa explained in a letter to Yelverton, "would have been algebra to her. The French have no imagination." A French girl, Theresa wrote (although the description could just as easily be applied to most English girls), was closely watched until she became engaged and all financial matters were settled. "I wonder if they are any better for all these precautions?" she asked. Though a romantic, Theresa was practical when necessary. She had no choice but to remain at the convent, not only because she had nowhere else to go, but also because her withdrawal would "give a shadow of truth to any rumours there may be afloat."[70]

Theresa's brush with infamy had impressed upon her the importance of respectability. The mother superior had identified "the point where she guessed I should prove most weak and sensitive"—her good name—and Theresa was now on the defensive. But she was still willing to place the ultimate responsibility for her protection in

Yelverton's hands. If, she wrote, Yelverton really was the man she had described to the nuns as her *"attaché mondaine,"* then she felt her "faith [had] indeed been well planted." She had never had such a protector—her father certainly didn't count—but she had been in love "with such a one from the age of ten years, when I formed my first conception of an ideal man from Scott and Cowper."[71]

A chivalrous savage was everything she wanted: "A man who has a sound mind and warm heart, unclouded by sophism and subtle refinement . . . who is bold, brave, and gentle and kind . . . who knows no other bonds but those of honour and affection . . . the guardian of justice and honesty—too noble for a tyrant, too generous to be selfish—a man realizing the intentions of the Creator, and worthy of the glorious gifts bestowed upon him." But, she continued, "if your phrase did not read exactly so, but as though you would warn me not to trust too much . . . I have but one answer to make—*I must trust all or not at all with you, I can have no half measures;* and come weal or woe of it, *I am prepared to meet it, and will make the best of it."*[72]

When a truce was arranged in March 1856, Theresa went to the Kamiesch Bay near Sevastopol where her friends, Colonel Straubenzee and his wife, were living. Theresa enjoyed the company, especially since relations with her companions at the convent had become strained. Yelverton learned where Theresa was staying, and about two weeks after her arrival he called upon her. He became a frequent visitor, introducing himself, according to the Straubenzees, as Theresa's fiancé. Mrs. Straubenzee did not like Yelverton at first, but she warmed to him during the evenings that the two couples spent together.[73]

When Theresa's six-week visit with the Straubenzees ended, Yelverton and the colonel accompanied Theresa to the steamer that was to take her from Balaklava to Istanbul. Before the boat left, Yelverton stole on board to bid a private farewell to Theresa. He may have spent the night, or he may have just watched over her as she fell asleep. If their entire relationship was a "mythic incidence," this was one of the events that swelled with prophetic importance when Theresa was left alone to contemplate their affair. "Saturday night, Carlo mio, was our *second* steamer scene," she wrote. "God grant the third be not far distant—and the consummation of all. What a most eccentric phenomenon that our destiny should hang by a steamboat. Did I go to sleep and dream it—that you watched over me all night, for [in] the grey dawn I woke and thought I saw you?"[74]

Whether or not Yelverton spent the night with Theresa—and whatever Theresa meant by "consummation"—the second steamer scene echoed their initial meeting. It was the type of coincidence that solidified Theresa's belief that their destinies were inextricably bound together by the type of luck that only struck in cases of true love. No matter what games Yelverton played, no matter the extremes to which her faith was stretched, she believed that fate would overwhelm the misguided waters that set them adrift—if only they were patient. He had told her that they should submit themselves to the "haze, vapour, and fog" of forces beyond their control, sink "with calm philosophy on the couches of [their] respective *caiques*," and float "down [their] respective streams." Obstacles were surmountable; "the ocean [was] not distant, and both streams must end there, and the occupants of both *caiques* may be again fellow-passengers."[75] It might not shine brightly, but the lamp of true love would illuminate a path across the channels that divided them.

CHAPTER TWO

Pursuit

In the ill-judged execution of the well-judged plan of things
the call seldom produces the comer, the man to love rarely
coincides with the hour for loving.

—Thomas Hardy, *Tess of the D'Urbervilles* (1891)

After she left the Straubenzees, Theresa idled in Bebek, with a mixed crowd of well-to-do Turks, Armenians, and Europeans. Theresa's house was painted yellow and stuck out into the road, features that would make it easily identifiable, she hoped, if Yelverton came to find her.[1] From her house, she could see and sketch the Bosphorus, a wide, gray-blue strip of silk in the morning, by midday reflecting the azure sky above it. It was a "delicious little nook . . . and only wants *somebody* to make it a *paradise*," she wrote.[2] In this enclave of tranquillity, Theresa's heart quickened whenever she heard news of departing British troops.[3] Yelverton was still stationed at Sevastopol and could send word if he desired, but news was scarce. When letters finally came, they continued in the same flirtatious but painful vein. Yelverton was clearly beginning to tire of the liaison. Sensing that Theresa's affection would not dissipate with time or distance, he began to summon more concrete obstacles to stand in the way of their union.

Any wealth that the first Viscount of Avonmore had secured for his family was exhausted by the time his great-grandson, William Charles Yelverton, was in line for the peerage. According to what Yelverton told Theresa, he lived off an allowance provided by his uncle. Eager to secure the title for his son, the uncle would only continue the stipend if Yelverton remained childless and unmarried. Yelverton had an older brother, George Frederick Williams, who stood ahead of Yelverton in the line of succession, but Yelverton never mentioned similar restrictions applying to his older sibling—a fact that casts doubt on the veracity of his excuse. (Years later, when the communications between Theresa and Yelverton were widely known, Yelverton's uncle openly refuted Yelverton's story: "Whenever this unfortunate case is brought before the public, whether in the courts of justice, or by the comments volunteered on it in the public prints, the story of the cruel uncle who held the bond of his nephew, the Hon. Major Yelverton, for money lent with the view of preventing his marriage until the bond was paid, is treated as though it were a fact." The uncle wished "to state that this story is altogether a fabrication.")[4]

Though she did not know of Yelverton's older brother at the time, and the uncle's true position had not yet come to light, Theresa thought the situation was suspicious. The bond his uncle had allegedly placed upon him was "unrighteous and iniquitous" she told him, and "the non-fulfillment can leave no stain on your honour or conscience."[5] There must be a way around it. "I feel persuaded I can manage it," she wrote to Yelverton, "women have far more ingenuity and resource than men."[6] She consulted her sister Sara and her brother-in-law, a lawyer, whom she called by his last name, Bellamy—"a sort of Mr. Jarndyce, who growls when the wind is in the east—is always doing kind and generous actions, but terribly afraid any one should think so," as Theresa described him.[7] She was sure they could devise a way out of the "labyrinth" of obligation that had placed Yelverton "on the high road to ruin." The future was bright for her; "by Bellamy's last accounts, there is every prospect of our doubling our income in two or three years." And if that did not happen, she would find employment. Her cousin Alcide had offered her a position: "£100 a year, if I would go with him and be his secretary, write his dispatches, and read up the Blue Book. This occupation would just suit me, and there I should not *be able* to spend sixpence."[8] Coquetry was not the only relief for idleness; she was willing to work.

Theresa's plan to find work was both part of a trend—increased employment among women outside the home—and an act of resistance to it. By 1851, half of the six million adult women in England "laboured for their subsistence," two million of whom were unmarried.[9] The men of Britain had been displaced to "all ends of the earth seeking their fortune," leaving a surplus of women behind, wrote *Blackwood's* magazine.[10] In England, 15 percent of women reached their fiftieth birthday without a mate.[11] Teaching was an option for unmarried women, as was nursing or midwifery, but respectable occupations were limited to those that retained the semblance of domesticity.

Theresa had already tried nursing and now wanted to do something different. "It is clearly demonstrated in the purest logic that something is better than nothing," she wrote.[12] But unlike many of her female contemporaries, she did not see a career as a means to obtain greater independence. Nor did she think herself part of the "superfluous" population of women who would spend their adult lives as spinsters. She saw work as a way to secure a husband.

In the end, however, her scheme did not progress very far. Yelverton did not encourage her to take the job with Alcide. Was there "something more than the money difficulty which you have not the courage to tell," she wondered—"family feelings and considerations, pride of birth" perhaps? She was from a manufacturing background, after all, and the family title was clearly still important to at least some members of the Yelverton clan. If that was the case, Theresa wrote, "*for God's sake let this be the end*. I am [from] an old and good family . . . and will never be a firebrand in any family." She even offered to introduce him to a rich, available young woman, although the offer was probably a roundabout attempt to highlight her own selfless virtues. "In your position," she wrote, "it is the simplest thing in the world to find a woman ready to pay your debts." The ostensibly eligible young woman she had in mind was not from aristocratic stock, but "money covers a multitude of sins," Theresa said, tweaking the biblical phrase ("charity covers a multitude of sins").[13] The real sin, she reminded him, was caring about it.

Through the spring and summer of 1856, Theresa's cravings for attention intensified. She accepted that Yelverton was not going to entertain her plan to support him, but refused to give him up. "Your silence causes me the deepest pain," she wrote. "It is dreadful to have to confess myself such a child, but it is true." When these self-punishing statements went unanswered, her hysteria grew. "Why must I live in spite of myself? Why was I not taken, when so many were going around me?" she wondered. "I never feared death, and prefer it to misery."[14] Theresa was prone to hyperbole, but her exaggerations did not unhinge her perspective. She knew she brought this suffering on herself. "I am disgusted with myself," she wrote. "I am not what I thought I was. I am beginning to hate myself for being such a miserable, wretched thing."[15] Her threats of suicide seemed sadly genuine, the only alternative to her hopelessly enamored but unloved existence: "I want to go—to go anywhere out of the world; to forget, to get rid of myself."[16]

Even to this, Yelverton's response was delayed. "My dear child," he wrote, "you must have mistaken the terms of my promise . . . I do not expect to be my own master for some days yet." She had obviously assessed his character and availability inaccurately, but he was not about to apologize for his inconstancy. "Who is consistent?" he asked. "If you are, and know what it is, you can amuse yourself throwing stones as long as it pleases you."[17] Beyond the expectations that Theresa imposed on him, Yelverton claimed that he carried a heavy, although vaguely defined, load of obligations. These burdens had tamed the savage who had pursued her at Galata. "I fear my self-command," he wrote, "will almost annoy you as much as my want of it" when they last met. He was becoming more attuned and sympathetic to the demands of civilization. She should focus on suitable marital prospects for herself.[18] "I still cannot counsel you to wait for me," he wrote in May.[19]

This time, there was a certain amount of resolve behind his words. On June 18, 1856, he left the Crimea via the Danube to avoid a prearranged meeting in Bebek. From Vienna, he explained his deliberations in a letter containing a bizarre dialogue between his Brain and his Self, a pre-Freudian battle between the id and the ego.

(Brain) Why are you going?

(Self) I promised.

(B.) Why did you promise [?]

(Self) We wished to meet again.

(B.) What for? To make a beginning to the end, or to add to the endless?

(Self) For my part the former.

(B.) Fool! Then the end will be all of your making.

(Self) True, if there be one.

(B.) That must not be.

(Self) No, I'll go by the Danube, or Moscow.

(B.) A steamer goes to Odessa to-morrow.

(Self) H'm a *steamer* to Odessa to-morrow.[20]

Yelverton's action was decisive. Theresa had been jilted. But as usual, the message was mixed. The "Self"—the base part of him that desired to see Theresa—was also the part that intended to "make a beginning of the end," while his "Brain" instructed him to stay away, foreclosing the possibility of physical interaction. He could not resist mentioning that a steamer—the type of ship that had hosted their most meaningful encounters—was sailing for Odessa. Perhaps Theresa understood this impulse: "[You] never cared to win me until there was danger of losing me,"[21] she told him.

Yelverton's letter did not reach Theresa until several months later. Whenever a ship of soldiers would depart from the Crimea, she would sneak on board, pretending to be looking for Mrs. Straubenzee, but really searching for Yelverton.[22] She finally gave up, left Bebek, and made her way to Malta, where she thought he might have headed. On the hot, dry Mediterranean island south of Sicily she looked for him during the day, ducking in and out of the churches built of limestone, wandering along the bastions lining the harbor. At night, she entertained expatriates with piano recitals in balconied apartments. Halfway between Europe and Africa, Malta had obtained new prominence in the latter half of the nineteenth century as a stopover for ships passing through the Mediterranean, and the British population had grown accordingly. But Theresa didn't settle down among her compatriots. Adrift in the company of strangers, she felt more powerless than usual. "I have no more command over myself," she told Yelverton, sending her letters to military headquarters in the Crimea and his home in London, hoping that they would eventually reach him. He had "obtained boundless empire" over her.[23] The rest of the world no longer held any meaning: "Life's torrent, boiling, toiling, goes rushing on; scenes and people glide before me like as in a panorama. I have nothing in common with them; they are an empty pageant."[24] His control over her was "like opium to the Dervish, the more dangerous it becomes, the more sweet."[25] She could no longer dampen her obsessions for the sake of propriety.

Yet this detachment from civilization strengthened her resolve. If conventional society prevented their public convergence, she would settle outside it and bring Yelverton with her. "The strongest and most prominent point of my character is the extreme *tenacity* of purpose," she once wrote, "and . . . the incapacity to relinquish an object once fairly sought." Nothing would deter her: "No obstacle daunts—no sacrifice appalls me—no means, however trivial, escape me, and struggle only augments my courage."[26] The lethargic but desperate inactivity of her suicidal phase had vanished.

A month of scouring Malta in the fall of 1856 yielded no information of Yelverton's whereabouts.[27] She left the East and headed for England on the *Stromboli*, still writing letters to a man she now feared might be dead, so absolute had his recent silence been. The ship took twenty days to cross the Bay of Biscay—she claimed—rolling from side to side the whole way. It was the height of "physical wretchedness," wrote Theresa. When she went outside for fresh air, the wind whipped around her so intensely that she felt as limp and useless as a "rubbish bag" when she returned to her stuffy indoor quarters.[28]

In January 1857, Theresa arrived in England and discovered two letters from Yelverton waiting for her at the Regent's Park house of her friend, the Marchioness de Belinay. He told her that he was stationed in Leith, a seaside suburb just north of Edinburgh. The second letter was especially brief, even for Yelverton. It read, in garbled Italian: "Carissima she cosa vuoi—Addio, penso a te. Sci la ben venuta."[29] Roughly translated, the message conveyed: "Darling, whatever you want—Goodbye, I'm thinking of you. Be welcome." Theresa had promised to visit her sister Sara in Wales, but she vowed to make her way north as soon as possible and stay there until the spring.

Before she left London, she wrote to Yelverton, making the terms of their situation as clear as possible: their mutual transgression— whether it was merely a secret liaison or a more substantial violation of conventional morality—bound them together. She, at least, was unwilling to remain quiet: "I am so situated now in the game that you are the only person to whom, as the law says, I can speak the truth, and the whole truth."[30] Theresa had attempted to retain Yelverton by showing her undying affection. Now, she took a more offensive stance, reminding him that "the truth, and the whole truth" might cast an unfavorable shadow on Yelverton's reputation if it were to emerge.

Theresa had never denied her relationship with Yelverton, but upon Yelverton's urging, she had promised to stop speaking to her family of their affair. The promise was less a concession to him than a reshuffling of her cards. "It is bitter to give up all those we love," she wrote of the loss of her confidants, "but if there is one left to love me, it will compensate me for every other ill."[31] Shifting the burden of her happiness to Yelverton, she used his anxiety to her advantage. If she seemed unpredictable, he might be forced to keep a closer watch. "Do not forbid me *anything*," she instructed Yelverton. "You must let me talk—it is a woman's privilege *et da vera*." The only way he could silence her would be to confront her in person: "I only know one legitimate mode of stopping her mouth, and that you cannot practise by letter, sir."[32] The "legitimate mode"—presumably—was a kiss, but whether it was meant to silence her with reassurance, or suffocate her with menace, was unclear. Whatever test she intended to create, she would soon try it in person.

In February, Theresa and her friend Arabella MacFarlane traveled to Edinburgh. MacFarlane's father, a Scottish writer, had known the Longworth family for many years, and so the girls arrived equipped with letters of introduction to the city's leading lights: the Scottish publisher Robert Chambers (of *Chambers's Journal*), the editor J. H. Burton, and a Mr. J. Hunter, whom they visited at Craigcrook Castle, where Sir Walter Scott had once been a regular visitor.[33] After a brief stay at the Ship Hotel in Leith, Theresa and MacFarlane moved into a three-room flat on the top floor of a townhouse on St. Vincent Street. They were boarders, but respectable, having been referred to the landlady, Mrs. Mary Gemble, by a mutual friend. The house was located in New Town, only a few miles from Yelverton's barracks in Leith.

New Town was separated from Old Town—the jumbled, medieval part of the city—by a deep loch. The loch had prevented northern expansion of the city in its earliest years, forcing it to be built on the descending slope east of the castle. By the mid-eighteenth century the city was overwhelmingly crowded. Many of the original buildings had been divided into flats, or "tenements," which housed all but the wealthiest of the city's inhabitants. (In London, by contrast, as in most of England, flat dwelling was generally uncommon even among the poor.) The city council responded by planning a "New Town," a residential suburb for the upper classes and a refuge from the increasingly hectic quarters of what became known as Old Town.

New Town would fill the city with spacious streets and large buildings—features designed to attract merchants and other people of rank.[34] The stately streets were laid out in an orderly east-west

Edinburgh.

orientation, with public buildings incorporated throughout and churches at the end of each axis. To a certain extent, the green spaces built into New Town were meant to echo the confrontation of nature and civilization that gave Edinburgh as a whole its distinctive character. The city and landscape had coexisted for centuries; as one commentator put it, Old Town had grown "and adapted itself as naturally as the ivy to rock or ruined tower."[35] New Town was a clear imposition on nature, but it did not seek to efface it. "In this singular city," Robert Chambers wrote, "instead of what is common in all others, a dense unvaried assemblage of mere streets,—we have . . . projected into the midst of the travelled and crowded ways of men, mountainous places, never yet touched by human foot . . . unfailing supplies of the primitive commodities of nature."[36] This city of confrontations— between medieval and Enlightenment architecture, the past and the

Edinburgh from the castle.

present, disarray and order, design and nature—most likely appealed
to Theresa. She knew all too well that pleasure and pain were never
very far from each other and midcentury Edinburgh was filled with
darkness and light. Tree-slung lanterns illuminated gardens during
evening fetes, while overgrown labyrinthine paths—"the constant
and favorite promenade of those favored with a right of entry"—
provided opportunities for clandestine rendezvous.[37]

Theresa and Yelverton began to see each other daily. Yelverton
accompanied MacFarlane to church on a few occasions when Theresa
was singing in the choir. Sometimes, they would ride through the
streets together. Most of their meetings, however, took place at Theresa's top-story apartment, where the small dormer window looked
out over shingled rooftops. Just as in Galata, Theresa's immediate
presence overwhelmed Yelverton's professions of disregard. When a
fall from his horse left Yelverton injured and unable to walk or ride,
he sent his carriage for Theresa and she visited him at his barracks.
He was solicitous and appreciative of her attention, concerned about

William Donaldson Clark's image of the Cowgate Arch of George IV Bridge in Edinburgh shows the juxtaposition of old and new architecture.

what she wanted to eat, and when: "I am on fever diet, so will give you some tea at about six o'clock and send you back safe and sound at whatever time suits you."[38]

His notes were brief but arrived frequently, arranging their meetings to maximize their time together. On the mornings when he did not appear at the apartment, he sent his servant in his place with messages and books for her to read. He wrote in Italian and was more affectionate than ever before. He was thinking *Sempre a te* (always to you), he wrote to her, and the regularity of their meetings cast no aspersion on the sentiment. For the first time, he showed a genuine desire to accommodate her wishes and desires. When she was unsure if she could manage to meet him, he wrote to her that she should not worry: "no character suffers, except mine, which is utterly unimportant."[39] On days when he did not see her, he would write to her that he was "sulky," claiming to "hate uncertainties, and believe

in nothing."[40] Despite this unprecedented attention, their committ-
ment was still not commensurate and Theresa grew impatient with
Yelverton's fears.

Her unhappiness increased until April 12, 1857, when, according
to Theresa, Yelverton declared himself her husband with his hand on
a Book of Common Prayer. There were no witnesses; MacFarlane (if
she was in the apartment at all) was not in the room. Her landlady did
not venture into Theresa's quarters. No religious or civil authority
presided over the ceremony. But, according to Scottish common law,
Yelverton's alleged declaration constituted a marriage. Such "irregular" marriages were not uncommon in Scotland, which had a long
common law history. While a "regular" marriage required the procla-
mation of banns before a clergyman, an "irregular marriage could be
forged by a mere declaration of vows between two people, requiring
neither witnesses nor written documentation," according to a contemporary legal authority.[41]

The "marriage" did not put Theresa at ease. Though she would
later say that she believed in its legitimacy, she would also claim that
her religious scruples prevented her from immediately sleeping with
Yelverton. Apparently alarmed by his sudden demands (Yelverton
would claim later that they were already having sex), she left Edinburgh for Hull only a few days after the makeshift ceremony and
sought refuge with her friend John Thelwall, an ironmaster, and his
wife. She was in a miserable state of mind, "half married and not
married," as she later put it.[42]

"Oh, for those blessed days when I could trust you," Theresa
wrote to Yelverton from Hull. Yelverton had countered Theresa's
retreat with his own, traveling to Belle Isle, his family's ancestral
home in Ireland, now the residence of his newlywed brother and his
wife. He stayed there through June 1857 while Theresa continued to
write to him. If Yelverton gave any credence to the Scottish "marriage," he did not want it advertised and told her to keep quiet about
it, a command that—as always—did not sit well with her. "What is
the use of . . . saying 'you must keep quiet,' when I cannot trust—

when by trusting I may lose . . . the fruits of a life of patient suffering." Should she give him up? she wondered. "Give you up now! Even writing about it, I have little sharp nipping pains at my heart. If I made my hand write a farewell, I should have a palpitation there and then. I shall die without you. Is it worse to die by you? I am in a bad state of mind, I am afraid, or I should not be seriously weighing which death I like best!"[43]

She became ill, and Mrs. Thelwall forced her to rest in bed. She wrote letters to pass the time, and in one she included the wedding card of an old friend, Mr. Shears, whom she had first met in the Crimea.[44] Shears, then a lieutenant in the navy, had proposed to Theresa when they first became acquainted. When she informed Yelverton of the offer, he had encouraged her to consider it, eager—at that point—to have her off his hands. She had brushed aside the suggestion. By including the wedding card of Shears, Theresa meant to indicate that a union between her and her former suitor would now be impossible, although she did not explicitly say this. Yelverton took the card to mean something else entirely: that Theresa had married Shears. "I congratulate you on the step you have taken most sincerely, as [it is] the most likely course to render your future life a contented one," he wrote, apologizing for addressing her by the old familiarity "Cara Theresa." If "ever a remembrance of me crosses your mind in your new sphere of duties and pleasures," he hoped that she would spare him "a place in [her] prayers." Conveniently extricated from responsibility, Yelverton was more eloquent and more honest than ever, finally willing to admit his own fault in creating their uncomfortable union: "By your marriage you have earned my lasting gratitude . . . On reflection I found that I had placed myself in a false position with regard to you . . . that I had promised to you to do more than I could have performed when the time came."[45]

Theresa was horrified. "Are you mad, or am I?" she wrote to Yelverton upon receiving his letter. "The first reading of your letter brought me to a stop, mental and physical. My present weakness could not stand such a shock; my heart went still." As she was writing her previous letter, the Thelwalls had noticed she was tiring and had made her curtail her letter before she could explain the significance of the card she had enclosed. She had not dreamed that the inclusion of the card would be taken as evidence of her own marriage. Though she did not believe that the irregular marriage had lawfully united them—she was, after all, a Catholic—she had committed herself to Yelverton long ago. "Oh, *Carlo*, to suspect me of such a thing. I whose very life is ebbing away for you; I who have sacrificed all but God to you . . . That you should judge me guilty of such an infamous thing!"[46] With this supposed mistake, Yelverton forced Theresa to confront the extent of his disregard for her. She may have wondered whether it was worth it to continue the pursuit after this transparent ploy to get rid of her. But she had few alternatives and seemed, despite it all, to still love him.

In her next letter, Theresa had calmed down, and she teased Yelverton for his misunderstanding while reminding him that she could not be so easily dismissed. "Earn your eternal gratitude by marrying Mr. Shears. So sorry can't oblige you. Had you only spoken sooner, especially at Malta"—where he had completely disappeared—"we no doubt would have been happy to come to an amicable arrangement on the point and relieved you of your burthen. To earn your eternal gratitude what might I not have been Quixotic enough to do?"[47] Marriage to dull Shears would have been a trial, both mental and physical: "Imagine my being content with Shears after having been loved by *Carlo* . . . it is against nature." Though Theresa would later claim that they had not slept together in Edinburgh, her letters from this period hint otherwise. "Love" was often used as a euphemism for intercourse, and to be "loved by Carlo," Theresa wrote in one letter, was unsurpassable.[48] Though their relationship played out mainly at a distance, physicality was ever-present: "It is bad to forget one is flesh and blood. Don't you think so? You cured me of that but the cure rendered me helpless without the constant care of the physician."[49] She had found a doctor for her troubled mind, and she wasn't about to give him up; the treatment was both painful and exquisite.

Yelverton's rapid concession to an imagined competitor most likely inspired Theresa to plan an official union. With the Scottish marriage Yelverton had committed himself according to his terms; why should he not do so again according to hers? She even devised an informal honeymoon, a "Highland expedition," to take place in the autumn. The Thelwalls might accompany them, but she reassured Yelverton that they were "true and silent. Moreover, they live entirely out of the world, and know no one person belonging to either of us."[50] The risk of exposure was a constant concern to Yelverton; Theresa assured him that the ironmaster circulated in different circles. Yelverton deflected the invitation, claiming that it was near impossible to obtain leave, and that his family's concern and inquisitiveness increased each time he excused himself due to a supposed illness. "I am not a free agent, and never shall be," he reminded her; "or not for many years," he characteristically hedged.

In July, Theresa wrote to Yelverton, who had moved temporarily to Dublin, to let him know that she would be making a trip to Manchester with her sister Sara. She had left Hull earlier to live with her sister in Abergavenny, Wales. If Yelverton might be able to meet her in the northern city, she would stay on after her family left. They could reunite in the cathedral where her ancestors were buried and complete their "other project" of making Yelverton a legitimate Catholic. (Theresa had heard rumors that there were Catholics in his family.) Since Yelverton was unknown in those parts, "it would be without any particle of risk," Theresa wrote. He merely had to "be present at mass" for the conversion to take place.[51] The plan never materialized, but Theresa did not allow the setback to dissuade her. She began preparations to travel to Ireland, where she would pull Yelverton away from the "midnight crushes—misnamed balls" that he had described for her. More important, she would separate him from the "great many pretty girls" and heiresses that, he had told Theresa, were pointed out to him "with the usual recommendations."[52]

Later in July, Theresa sailed to Waterford on the southwestern shore of Ireland, where she expected Yelverton would be waiting for her. He had not yet arrived so Theresa lingered, impatiently, at the

Waterford, Ireland.

Cummin's Hotel. Ships crowded into the harbor from the Atlantic Ocean and the Irish Sea, but none brought Yelverton. "All day I have waited in a fever of listening—every step or sound approaching making me breathless with hope—all to melt in despair as night comes on . . . What am I to do next? If you cannot come will you send me a telegraphic message where I am to go? I shall never return home. It is all over there."[53] His impending arrival hardly assuaged her anxieties. Yelverton finally met Theresa at Waterford, and they set out northward, toward the less populated regions where neither of them would be recognized.

By August 10, the couple had reached Rostrevor at the foot of the Mourne Mountains, about halfway up the eastern coast of Ireland between Dublin and Belfast. Sloping directly into the sea, the Mourne Mountains provided a dramatic landscape for their excursion. Until the late eighteenth century, when roads and transportation improved

access to the region, the area had been practically self-sufficient because of its isolation. Tourists had been content to view the peaks and
precipices from a distance and the Mourne locals were used to a hard-
scrabble life. A shipwreck off the craggy coast was no tragedy, but a
gift of unanticipated bounty. "God bless daddy and mammy, / And
send the big ship ashore in the morning" went a local ballad.[54] The
rocky granite shore was cut by inlets, convenient hideaways for smug-
glers who brought their wares to the region and hawked them alongside the "cadgers" (fish sellers) carrying baskets of herring and
mackerel through the hills. By the time Theresa and Yelverton visited the region, the area had gentrified to a certain extent. Rostrevor
was known for its healthful air, a "romantic retreat" and a place of re-
tirement for the "merchants, lawyers and others of the wealthy classes,
who tread on the heels of the aristocracy."[55] But well-heeled expansion
was limited; the towns remained tiny, and secluded churches were
only disturbed by winds off the Irish Sea.

In Rostrevor, they made plans for their wedding at one of these
quiet thatch-roof churches. On August 11, Yelverton went to Dublin
to visit a jeweler and buy a plain gold ring. While he was gone, Theresa met with Reverend Bernard Mooney, the parish priest of Kilbro-
ney, who ran a church at Killowen, a small town about two miles
from Rostrevor. Theresa and Reverend Mooney went together to see
the bishop overseeing the diocese. The bishop gave Mooney permission to renew the consent of the marriage in Scotland, and so Theresa
planned to appear before Reverend Mooney with Yelverton at her
side a few days later.

When the moment Theresa had anticipated for so long finally came,
she and Yelverton were late. They had traveled by boat along the coast,
and they had misjudged the amount of time it would take them to reach
the church. Once they docked, they had to rush through the rocky
fields. By the time they reached the church, the reverend had been
waiting for several hours. Theresa apologized profusely, acknowledging that the reverend had already made so many concessions—
agreeing that no person was to witness the marriage, and to only record

the marriage in his private register. Theresa had explained the need for secrecy by telling the reverend that Yelverton's family was Protestant and would not look kindly upon this union with a Catholic.

When the ceremony began, this last condition caused Mooney to pause. Was Yelverton himself a Catholic?

"I am not much of anything" Yelverton responded, which startled the reverend. It was a punishable offense (or so Mooney thought) for a Catholic priest to marry a man and woman who were not both Catholics.[56] Theresa jumped in to clarify; Yelverton had yet to be confirmed, but he had gone to mass with her several times.

"What are you?" Mooney asked Yelverton again.

"A Protestant Catholic," Yelverton responded, and despite its ambiguity the answer satisfied Mooney.[57] According to his understanding of the situation, Mooney had merely been asked to renew the vows the couple had exchanged in Scotland, not to create a new union.

Theresa and Yelverton knelt before Mooney on the cold stone floor, and they pledged their devotion to each other. The couple had now been "married" twice: once in the cosmopolitan center of the Scottish Enlightenment, once in the backwaters of Ireland; once according to custom, once according to religion. Neither wedding was exactly conventional and both were of dubious legitimacy, but as Theresa had once insisted in a letter to her lover, "Conventionality is *not* the question between us. I dislike every shadow of it as much as yourself. My whole life, you know, has been a protest against it, and in my relations with you it has never been brought to bear or wished for."[58]

Despite Theresa's flippancy toward convention, her bohemian abandon did not run as deep as she claimed. With these two unions, she hoped to gain a level of legitimacy that would allow her to live a less secretive life. But before Yelverton gave her the ring that he had bought in Dublin, he asked for something in return: another ring— one with his seal—that he had given to her much earlier. She had worn it for years with the seal turned inward, his imprint hidden to the world and nestled in her palm when she made a fist. Now, a plain band devoid of personality replaced his imprimatur. The new ring should have sealed their union, but, like the wedding itself, it almost seemed to loosen the terms of their relationship. They were clearly more than correspondents—more, perhaps, than lovers—but were they man and wife to the rest of the world? There were few people to whom they could permit that impression. They were not given much time to test the new boundaries. By the end of August, they had parted ways again.

CHAPTER THREE

Betrayal

*The idea . . . is that of a young person . . . passionately desiring
to "put in" before extinction as many of the finer vibrations
as possible, and so achieve, however briefly and brokenly,
the sense of having lived.*

—Henry James, preface to *The Wings of the Dove* (1902)

Theresa spent the time immediately after the Irish wedding in Wales, where she did not bear the separation well. "The eyes yearn to see you, the ears are distended to catch the first sound of your voice or footfalls, the hands throb and tingle to touch you and feel you once more safe within their grasp," she wrote. "As to there being any conditions about the arrears of petting, I am crabby. I *must* have it, or I shall hate you."[1] About six weeks after the ceremony in Ireland, Yelverton and Theresa reunited in Edinburgh, where Theresa had moved into an apartment at 31 Albany Street owned by a woman named Mrs. Stalker. Arabella MacFarlane was still Theresa's primary companion, and Theresa and Yelverton kept a low profile. But Theresa's closest friends assumed they were newlyweds, and it was no secret to Stalker and her staff that they slept together at night.[2]

They did not remain in Edinburgh for long, perhaps because Yel-

A Highland landscape. Theresa and Yelverton spent their
"honeymoon" after the Irish wedding in the Highlands.

verton wanted to prevent his friends from forming the same impression. As October approached, they made plans for a trip through the
Highlands, and in early November they began a twelve-day tour, visiting Doon Castle, Linlithgow, Dunblane, and Dunfermline. They un-
wittingly left a trail of witnesses: hotel owners, maids, and waiters who
would later testify that they had lived together as man and wife, at least
while staying at the hotels. At Doon Castle they provided more tangi-
ble evidence, signing their names "Mr. and Mrs. Yelverton" in the visitors' book.

Theresa and Yelverton may have felt freer in the Highlands than
elsewhere in Britain. Visits to continental Europe yielded cultural ac-
creditation; Scottish tourism, on the other hand, particularly in the
Highlands, offered raw exposure to nature and a glimpse of an antique way of life. A visitor remarked, "To a stranger from the far

south, the scene presented to his gaze . . . seemed quite unique, stirring, and interesting, and apt to make him fancy that he had been suddenly transported to some far off region of the world."[3] Theresa and
Yelverton had already seen much of continental Europe. Theresa in
particular had acquired perhaps too great a cultural pedigree as the
result of her foreign travels. A Highland expedition was a fitting honeymoon for this couple who had always sought a semimystical "far off
region of the world" to call their own. They had failed to find it in the
East and now, perhaps, were seeking a refuge closer to home. Highlands communities—according to the lore—lived with disdain for
conventional civilization, just as Theresa and Yelverton had throughout their secret romance.

Their trip through the Highlands provided only a brief respite
from the difficulties that had plagued their relationship all along. In
late November, Theresa went to the Thelwalls' house in Hull. Yelverton came to visit her in Hull later that fall, and they made plans to
travel through the Continent together at the end of the year. Late in
1857, Yelverton sent Theresa a passport that he had procured in London, telling her to "sign it and (take care with the right name)"—an
instruction that would be extensively analyzed when Yelverton later
claimed that they had never been married.[4] Did he want her to use his
name or her maiden name? Such fragments and phrases would come
back to haunt him.

Their nomadic proclivities were not the only impetus behind their
plans. They thought that Theresa might be pregnant, which would
raise a whole host of issues that would affect their curious, quasi-secret
arrangement. Yelverton was somewhat less eager for her to leave England immediately, advising her to "stay quiet until the first week in
January."[5] He warned her, "[It is] not *quite* certain that I should be able
to follow, and I have something to say to you, in case your fears are
well founded." He hoped—if in fact Theresa *was* pregnant—that she
would terminate the pregnancy, and feared that he would only be able
to persuade her to commit what was then considered a crime in person,
if at all.

He had good reason to anticipate her reluctance, just as Theresa had good reason to feel anxious about her predicament. Since 1837, aborting a fetus at any stage had been declared a criminal offense.[6] The 1861 Offense Against the Person Act would make it a crime punishable by penal servitude to even attempt to procure a miscarriage for someone else.[7] Punishments were justified on several grounds: the harm likely to be done to the woman (anesthetics and disinfectants were rarely used), concern for the fetus, and a fear that acceptance of abortion would lead to greater licentiousness. Of course, these deterrents did not stop abortion from taking place, and the rate of induced abortion increased throughout the second half of the nineteenth century.[8] One Scottish physician practicing in Glasgow in the 1870s said that he knew of nine professional abortionists and could find more if pressed.[9]

Giving birth to a child came with its own extensive risks: almost all women delivered at home, sterilization was not common, and bathing was not recommended for eight days after giving birth, which increased the risk of infection.[10] Beyond these hazards, a child born out of wedlock—as Theresa's child would appear to be—cast a profound shadow of disgrace over its mother. Literature provided abundant examples of women who were outcast—or faced the threat of exile—from respectable society because of an illegitimate pregnancy (Hetty Sorrel from *Adam Bede*, Lady Dedlock from *Bleak House*, Tess from *Tess of the D'Urbervilles*), and real-world society was no less harsh in its treatment of unwed mothers. In an effort to reduce the "profligacy" of young women, the bastardy clause of the 1834 Poor Laws placed full responsibility for the welfare of illegitimate children on their mothers. The law had been amended somewhat in 1844, but the process by which mothers might coerce putative fathers into accepting responsibility for their children was convoluted. The death rate of illegitimate children was double that of legitimate children under the age of one, and unwed mothers were often subject to allegations of infanticide.[11] "No one could tell how many lives of innocent children were sacrificed by the hardheartedness of mothers, in endeavoring to hide their shame," said a judge trying a woman for murdering her newborn son in 1853.[12] It was all too easy to hold women who had already disgraced themselves culpable for additional sins.

Even though he might have been able to evade legal responsibility for the child, Yelverton must have sensed that a pregnancy would not be easily resolved when dealing with a woman like Theresa. Perhaps he hoped merely to delay any decision making by keeping her close at hand. He continued to urge Theresa to postpone the journey until she could be absolutely certain that she was pregnant. "False alarms often do not declare their falsehood before a period." He cautioned that the "cat *must* be kept in the bag just now; for if the fiery devil gets out now, she'll explode a precious magazine and blow us all to the d——l."[13] Theresa had previously written of her strong "resolution in case certain events should occur."[14] She would not suffer through either the ordeal of an abortion or the scandal of giving birth to a child who would be considered illegitimate. In such a scenario, they would have to fully publicize their marriage—an action they had yet to take.

Late in December of 1857 Yelverton wrote to Theresa, "Your *resolution* is founded on false views . . . I have never intentionally deceived you, and have done more than I promised (at great risk)." Sounding eerily like Theresa at her times of deepest despair, he appealed to the secret covenant into which they had entered: "If you break with me, you will never from that moment, have one [day] of even tolerable content during the rest of your life."[15] Despite his forcefulness, Yelverton's letters were not devoid of affection. He addressed her "carissima mia" and "tooi-tooi carissima," invoking a bird that reminded him of her. He reported on his daily life in Edinburgh and reassured her that she was always in his thoughts. "I arrived here [in Edinburgh] in due course, having sat in the coffee room at the Railway Hotel, York from eleven to two, without a single nap, thinking of you, and reading the *Times*," he wrote to her.[16] One evening, he fell asleep sitting before the fire. "[I] dreamt you came and awoke me . . . I never recollect having so real seeming a dream. What do you mean by it? Disturbing my slumber in that way . . . You're a

Edouard Manet, *The Port of Bordeaux.*

dearest darling darling." After signing the letter, he added one last indication of his affection: "I forgot to mention that I wanted you to be with me once since we parted, and that once was ever since."[17]

But, as in so many of their seemingly loving exchanges, the flirtation was inextricable from the power play. Yelverton did not like the idea of spending New Year's Eve at the Thelwalls', which Theresa had suggested, and proposed instead that she come to Edinburgh. "I'll have a cage for you," he told her, a fitting place for the mistress he wished to keep captive. And though he never said it outright (at least in his letters), he was increasingly clear about his reluctance to have a child. "The event we fear could be avoided," he wrote. "And you certainly cannot doubt that it is equally unwelcome to me as it can be to you."[18]

In February of the following year, when they finally embarked on their continental trip, they met in Dunkirk, then traveled through Paris and Rouen, ending their journey in the southwestern town of Bordeaux, where they took rooms in a house owned by a woman named Madame Andre. The elegant port city of wine merchants and traders, with its wide streets, castlelike châteaux, and ornate cathedrals, was built on the Garonne River. Theresa and Yelverton had always gravitated toward towns near water (Istanbul, Naples, Leith), but they may have stopped in Bordeaux out of necessity. Theresa was ill. The end of Yelverton's leave was fast approaching, and so they agreed that she would send for her sister Ellen, who lived relatively nearby, if Theresa got worse after he left. In the meantime, they lived quietly, eager to avoid arousing the suspicions of Madame Andre, who was more inquisitive than their previous landladies.

It is impossible to know whether or not Theresa was actually pregnant when the couple arrived in France, or if she had ever been pregnant. There is no explicit discussion of pregnancy in the surviving letters; nor are there references to her "condition" or other such euphemisms. Theresa, however, allowed a few individuals to form the impression that she was expecting. She wrote a letter to Reverend Mooney to ask him for a copy of their marriage certificate in order to satisfy the conditions for baptism in a foreign country. "Dear Rev. Father," she wrote, "I trust that you have not forgotten the lady who last autumn had the pleasure of making your acquaintance, and to whom you rendered such inestimable service and deeply valued kindness." She continued to flatter him.

> I can never forget you, my dear sir; for in you I recognize one of those true ministers of the Almighty, who tread in the ever charitable, kind and merciful steps of our Saviour, rejecting none who come with a sorrowing heart. You made mine a happy one in your little church of Killowen, last 15th of August, the Feast of Our Lady. In our rambles on the Continent how often we have thought and spoken of that day! I have now an arrival to look forward to; and, finding some little difficulty about the baptism abroad—they require a certificate from the priest who united the parents,—I wish to take my precautions in advance.[19]

She told him Yelverton's last name, which had previously been kept a secret, and asked that he add it to his private register. While he might not yet be a good Catholic, Yelverton, said Theresa, was gradually moving toward the faith: "You will be glad to hear that I have much hopes of my husband."

The obliging Reverend Mooney sent a certificate that declared: "From the book of marriages of the parish church of Killowen, in the diocese of Dromere, in Ireland, it appears that William Charles Yelverton was lawfully joined in matrimony with Marie Theresa Longworth, according to the rites of the Holy Roman Catholic Church, on the 15th of August, 1857; the witnesses being Richard Sloane and Elizabeth Brennan. This I testify."[20]

These letters, of course, do not prove that Theresa was pregnant, and by the spring of 1858—when a child should have arrived—there was no delivery. As one of the judges who later took a critical view of Theresa pointed out, the letter to Reverend Mooney might have been written *after* Theresa had a miscarriage—if, in fact, she had one at all. Mooney's response was dated June 15, 1858, although Theresa claimed that she had written to him in April. Nor did the certificate provided by Reverend Mooney hold much weight when it came under scrutiny. Theresa and Yelverton had insisted that no witnesses observe the ceremony. Elizabeth Brennan, a woman who cleaned the church, might have been just outside the chapel, but this was the first anyone had heard of Richard Sloane. Since no child appeared, Theresa's supposed pregnancy was less important than the reactions it provoked. Theresa's ostensibly maternal instincts—whether feigned or actual—would provide one of her greatest defenses, while Yelverton's criminal suggestions would come back to haunt him.

At the start of April 1858, Yelverton returned to Edinburgh from Bordeaux. He claimed he was miserable at leaving her and that she remained on his mind.

Next time we have to part we must both start to travel in different directions, for the necessity of doing something is naturally a relief to the mind. I began to cry again when in the railway, to the amazement of a *bonne* and two pretty little girls in her charge. One of the latter, a small fairy of about twelve years old, found me out in the fact, and announced it, at the same time wanting to console me. Good-bye, *carissima mia*. Write, or get Madame to do so. *Sempre a te,* Mille baccie, Carlo[21]

He continued to write to her regularly, filling her in on life in Edinburgh—the pups his dog had given birth to, the frost that lingered—and checking on her health. If Theresa responded at all, her replies did not match Yelverton's in their frequency. He grew stern at her reticence, scolding her as she had so often scolded him. "I *must* hear of you," he wrote. "Do not forget that, and do not fancy that I do not care, for I never feign a feeling . . . and what I do feel, if it does not equal the intensity of your wishes and expectations, is perhaps all the more lasting on that account. Recollect that the hardest substances when impressed keep the most lasting impression."[22]

By the end of April, Theresa had still not answered him, and Yelverton began to worry. "Please write me a line to say how you are, I am so afraid you must be worse, as you have not answered my last letters—have you received them? DO write, or make Madame Andre do so."[23] By this time, he had already appealed directly to Madame Andre. She had informed him that Theresa's situation was grave. Yelverton's anxiety and guilt began to grow.

In the first place, send for a nurse at once. That old woman in our old house would do, would she not? If not, tell the doctor to engage you one then send for your sister, if you wish. I have tried to get leave, but have not succeeded; still, if you would rather that I should come, you must make your doctor write a few lines *that I can show*; and just write at the end of his ("pray come, I am no better"). He must not speak of you otherwise than as my relation, or I dare not show the letter, and cannot get leave without . . . it. Make him write to me *privately*.[24]

Yelverton's concern was justified. Theresa's health was rapidly declining, and Madame Andre, increasingly suspicious of the single (possibly pregnant) woman who had been abandoned, was of little help. Theresa wrote to her sister Ellen Lefebvre, who tracked down the location of Madame Andre's boardinghouse. When she arrived, Lefebvre asked for Miss Longworth. There was no such person staying at the house, Madame Andre replied, only an Englishwoman whose husband had left several weeks ago.

"Then it is not my sister," Lefebvre said. "My sister is not married." Madame Andre brought her inside and showed her Theresa, who was lying in bed. Theresa could not see her sister and the landlady enter the room; her eyes were infected and swollen shut. The dirty sheets were twisted around her, and the room was hot and airless. Lefebvre caught her breath and ushered her husband's brother into the room. Together they lifted Theresa from the bed and packed the few belongings she had brought with her. Madame Andre stood by the door, watching with folded arms. With the help of her brother-in-law, Lefebvre moved Theresa to a hotel and then to her house in Boulogne. Theresa was so weak that she had to be carried from carriage to carriage.[25]

Theresa's sister wrote to Yelverton to tell him that she had taken Theresa to her home to nurse her back to health. According to Lefebvre, Theresa had lost the use of almost all of the right side of her body.[26] "Please tell your sister how very much I am obliged to her for the bulletins she so kindly sent to me," Yelverton responded via Theresa. "I hope she will continue to act as your amanuensis until you feel able to write yourself, as I still feel very anxious on your account."[27] He was not unaware of the blame he shouldered, but he was unwilling to make amends. The real fault lay with Madame Andre, who had seemed such a charming proprietress but had refused to aid Theresa in her illness. "What a she devil that Bordeaux woman is!" Yelverton wrote. "I can hardly believe it possible, when I think of her smoothly affectionate manner. Perhaps it is fortunate that I could not go to you, as I certainly should have abused her, and probably caused a commotion in the house, which would not have been good for you."[28]

In Boulogne, Theresa was slowly recovering. Some days, she may even have felt strong enough to walk along the docks of the harbor, look out over the fishermen at the white-capped waves, and remember the Channel passage that had changed her life six years ago. She had trusted the water, believing that it would breach the divisions between the lovers. But now, the benevolence of the Channel seemed dubious; it was more like a yawning chasm that would seal her in solitude.

Yelverton waited for a letter from Lefebvre, but the next missive he received was from Theresa. It was perhaps the saddest of their correspondence, revealing the desperate position in which he had left her. While his solicitous inquiries about her health might have been motivated by genuine affection, they did not diminish the fact of his absence during her struggle. Her illness had left her temporarily blind, but it had clarified her vision in other ways. Her sister, not Yelverton, had been the one who had protected her from the insinuations of Madame Andre and restored her health. Throughout her life, her friends and lovers had been as important to her as her family; but it was her family who came to her defense when she most needed protecting. It went without saying that she would forgive Yelverton, but he must acknowledge the severity of his misconduct.

> There is now no need of excuses, or disguising of facts, which medical men who have attended me have confirmed. Neither was the malady a *slight* one, as you are trying to persuade yourself. My sister is witness, and you may be convinced by coming to see the wreck I now am. I shall not *die*, as you say! She has saved me; but it is somewhat hard to lose health, eyesight and every beauty in the prime of life.

Although incapacitated by her illness, she was emboldened by the ordeal and suggested, in a mix of despair and hope, that Yelverton finally reveal to his mother, if not the wider world, that he had broken his promise to his uncle and had married.

Surely she will forgive, and help you. She has a mother's heart, and a clever head. Do not, in the hope of patching matters up, throw away our last chance of united happiness. Events have rushed so swift to a crisis it is not possible to stem the tide. We must cling fast together or we shall be lost to each other. Our past cannot be reacted in the future. Do not for the sake of a mere chimera give up a real life long enjoyment. You have already broke the *spirit* of your promise. What is the bare letter good for; I do not ask you to rush on to immediate ruin; but your mother will keep the secret for your sake.

She had surrendered her hopes for a warm welcome into the Avonmore clan, but she would not suffer through accusations like the ones she had endured in Bordeaux. "Imputations in open courts upon my fair fame as a woman are not to be borne," she told Yelverton with chilling foresight. "That vile thing wanted to make a claim on the plea that you had deceived her and introduced an improper person into her house in order to abandon her. Imagine if you can the misery I have gone through—think of your own sister in such a position."

Her determination, however, was coupled with profound uncertainty. How could the man to whom she had devoted years of her life leave her in such a state? Could this secrecy continue? And what would become of her if it did?

You think, perhaps, that it would be better for us to keep apart for a long, long time, until circumstances remedy themselves? This may be wise, but it is very hard. Even now time hangs like an *incubus* upon me. *Tempus fugit* seems a fallacy. I should be tempting you to come over, only I am so very ugly that you could not love to look at me. It is strange you do not miss me more. We have never lived together long sufficiently.

The only thing she had to look forward to was Yelverton's letters. "I often lie awake from daylight waiting for the postman," she wrote. She ended her letter with a plea.

Caro mia, think at least of the happiness we have known together—
so entire so unbounded. Is there any other joy in the world to be
compared to reciprocated love? [Everything] on earth became in-
different but our two selves! You said I was the dearest small *Tooi-
Tooi* that ever lived, and I thought there was not in the wide world
another *Carlo* like mine.[29]

She signed it with uncharacteristic, declarative formality: Theresa
Yelverton.

Theresa waited for an answer and heard nothing. Yelverton, in the
meantime, was continuing life as usual in Edinburgh, and—despite his
ostensibly concerned letters during her isolation in Bordeaux—was
seemingly untroubled by Theresa's distant struggles. Early in June, he
encountered Mrs. Stalker, Theresa's former landlady, on Albany Street
while he was riding on horseback. He told her that he had delivered a
present to her house: two candlesticks from the south of France.
Stalker asked if they were from Mrs. Yelverton. Yelverton balked and
asked to speak to Stalker privately. He was not married to Theresa, he
told her.

"I ought to have told you that long before, but was afraid it would
bring evil to you of your house," said Yelverton, according to Stalker's later testimony.[30]

"God Bless me, she was a lady," said Stalker. "Why did you bring
a lady here and behave so to her? For she was a lady, and if you
wanted a woman, you might have had another, and not ruined her."

Yelverton agreed but did not apologize. Stalker asked where
Theresa was now, and Yelverton replied that she was still in France,
was very ill, and that it was doubtful that she would live. Stalker an-
grily told Yelverton that he had broken the laws of God and man. He
knew not about the laws of God, he replied. But he knew the laws of
men, he said with a laugh, and departed.[31]

When Theresa had sufficiently recovered, she made her way back
to Edinburgh, where, on June 25, she met with Yelverton at the Ship
Hotel in Leith. He told her his position was more uncertain than ever
before and urged her to go to live with her brother Jack in New Zea-

land until he was able to secure his finances. Theresa refused, and Yelverton urged her to at least leave Edinburgh. "You must go to Glasgow," he told her the next day in a note. His brother would meet her, and they would devise a plan from there. Yelverton even suggested—after professing such genuine-seeming care and affection during her illness—that she might captivate another, wealthier man and live a happier, more stable life. On June 26, Yelverton's brother visited Theresa and urged her to come with him to Glasgow, saying that Yelverton was already waiting there. The claim was a blatant lie. Earlier that very same day, Yelverton had married a woman whom he had been courting for months.

At the same time that he was writing grateful notes to Theresa's sister and sending Theresa his wishes for her speedy recovery, Yelverton had been pursuing Emily Marianne Ashworth Forbes. What little is known about Emily Forbes—born in 1825, the daughter of a Sir Charles Ashworth and Mary Anne Rooke—is due to her first marriage to Edward Forbes, a botanist and geologist renowned for his studies of the marine creatures surrounding the British Isles. Although Edward Forbes did not marry until he was thirty-three, he, unlike Yelverton, longed for a wife. "Surround a bachelor with every possible comfort . . . feed him among the luxuries and comforts of the snuggest of clubs, do all these things and more for him and he will nevertheless be unhappy."[32] When he met Emily Ashworth, he was smitten, and convinced her to abandon her plans to sail for Canada and to marry him instead.

She became a willing companion on his travels. In a cottage in Llangollen, she tended the cabbage patch while he went out on his daily expeditions. "I have every reason to be more and more pleased with her every day," he wrote to a friend.[33] Forbes's friends were not as pleased with his new domestic bliss. Charles Darwin wrote to the botanist J. D. Hooker to lament the passing of an era: "I . . . grieve to think I shall have no more of the old *bachelor* parties."[34] Forbes's pleasure, however, continued unabated: "It is now above a year since I have tasted the happy cup of matrimony, and have found it grown sweeter every day."[35]

In the early 1840s, Forbes took a job with the Geological Survey in order to secure his finances, but his ultimate desire was to retire someplace where he could think uninterrupted.[36] In 1853 he became the president of the Geological Society of London and a year later he became a professor of natural history at the University of Edinburgh, a position he had long coveted. He was only to enjoy the post for a few months before he passed away in November of the same year.[37]

Emily had some money of her own, but whatever her financial assets at the time of her husband's death, they could not have been so great as to overwhelm all other considerations. Other forces of attraction were at work between her and Yelverton, evidenced by the birth of a child only seven and a half months after their wedding. Adhering to family tradition—the same family that had supposedly forbade Yelverton from marrying and having children—they called their first child Barry Nugent Yelverton. Emily was not an obvious match for Yelverton. She had several children from her marriage to Forbes, and according to Forbes's friends, she was not an affable woman. Darwin "did not like what little [he] saw of her" and agreed with Hooker's assessment that she was "cold, unsympathetic."[38] When the geologist Sir Archibald Geikie took over the writing of Edward Forbes's biography (the original author having passed away), Emily insisted that he return all the materials she had previously lent to the project.[39] (*The Memoir of Edward Forbes* was eventually published in 1861.)

But Yelverton seems to have genuinely cared for Emily, and strangely—or perhaps just hypocritically—to have had no qualms about committing to her. He never attempted to hide this marriage, and he remained married to her until he died. The marriage took place in the Episcopal Trinity Chapel, a church by the sea, just a few miles from Edinburgh, and was publicized in the conventional manner.[40] Yelverton later claimed he could not remember the name of the church where the ceremony took place, but what he lacked in sentiment, he made up for with open acknowledgment of the union, reversing the attitude he had held toward Theresa throughout their affair.

Yelverton's brother wrote to Theresa the day after the wedding, again urging her to go to Glasgow and telling her that "this present storm must be allowed to blow over." Theresa was confused but unshaken. "My dear Sir," she wrote. "If you would kindly inform me of the true motive of Mr. Yelverton's sudden and extraordinary conduct, also the nature of the storm which you say must be allowed to blow over, I should not doubt your friendly intentions toward me. But so long as I am kept in the dark on this point I can not form any views or plans for the future."[41]

Theresa did not go to New Zealand. She did not go even so far as Glasgow, so it did not take long for her to discover what had happened. When she visited Mrs. Stalker, her old landlady confirmed the terrible truth by telling Theresa about her interaction with Yelverton earlier that month.[42] Although Theresa still had not fully recovered from her illness, she took immediate action. She had spent years appealing to Yelverton's sense of duty and obligation to no avail, so she did not bother tapping those apparently dry wells now. On July 1, responding to a telegram they had received the previous day, Theresa's sister Sara and her lawyer husband Mr. Bellamy arrived in Edinburgh. Theresa appealed to the public prosecutor of Edinburgh and accused Yelverton of bigamy on the basis of the Irish marriage.[43] Yelverton was suspended from the military.

Since the legal power of women in nineteenth-century Britain was more limited, in many respects, for married women than for single-women, Theresa found herself in a tricky position. Asserting her marriage would immediately limit her legal rights. When a woman marries, the reformer Barbara Bodichon wrote, "the law immediately steps in, and she finds her self legislated for, and her condition of life suddenly and entirely changed . . . She loses her separate existence, and is merged in that of her husband."[44] In 1858, when Theresa was assessing her situation, a married woman did not retain control of either the assets with which she entered the marriage or her subsequent earnings. She became a *femme covert*, a woman with no separate legal status, who could only act under the guidance of her husband.[45] She could not bring legal action before a court unless her husband's name was joined with hers, and she could not testify against her husband. So how was a woman whose "husband" denied her status as his wife meant to proceed in a court of law?

Theresa was going to have to tread very carefully if she was to avoid discrediting her own arguments before she even began them. Merely seeking evidence violated the wishes of her supposed husband and could be held against her. If she was not directly violating the law by bringing suit, she was at least asserting herself contrarily to the wishes of her husband. A married woman, wrote the writer and reformer Francis Power Cobbe, was taught that her "whole life and being, her soul, body, time, property, thought, and care, ought to be given to her husband; that nothing short of absorption in him and his interests make her a true wife."[46] A man and his wife were "one person in law," according to the eighteenth-century lawyer William Blackstone, and that one person was the husband.[47] Her effort to prove herself a wife would make her less of a wife in the eyes of the law. The standards by which she would legitimate her position would require finesse.

In the months after Yelverton's marriage to Emily Forbes, Theresa and Yelverton communicated through the courts. Yelverton countered Theresa's accusation of bigamy in Edinburgh by asking for a legal declaration stating that he was not married to Theresa. Theresa responded with her own plea that the court deliver a decision regarding her marriage. In 1860, the Scottish court combined the cases and delayed them. In the meantime, Theresa applied to the newly created Court for Divorce and Matrimonial Causes in England for restitution of conjugal rights. But again, Theresa found herself in an unfortunate position. Because Yelverton was an Irish citizen and had never really lived in England, the court had no jurisdiction regarding his affairs. Although she was English, if Theresa was assumed to be Yelverton's wife, she had no domicile of her own, and so her case would not fall under the jurisdiction of the English court either.[48]

For almost two years, as these cases started then stalled, Theresa and Yelverton traveled between Edinburgh, London, and Ireland, independently retracing their path and gathering evidence that would support their respective positions. Yelverton and his attorney made their first trip to Ireland almost immediately after the marriage to Emily Forbes. He returned to the places he had visited with Theresa and even saw Reverend Mooney from a distance at a railway station.

Later that autumn, with another lawyer, Henry Dwyer, Yelverton returned to the villages in Ireland with a lock of hair cut from the head of a six-year-old child and a scrap of fabric from a dress. The lock of hair, similar in color to Theresa's, and the swatch of fabric were meant to "point out to people what sort of person [his interviewees] had to describe" and to confirm that she had stayed at the hotel.[49] Yelverton knew it would be impossible to deny his connection to Theresa, so he wanted to establish that she had entered situations that would compromise her claims of virtue and chastity—the foundations of her credibility. The props served their purpose. Rose Fagan, a chambermaid who had briefly worked in the Malahide Hotel in 1857, told Yelverton and his lawyer that she remembered a woman with fair hair who had visited the hotel two years previously.[50] Yelverton and his lawyer visited other hotels, examined the registers, produced bills, and built their case.

Theresa also began evidence-gathering excursions, aware that the impressions of innkeepers and maids would be critical if the case ever came to trial. An assistant, Emma Friedland Crabbe, was hired in January of 1859, to be Theresa's "companion," for a salary of fifty pounds a year.[51] At first the responsibilities—accompanying Theresa on her trips between Edinburgh and London—were mundane, intended to stave off further risks to her reputation. (Arabella MacFarlane was no longer available to play the role of informal chaperone, having entered a convent in Edinburgh.) But Theresa had never had much use for female companionship, and there were more important things to which Crabbe could attend. She sent Crabbe to Leith to observe Yelverton. On three occasions Crabbe and Yelverton even spoke directly, although nothing of consequence appears to have passed during their conversations.

Crabbe was then dispatched to track down Rose Fagan, who had

left the Malahide Hotel and was living with her brother in Rathcof-
fey, near Kildare. She asked if two men had visited Fagan and offered
a bribe concerning a certain female guest from two years earlier.
Fagan remembered the two men but, suspecting some "rascality
[from them] in wishing her to remember" the woman who had stayed
at the hotel years before, she denied taking any bribe.[52] Crabbe then
visited a hotel maid named Bridget (Biddy) Cole, who told Crabbe
that she remembered making up one bed for a lady and a gentleman
who had visited the hotel a year and half earlier. According to Cole's
later testimony, Crabbe quickly responded with an excuse for the im-
modest sleeping arrangement; the gentleman suffered from an illness
that forced him to sleep upright, and he usually spent the night in a
chair. Crabbe made her way through Ireland and the Highlands, lining up women who would back Theresa's story.

At some point in the midst of evidence hunting, Theresa realized
that a direct attack upon Yelverton was unlikely to yield the result she
wanted. Her accusations of bigamy had caused Yelverton's dismissal
from the Royal Artillery in the summer of 1858, but little else. She
decided instead to relinquish her position as the righteous wife and assume the mantle of the deserted wife. Women in this position were
considered married but had slightly more legal recourse than the average married woman, particularly with respect to property disputes—
a common, if not always an easy, path to judicial intervention.[53]
Abandoned wives often filed suits for restitution of conjugal rights
that—if successful—mandated cohabitation and an allowance for the
wife. Since the wife was entitled to interim alimony as soon as the petition was filed, financial security was often a primary motivation.[54]

Theresa did not seem to care about money, but she found her
standing through it. In February of 1860, Yelverton agreed to pay a
tradesman, Mr. Grant, for dresses that Theresa had purchased. His
counsel assured him that the debt could be squared away without
entering into the status of his relationship with Theresa. This was the
first concession Yelverton had made since abandoning Theresa, and
she must have sensed that she had found an indirect route to the outcome she desired. She would reenter respectable society not by dem-

onstrating that Yelverton was her husband, but by proving that—as her husband—he was financially responsible for her. When newly married women lost control of their property, the argument went, they gained the protection of their husband, who became responsible for their financial well-being and solvency. A strategy was hatched: the sacrifices of married women, and the recompense they implied, would deliver her redemption.

CHAPTER FOUR

The Dublin Trial

*For its own sake . . . the world should throw open all its
avenues to the passport of a woman's bleeding heart.*

—Nathaniel Hawthorne, *The Blithedale Romance* (1852)

In January 1861, word spread through Dublin that an Irish aristocrat had been accused of bigamy. He had carried on a secret correspondence with the woman who now called herself his first wife,
had met her in cloistered convents and sultry harems as the Crimean
War raged. There had been gallivanting rides though the Scottish
Highlands and recurring passages across the English Channel. Mur-
mured conversations and market-stall gossip circulated the story, each
layer of secrecy making it more irresistible. A few Dubliners claimed
to have seen the abandoned first wife walking through the streets, dif-
fidence echoing in her footsteps.

On February 21, 1861, when the trial of *Thelwall v. Yelverton* began, the entrance to the Four Courts in Dublin was packed. The
Court of Common Pleas, one quarter of the Four Courts, filled with
observers in the early hours of the morning, and the overflow stood
in the copper-domed foyer, straining to hear if the trial had begun.
The room grew warm, snowflakes melting into pearly drops on coat

The Four Courts, Dublin.

lapels. Outside, walking along the Liffey, ignorant passersby saw the crowd spilling out onto the arcaded front passage and wondered what was going on inside.

At nine in the morning, Sergeant Edward Sullivan, officially representing John Thelwall, stated the case. "The action," he said, "rested on the well-settled principle of law that if a husband turned his wife out of doors without cause he sent her into the world as his accredited agent, and he was responsible for her reasonable support." Yelverton owed Thelwall 259 pounds 17 shillings and 3 pence, the sum of Theresa's expenses during two recent visits. The charges issued by Thelwall included board for Theresa and her maid, use of a horse and carriage, payments for washing, the purchase of a hat, and medical bills.[1] Because there was no question that Yelverton—in line for the Irish peerage—resided in Ireland, the Irish court had jurisdiction over the matter.[2]

Despite the mundane litany of expenses, "this was not an ordinary kind of case"—no banal property dispute—Sullivan stated. In this case, "the relationship of the defendant, as the husband of the woman to whom the goods and necessaries were supplied, was disputed." This woman, he said, had been "mercilessly abandoned." Her husband had "driven her on the world without the means of support." Money was only the immediate point of contention upon which the larger issues—Theresa's status and honor, the substance of marriage, the tangled effects of love gone awry—rested. The cause of the plaintiff, Sullivan boldly stated, was "the cause of virtue"; much more than £260 was at stake.[3] From its first day, the trial became a public melodrama, indulging in the trademarks of the genre: extremes of emotion, moral polarization, villainy, extravagant expression, and suspense. The entertainment—the best to be found in Dublin for those ten days—was both high and low: deep spiritual matters would be examined; scandalous stories would titillate.

As exceptional as Sullivan wanted to make it seem, the Yelverton trial—with its crowds of observers, thorough coverage in the newspapers, high-flung rhetoric, and subsequent literary spin-offs—was an example of trends that had recently changed the public face of justice. In the early part of the nineteenth century, punishment centered on the scaffold and public executions. By midcentury, however, the large vengeful crowds that gathered around the gallows were beginning to seem uncouth and dangerous to bourgeois observers. The increasingly vocal middle class was concerned that spectators had lost track of the significance behind public punishment, overwhelmed by titillation. At public hangings at Newgate Prison, critics complained of the multitudes of onlookers, "it is the spectacle, the spectacle purely, that they love."[4]

As the number of outdoor executions and punishments declined, the crowds began to move indoors and participate in the earlier judicial processes. Large courthouses, such as the Manchester Assize Courts (built in 1864) and the Royal Courts of Justice (built in 1882) accommodated observers, who were still seen as crucial public guardians of justice. As the judges in *Rex v. Wright* (1832) had declared, "It is of vast importance to the public that the proceedings of the Courts of Justice should be universally known."[5] Thirty years later, the atti-

The interior of the Four Courts.

tude toward the crowds at the Four Courts in Dublin was no different. "An immense crowd of respectable persons filled the court to capacity," wrote one reporter, careful to call the crowd "respectable," not threatening or unruly—attributes that had made the scaffold-scanning hordes seem lately unappealing. "The galleries, the side benches, and approaches were thronged to excess" with citizen-watchdogs of innocence and guilt.[6]

For those who could not squeeze into the courtroom or the Four Courts' hall, newspapers recorded the proceedings. The Yelverton case might not have received any attention in the first half of the nineteenth century, but now this type of case had become a mainstay of the press's coverage. With the end of the Napoleonic wars, battles on the seas were replaced by skirmishes on the streets, murders in mansions, and courtroom trials. Urban and domestic violence sold papers, and the burgeoning newspaper industry needed the income. The *Newgate Calendar*, a monthly bulletin of sensational crimes "that made the blood run cold; of secret murders that had been committed by the lonely wayside; of bodies hidden from the eye of man in deep pits and wells," as Charles Dickens described it in *Oliver Twist*, was common reading material.[7] The young Dickens was just one of many reporters sent daily to observe the goings-on at Chancery and lesser courts.

Each newspaper that covered *Thelwall* claimed to deliver a precise account of the events as they unfolded. For the most part, only slight

EDWARD BEAZLEY,

WHIPPED FOR DESTROYING WOMEN'S APPAREL.

UNTIL the severe examples made of this boy, females often found their clothes drop to tatters, and such as restricted themselves to mere muslin and chemise were frequently dreadfully burnt, in a way invisible, and almost unaccountable. A set of urchins, neither men nor boys, by way of a 'high game,' procured aqua-fortis, vitriol, and other corrosive liquids, and, filling therewith a syringe, or bottle, would sally forth to give the girls ' *a squirt.*'

Of this mischievous description we find Edward Beazley, who was convicted of this unpardonable offence at the Old Bailey, the 11th of March, 1811.

He was indicted for wilfully and maliciously injuring and destroying the apparel of Anne Parker, which she was wearing, by feloniously throwing upon the same a certain poisonous substance, called aqua-fortis, whereby the same was so injured as to be rendered useless and of no value.

He was also charged upon two other indictments for the like offence, on the prosecution of two other women.

It appeared that the prisoner, a little boy about thirteen years old, took it into his head to sally into Fleet Street, on the night of Saturday, February 16, and there threw the same upon the clothes of several of the Cyprians who parade up and down there. He was caught, carried before the sitting magistrate at Guildhall, and fully committed on three several charges.

Three ladies appeared, and proved the facts stated in the indictments, and exhibited their burnt garments, such as pelisses, gowns, and other articles, which were literally burnt to riddles.

He was found Guilty.

His master, Mr. Blades, and an eminent chymist on Ludgate Hill, gave him a good character for honesty; he never knew any thing wrong of him before; but he acknowledged that he had access to both vitriol and aqua-fortis.

The Court having a discretionary power under the act of parliament, instead of transporting him for seven years, only ordered him to be well whipped in the gaol, after which he was returned to his friends.

MARY GREEN,

CONVICTED OF PUTTING OFF BASE COIN.

COINERS of base money employ low people to go from shop to shop to put off their counterfeits; and in doing this every stratagem that can be devised is employed. One of these tricks is to ask change for a good dollar; and, in counting the shillings given for it, they secrete one or more of them, and substitute counterfeits. Then they pretend that part of their change is bad; and the tradesman, unconscious of the deception, takes their base coin,

and gives them good money in return. This the rogues, among each other, call ' ringing the changes.'

At the Sessions for Middlesex, held the 5th of April, 1811, Mary Green, a decent-looking girl, was found guilty of putting off two bad shillings to Mr. Harris, a linen-draper, in Pickett Street, Temple Bar.

She went into Mr. Harris's shop, and asked for small silver for a dollar; Mr. Harris gave it her. She walked two or three yards up the

A page from the *Newgate Calendar*, a record of sensational crimes.

variations distinguished the different versions, except when it came to editorial introductions. Despite their faithfulness to the spoken substance of the trial, the reporters made little attempt to temper the tenor of their prose in these sections. "In the following pages we present the public with a full account of one of the most memorable and important trials it has been our lot to read." This was a trial that, "for the extraordinary amount of interest taken in it, and the importance of the principles it involved, has never, we believe, been surpassed, if even equaled . . . Among all the *causes celebres* taken down, we venture to say, not one of them will bear comparison, in the importance of its character, with the trial which has just been concluded in the Court of Common Pleas."[8]

Nor was there much effort to maintain neutrality toward the parties involved. Twenty-six-year-old Theresa was the clear favorite. She had a "dignified and lady-like manner" and was "a lady of superior attainments," embodying female beauty as depicted by the Renaissance masters: "thorough blonde, with that rich and glowing golden hue in which Titian and the painters of his school used to portray their ideal beauties." Theresa's blondness—a stereotype of Victorian purity—combined with the generally laudatory tone of the description seemed to overwhelm the potentially damaging fleshly implications of the Titian comparison. While her features betrayed the experience she had endured—the "harrowing and distressing workings of her soul"—they were revived "when lit by the higher sentiments of her womanly nature." Most important, she was discreetly attired, wearing a modest black silk dress, a velvet mantilla, and mauve-colored gloves.[9]

Yelverton, on the other hand, received no recommendation through his features. His physiognomy—a crucial measure of moral worth in the Victorian era—betrayed his rapaciousness. "His mouth is well shaped and rather voluptuous, clearly evidence of his strong passions." Like fictional villains of the time, Yelverton advertised his sinful tendencies on his face. Strong passions boded not only brutishness but also, as Coventry Patmore warned in *The Angel in the House*, "weak will."[10] As the minister Isaac Taylor had written in *Self-Cultivation*,

"The main source of the miseries of human life is ungoverned passions."[11] Reporters stopped short of depicting Yelverton with a cape
and cane, although illustrators did give him in a mustache. They did
not condemn the more average aspects of his appearance—his medium height, slender build, and brown hair, rather "thin on the crown
of the head"—but they reviled his composure; "nothing could sur-
pass the self-possession, and deliberation with which he gave his
evidence." Unflappability would not win him any supporters; his calmness while delivering those "revolting" portions had "caused a thrill of
horror to run through the court."[12] Ice water, it seemed, had replaced
his blood.

The newspapers' rhetoric was fueled by the evocative liberties
taken by the lawyers. More than ever before, lawyers in the mid-
nineteenth century had become storytellers. Early in the 1830s,
criminals were generally not given legal counsel, and the average
trial lasted a total of thirty minutes.[13] With the passing of the Prisoner's Council Act of 1836, defendants in criminal trials gained
full representation. Lawyers now had much more freedom in their
speeches—permission not only to present the facts, but to probe the
origins of their clients' transgression in order to make them sympathetic to the judge and jury. The shift affected noncriminal trials as
well.

To some extent, the increased prominence of interior motives in
the courtroom was a response to literature that explored the psychol-
ogy of characters who had previously remained obscure. Novelists
who had spent time in courtrooms, such as Charles Dickens and
Wilkie Collins, believed that imagination, as well as juridical process, was necessary to whittle out the truth of the human condition,
and they said so in their novels. The law fell short when it was "still
the pre-engaged servant of the long purse," wrote Collins in the preface to *The Woman in White*. The full story was "left to be told, for the
first time," in the novel.[14] As readers began to expect and appreciate
more fully formed characters in fiction, they desired the same dimen-
sion in their real-life villains, victims, and heroes. Indirectly, lawyers

responded, fleshing out the people they were defending or accusing with histories and inner lives.

If the Yelverton case followed contemporary trends in the spectacle it provided to the public, the detailed and florid reportage it engendered, and the cultivation of courtroom narrative, there was one way in which the trial was unique. Lawyers regularly borrowed the techniques of novelists, and novelists borrowed characters from the courts, but this was perhaps the first time that the central evidence so closely resembled fiction. The correspondence was not quite an epistolary novel—Yelverton and Theresa *had* exchanged these letters—but the colorful trajectory of the love affair and the coded meanings of their words gave their exchange a distinctly literary feel. This aspect of the evidence was both a blessing and a curse. Private passions did not translate to clear-cut answers, but the interpretive latitude that the letters allowed gave the lawyers space in which to spin their tales.

Edward Sullivan, the lawyer ostensibly representing the plaintiff, John Thelwall, but really arguing on behalf of Theresa, was up to the task. He was born in Cork and educated at the same school that Barry Yelverton (Yelverton's great-grandfather) had attended several decades earlier, and then Trinity College, Dublin. In 1858 he became a queen's counsel and in 1860 a sergeant at law, the only level of attorney who could argue before the Court of Common Pleas. He was made attorney general for Ireland under William Gladstone's first administration, and he remained a trusted adviser to Gladstone throughout his tenure.[15] In 1881, Gladstone rewarded him for his years of service with the title of baronet. He was an erudite as well as politically minded man, amassing a large and valuable library.[16]

Sullivan's oratorical skill and literary interests (he would quote Shakespeare among other canonical texts in the course of his argument) served him well. His objective was to prove that Theresa was virtuous and Yelverton was villainous—a goal that suited the Manichaean simplifications to which the press was inclined. He would grudgingly accept certain nuances but generally adhered to the innocent-heroine-versus-traitorous-villain theme. The timing of the unfolding of this dynamic was critical; too early a description of Yelverton's misdeeds might remind his audience that Theresa had participated in the activities that he hoped would incriminate Yelverton. So Sullivan emphasized the letters that underlined Theresa's ordeal. When they first met, Theresa was "a lovely and accomplished girl . . . as lovely a woman as ever breathed the breath of life," he said in his opening statement. But now, "she was changed. Her cheek was paler and thinner than it should be for one so young."[17] Her suffering had become her stigmata.

Theresa's demise, however, would not win her any supporters if it seemed as though she had brought it upon herself. If *that* was the case, she was little better than a prostitute, a woman who had made poor decisions, but with knowledge of their consequences, deserving of sympathy perhaps, but not recompense. Her experience would not have been unique. As the novelist and journalist Bracebridge Hemyng had written in an essay, a soldier who "cannot afford to employ professional women to gratify his passions" would often "form an intimacy" with a woman who would "cost him nothing, but the trouble of taking her about occasionally, and who, whatever else she may do, will never by any chance infect."[18] The judge and jury, Sullivan realized, needed to believe that Yelverton's nefarious influence was the only reason that this woman had ended up in such a dubious, and apparently common, position.

Ambition—a desire to marry upward—was another potential blemish upon Theresa's reputation, so Sullivan set out to disparage impending accusations. "The defendant was a man of noble family, the heir apparent to the peerage of Avonmore," Sullivan acknowledged. But Theresa "was also of gentle blood," he asserted. "She belonged to an ancient and honorable family," he claimed, repeatedly reminding his audience that Theresa "always moved in the first society."[19] Her family did not possess the pedigree of the Yelverton clan, but the press accepted Sullivan's sketchy but estimable version of the Longworth history. A pamphlet published at the time of the trial claimed that the Longworth family was a most ancient one and highly respectable; and certainly would not sully the name or contaminate the blood of the oldest and noblest peerage in the realm, whatever may be the opinion of the Hon. William Charles Major Yelverton to the contrary. True, the Longworth's [*sic*] of Manchester . . . were tradesmen, but their business was quite as respectable as that of a foreign adventurer, or as that of a butcher or any other tradesman.[20]

The virtues of the middle classes were well established by this time—at least to those who valued political economy and personal responsibility. The "honorable" William Charles Yelverton might possess a title, but Theresa's family had shown hard work and industry, lauded characteristics in the age of progress.

If there was any lingering unease among the spectators about Theresa's origins, her religious devotion was offered as additional evidence of her moral character. "A more sincere or devoted member of [the Catholic Church] never existed than Theresa Yelverton," Sullivan stated, underlining her similarity to the largely Catholic crowd. "Her moral principle and sense of religion were so strong that no inducement could make her yield from her determination [other] than a priest of that religion which she professed should unite her in marriage." As Yelverton continued to insist upon secrecy, it was her "religious feeling" that made the ambiguity of her union unbearable.[21]

On top of this, Theresa's selflessness and self-respect further testified to her character. Her suffering stemmed not only from her own discomfort, Sullivan asserted, but also from the burden of obligation she felt toward others. When she believed herself to be pregnant, "she told [Yelverton] she had also a duty towards the child of which she was about to become the mother—that she had a duty towards society, towards her mother . . . towards a long line of ancestors whose name was never tarnished by disgrace."[22] Respect for family and motherhood—the natural concerns for a woman—had driven her decisions.

Sullivan's argument was punctuated by reminders that the outcome of the trial stretched beyond the few lives that were intimately involved. The trial was a test not only of one woman's honor, but also of the sexual standards that kept society stable by containing male impulse. It was the responsibility of the male jury to uphold the honor of their sex by protecting the weaker, to prevent marriage—that central institution in Victorian society—from becoming "the trick of libertines."[23] Sullivan addressed not just the jury but the spectators who lined the galleries and the side benches. "The execration of every man," Sullivan insisted, would hound Yelverton from the court if the crimes he admitted were the truth.[24] Yelverton's abandonment was an act, Sullivan claimed, slightly misquoting *Hamlet*,

> *As blurs the grace and blush of modesty;*
> *Makes virtue hypocrite; takes off the rose*
> *From the fair forehead of an innocent love,*
> *And sets a blister there: making*
> *Marriage vows as false as dicer's oaths, and*
> *Sweet religion makes a rhapsody of words.*[25]

A raving Hamlet directed these words at his mother, but the context was less important than the effect. In the face of such crimes against modesty, virtue, innocence, marriage, and religion, the validation of Mrs. Yelverton (as Sullivan referred to Theresa) "would earn the approbation of every honest man."[26] This was a trial of every woman and every man.

The same day that Sullivan delivered his opening address, Theresa took the stand. "My maiden name was Theresa Longworth," she began; "I was born in Chetwood, in Lancashire." She related the familiar story to the jury: the meeting on the steamer, the seductive correspondence, the two marriage ceremonies. As she told her tale, she knew which attributes of her behavior she should emphasize (her chastity before marriage and wifely behavior after) and those she should suppress (her vivacity, her adventurousness). After the Edinburgh marriage, which she claimed was not valid in her mind, she "did not consent to live with him as his wife"; "he wished to go to some hotel round Edinburgh, and that he would recognize me as his wife, and I refused," believing "it would be a sin to live together as man and wife except married by a Catholic priest."[27]

Once married by Father Mooney, however, Theresa showed her obedience to Yelverton's demands like the dutiful wife she believed herself to be. She revealed her marriage only to people Yelverton had approved as trustworthy confidants. She fully embraced financial self-abnegation, offering him her not-insignificant allowance (a few hundred pounds a year, a comparable income to that of doctors and barristers) from her father's bequest, and was willing to hand over any additional money she came across. At their last meeting in Edinburgh, when Yelverton reported that he was a "ruined man," she told the Dublin courtroom that she had pledged to "make any sacrifice" for his sake.[28]

Theresa knew she must temper the vivacity of her character with feminine weakness when she appeared in the Four Courts. Had she seemed determined to punish Yelverton, the impression of passive victimhood would have collapsed; had she seemed vindictive or bitter, her narrative of devotion would have seemed disingenuous. She assured the audience of her vulnerability on the second day of the trial when, spotting Yelverton across the courtroom, she began to tremble violently. She swooned; the crowd gasped. It was too much for Theresa to bear, her lawyer interjected, asking that the defendant leave the courtroom. The judge said Yelverton was under no obligation to do so, but Yelverton's lawyer encouraged him to go. "The witness [Theresa] was unable to answer Mr. James Whiteside [her lawyer] for some moments, owing to her continued trembling," wrote one observer.[29] She needed protectors, it seemed, to shield her from Yelverton's lascivious gaze and the memories of her mistreatment.

In addition to Sullivan (officially acting on Thelwall's behalf), Theresa's lawyer, James Whiteside, was one such protector. Like Sullivan, Whiteside had rapidly ascended throughout his career, becoming famous for his rousing defense of the Catholic liberator Daniel O'Connell in 1844, and serving stints as both solicitor general and attorney general of Ireland. By the time he began the Yelverton case he was well versed in the art of martyr building, and his eloquence was considered to be fearsome. A sketch in *Temple Bar* described "his scorn as withering; his sarcasm bitter, blighting, blistering; his love of the ridiculous irrepressible."[30] Over the next few days, under Whiteside's guidance, Theresa reiterated the points of her character that Sullivan had underlined in his opening statement: her esteemed position in society, her religiosity, her chastity, and her sense of duty and sacrifice.

When Yelverton's lawyer, Sergeant Abraham Brewster, began his interrogation of Theresa, he went straight to the weaknesses in her story. Brewster was as accomplished as his colleagues, having also already served as both solicitor general and attorney general of Ireland when he defended Yelverton. He was a consummate professional, later described as "one of the few fortunate lawyers who have risen to judicial eminence through professional services alone."[31] His followers acknowledged his rapid-fire ability to react and respond, but admitted that he was less rhetorically gifted than his peers. If he could not construct a compelling narrative to redeem Yelverton, he would try to detract from Theresa's. Did she *really* believe that Yelverton was a Catholic? Why did so many other men hover around her? Didn't her flippant attitude toward her father betray a shameful levity of character—even in the face of death? On each occasion during the cross-examination, Theresa rebuked his insinuations. Sullivan had laid the foundations of her innocence and helplessness; she had finished the portrait by filling in the details. Now she was free to dispense with Brewster's aspersions with a little more assertiveness.

Theresa was firm about her belief of Yelverton's Catholicism. "My impression [in the Crimea] was that that he was a Catholic; I first conceived that idea in Naples; after he had told me himself he was a Catholic."[32] She had seen him twice in chapel in Edinburgh, and when she asked him about his religion, having been told by his acquaintances that his relatives were Catholic, he confirmed the impression. "I entertained no doubt as to his religious belief up to the time of the marriage in Ireland," Theresa insisted.[33] In Ireland, when his religion directly bore upon the validity of the wedding ceremony, Theresa claimed that she had asked Yelverton into what denomination he had been baptized and he had responded that "he did not recollect." When repeated in the courtroom, this response generated laughter. But it was kind laughter, full of sympathy for her pitiful but charming naïveté.[34] Her ingenuousness did not reflect poorly upon her; it seemed an organic outgrowth of a pure religiosity that blinded her to others' connivances. Yelverton, on the other hand, lacked religious conviction entirely. His commitments were at best shaky and at worst blasphemous, manipulated to improve his chances of getting Theresa into bed.

As for the other male admirers, Theresa flatly dismissed Brewster's accusations of coquetry. He probed her over a certain Mr. Roe, a friend of Yelverton's whose path had crossed Theresa's while she was living in Naples and who had been mentioned as an suitor in her letters. Theresa confessed that a flirtation had taken place but insisted that she had always preserved the appropriate distance. She was invited onto Roe's yacht for a cruise one day but refused to go unless a chaperone came with her and Roe stayed behind. When Roe reneged on the conditions she had set, and decided to join Theresa, she backed out. "He said I was a prude," Theresa said, but the accusation didn't bother her; it was merely evidence of male irrationality. Roe departed, agitated, "in a gale of wind," and that was the last she saw of him.[35] Toward the end of her testimony she retreated somewhat from the harsher aspects of her caricature lest it reflect impertinence on her part. Roe was an honorable man, she stated; "he never said a word disrespectful to me," and "he was not the man they have represented him to be."[36]

The one matter that inspired contrition was her attitude toward her father. The disagreements between her father and his children, she admitted, "were of a serious character," as all "disagreement between a parent and a child must be serious."[37] Despite his unaffectionate temperament and his atheism, she "always entertained a filial respect for him" and was "prepared to do everything for him," her

rhetoric of self-sacrifice echoing her courtroom professions of devotion to Yelverton.[38] As the trial progressed, Theresa apparently began
to think that her criticism of her father's atheism might turn into an
unanticipated black mark. Toward the end of her testimony, she la-
bored to demonstrate that her religious quarrel with her father did
not prohibit her from embracing her daughterly responsibilities: "I
attended for fourteen days on my father during his last illness; I had
previously attended him in a very dangerous illness for ten nights,
during which I never slept or took off my clothes; I ran four miles to
fetch a doctor to him, for he did not wish to send for a physician himself." She formally apologized for disrespecting her father in her letters to Yelverton: "I wish here to publicly make the *amende honorable*
to my father's memory."[39] She was willing to show remorse for her
peccadilloes; it was now the jury's duty to force Yelverton to accept
his more weighty sins.

For the remainder of the fourth day, Sullivan brought forth additional witnesses to substantiate the points that Theresa had stressed.
Thelwall testified that Yelverton visited Theresa in her apartment
in Edinburgh and that the couple was later received at his house
"as man and wife."[40] He had helped with practical matters when Yelverton had asked him to obtain a ring for Theresa with a removable
stone and to assist with the procurement of her passport. The two
men seemed to be on good terms, according to Thelwall's testimony;
Yelverton had thanked him for his hospitality and assistance with a
gift of cheroots, square-cut cigars. "Please [smoke] the accompanying sheroots [*sic*]," he had written to Thelwall, "and make my conscience easier in the matter of the number of cigars of yours I have
smoked." Thelwall had presented the expenses Theresa had incurred
to Yelverton because he had assumed that Theresa was his wife: "I
had no reason to doubt that Mrs. Yelverton was Major Yelverton's
wife whilst they were in my house, nor had I any reason to doubt it
afterwards."[41]

Arabella MacFarlane then appeared, primarily to validate Theresa's
assertion that Yelverton was generally known as a Catholic. She testified that "Major Yelverton appeared always to have a leaning toward

Catholicity" but faltered when she was probed over the reason the marriage was kept a secret. It was "because she was a Catholic and he was not," she said. Brewster interrupted to press her on this point. She claimed she had made a mistake: "I should have said that it was because of the religion of his family it was desired to keep it secret, and not on account of his own religion." But Brewster wasn't going to let this opportunity to weaken Theresa's story slide. "You have no right to say that," he told her, "did you not say on the former occasion that the reason Mrs. Yelverton assigned for keeping the marriage secret was that she was a Catholic and he a Protestant?" "I did," MacFarlane admitted, "but I made a mistake." Despite Brewster's sputtering objections and the fact that MacFarlane had conferred with Theresa between her two appearances, the matter was dropped.

The most intense examination took place when Reverend Mooney took the stand. Rather than indulge the priest's lackadaisical assessment of Yelverton's religious affinities (or argue that Yelverton really was a Catholic), Theresa's lawyers sought to expose his carelessness. If there was any lingering uncertainty about Yelverton's faith, it was the priest's fault for not confirming his denomination, not Theresa's. "What is that mongrel thing called a 'Protestant Catholic'?" asked Whiteside. "Have you anything like it down in your part of the country?" Mooney attempted to clarify his position, but before he could speak, Whiteside resumed his attack:

"I ask did you ever meet a man of that particular religion before?"

"I heard—," Mooney began, before Whiteside cut him off.

"I am not asking what you heard. Did you ever meet a man that gave you such an answer as that?"[42] To defend himself, Mooney claimed that he had dispensed with some of the conventional procedures (confirming the denomination of each party, signing the registry, finding an official witness) because he had only agreed to renew a prior ceremony, not to consecrate a new marriage. When presented with the marriage certificate that he had sent Theresa in France, he claimed he gave it to her so that "her child might be baptised legitimately . . . If I had thought it would have been used for any other purpose . . . I would have cut off my right hand sooner than have given it."[43]

Believing that it was a crime for a priest to marry a Protestant and a Catholic, Mooney had reason to dodge responsibility for the union. Realistically, Mooney was in no danger of being prosecuted, but his anxiety and graceless testimony did little to win him any admirers. "Before you go back to Rostrevor answer me a question," Whiteside said at the end of Mooney's appearance on the stand; "is it the practice, or is it usual for Catholic priests to certify falsehoods under their hands?" Mooney responded with a single word—"No"—and stepped down. It was clear, Whiteside implied, that he was someone that Theresa should have avoided. But who could blame her, in her weak and desperate state, for grasping the first opportunity that emerged to legitimize her position? The case for the plaintiff closed with a reading of the marriage certificate that Mooney had provided.

In the first few days of the trial, Theresa had become the audience's favorite, met by crowds of cheering supporters when she left the courtroom each day. Defending Yelverton was not going to be easy, and Brewster began his opening statement by acknowledging the difficulty of his task. "I am fully conscious of the disadvantages under which the advocate of any man must labour before a court of justice to defend him under circumstances such as those in which my client is placed." The facts of the story, as well as natural prepossessions, favored Theresa's cause—the cause of female virtue over male misadventure— and Brewster "would be extremely sorry [if] it were otherwise." But for the short while that he was to be "performing [his] part on the stage"—for there was no doubt that what was taking place in the Dublin courtroom was a theater—he asked observers of the trial to look at this story through a slightly less purple lens than the one that Sullivan, Whiteside, and Theresa had offered. Behind the melodrama, there were some basic matters to clarify that would dispel not only the case of Mr. Thelwall—"a mere stalking horse"—but also the larger accusations of iniquity and villainy.[44]

Brewster's fundamental argument was twofold. First, "If there was clear, precise, and positive legal evidence in reference to the transactions that occurred, or are alleged to have occurred, in Edinburgh in April, 1857, it would have been unnecessary to do more in the case."[45] But such evidence was lacking. And second, had Yelverton been a Catholic on August 15, 1857, and on that day, had "the Rev. Mr. Mooney joined them in holy wedlock according to the rites of the Roman Catholic Church, there would be no further question in the case." But proof of Yelverton's Catholicism was similarly unclear. The whole point of Theresa's long testimony, Brewster told the audience, was to "place before you the relative position of these two parties, how they were circumstanced to each other," and to tug at the audience's heartstrings. The backstory, however, should not govern the outcome of a case in which so much material was missing.

Despite his cut-and-dry rhetoric, Brewster knew that the audience would not be won over by a mere dearth of evidence. So even while Brewster professed sympathy for Theresa and vowed not to disparage her character, he turned to her letters and testimony for indications that she was not as virtuous as she seemed. "I mean to present her to you as she presented herself to us all," he said.[46] *He* was not the one who would darken her character; she had already done it. "Everybody must see," he began, "that she is a woman of most extraordinary talents—perhaps of greater talent than you ever had an opportunity of seeing before." In the course of his opening address, Brewster would use the word "talent" six times in reference to Theresa, each repetition diminishing the ostensible compliment. "She is more than a woman of talent," he continued, "she is a woman who has had that talent cultivated to the highest possible pitch." The pitch, Brewster implied, was a shade too shrill for a world of moderate, mediated emotions. Theresa, according to her own representation, "was a woman of a determination the like of which was never seen." The jury must understand, Brewster asserted, that Yelverton "was not the wooer from the beginning." Her resolve had led her into "a sort of craze and frenzy that would make her stop at nothing for the purpose of obtaining her object." Such extreme states, especially in women, tended to obscure better judgment.[47]

Theresa was not to blame for her attachment or for the drastic measures it had driven her to take. "It is natural, it is laudable," to want to preserve one's virtue and honor, Brewster asserted. "The only consideration is whether she is not prepared to go a little further than she ought to maintain the first principle of her life." This indirectness characterized Brewster's tactic: posit a flaw, claim that the consequences were not entirely her fault, then wonder if perhaps she should still bear some of the responsibility. He knew where most sympathies lay, and so he was stealthy in his criticism, turning her into an example of the mistakes that society made in dealing with young women. If she had gone too far in pursuing Yelverton, they should not hold her liable but turn to those who had shaped her upbringing.

Theresa had been the victim of a French education, an experience for which they must make large allowances. It was her education that led her to use "expressions in French and Italian [that] are stronger than the usual expressions of English people." Brewster did not mean to suggest an innate superiority of one nation over the other—"There is nothing . . . more unworthy or more unwarrantable than national reflection," he opined—but it could not be ignored that the countries had given rise to two very different types of literature. In England, "we have had in the present century a race of authors the most remarkable for brilliancy of fancy and eloquence, who displayed their genius in romances and novels." France, on the other hand, was home to a "host of imitators" with very different motives.

> For the last fifteen or twenty years—just at the time that this young woman was likely to have books of amusement put into her hands—the French press has teemed with novels written with all the brilliance of Scott, but in which one would suppose the whole effort of the authors was to turn everything glorious in our nature into contempt and derision, and to advance, as it were, the cause of vice and the devil.

Impressionable minds were particularly vulnerable to such contamination. "There is always a danger of young people, without any evil intention on their part, having their minds tainted if books of this description, written with a talent and an eloquence not to be surpassed, happen to fall into their hands," Brewster claimed.[48]

Theresa had all the qualities—femininity, an active imagination, a foreign upbringing—that made her particularly susceptible to the corruptions of literature. A "plain honest woman" might "never go astray," Brewster argued, but "many an over refined one from excess of imagination, was precipitated to ruin."[49] The lascivious plots of French novelists had nurtured Theresa's risqué literary inclinations; the evidence had been produced by her own hand in the romanticized, melodramatic, and overly clever depictions of her life.[50] She had imagined herself as a vivandière—a traveling civilian nurse—"with a little barrel round her neck . . . marching at the head of a regiment with short petticoats and red stockings," scarlet underclothes revealing her immodesty. Immediately after the death of her father, she had shown off her wit, callously spinning her squabbles with the lawyers into an amusing anecdote. Withdrawal would have been more appropriate, Brewster implied. "For a woman, an educated pious woman, to sit down at such a moment, and write such a letter, entirely passes my comprehension," Brewster said. "Moreover, that she should have written it to a man that she had never seen but once in her life . . . and whom she had met under circumstances which in real life not unfrequently occur, must greatly surprise any one."[51]

Not only had her reading distorted her sense of decorum, but it had given her an acute understanding of the power of language, and the audience must take this into account when reviewing both the correspondence and her testimony. Theresa—in Brewster's assessment—was a woman who "understood the use of language as well as anyone that ever lived."[52] So why did she repeatedly mistake Yelverton's attempts to disentangle himself from her? "Social caution," Yelverton had written, "stands between us, staying your approach me-wards with grave advice and friendly-seeming forewarnings, and mine thee-wards, with loaded arms and stern command, 'stand back.'" How, Brewster asked, could this woman be "held up to the jury as a wonder, for her powers of language, her perception of the meaning of words" if she failed to understand Yelverton's meaning in a letter as blunt and direct as this one? Was the jury to regard her as "a simpleton incapable of understanding the sentences" he had just read aloud to them at the same time they were to praise her literary acuity?[53]

Theresa was no simpleton, Brewster argued. Her letters were the product of a consummate stylist, a woman determined to entice with her words when her body was of no immediate avail. "To-day I have been running about and have found the *bank of violettes* you were sighing for the other night," Brewster read from one of Theresa's letters. The bank was "entirely closed in by verdure; it overhangs the sea, impervious to human eye or ear; only the nightingale above would melodise our thoughts, too deep and sacred for mortal words to tell. I send you some of the violettes, charged with much that you might claim, if in their native bower."[54] This was not "the language of a woman who was engaged to the man she was writing to," Brewster asserted. Her letters "contained a variety of expressions that no married woman would have written to her husband."[55]

Although a less competent stylist, Yelverton wrote letters that similarly disregarded matrimonial propriety, describing his lack of restraint in her presence. What kind of man, Brewster asked, wrote "a letter of that kind to his betrothed wife"?[56] It was not just the tone of their exchange, but the absence of explicit reference to marriage that underlined the dubiousness of their supposed promise: "The word 'marriage,' in any of these letters would be worth a Jew's eye in the case, but the only letter in the whole correspondence in which it occurred was that written by her from Bordeaux, when she was beginning to doubt her condition, and when she wrote to Father Mooney."[57]

Brewster presented these violations of propriety while shying away from direct accusation, asserting that it was necessary only to keep in mind "views about the general conduct of a woman."[58] He did not know, for example, "whether it is customary for ladies who have never seen a certain gentleman before, especially if he be young and apparently gallant, to sit under the same plaid"—Theresa and Yelverton had shared a blanket, a "plaid," on their first steamer voyage—"and to spend the whole live long night in that manner." He did not deny "the fair sex the privilege of becoming wooers if they think fit." Such behavior did not befit "the habit of this country," and he thought that "the gentleman should follow the lady, and not the lady follow the gentleman," but it was not for him to make moral judgments for the rest of them.[59] If the jury did not think it exceptional and egregious to share a blanket with a stranger and for a woman to pursue a man, so be it. But he could not help but condemn the inappropriately revelatory tone of Theresa's letters, a window into her soul "at a time when she had no motive whatever to misrepresent herself." Even if her illegitimate desires only took shape in writing, this evidence of their existence should cast doubt upon her proclaimed virtue.

Lest the accusation emerge too forcefully, Brewster hedged his assessment. "Don't understand me as thinking that a woman should be a prude," he had said, earlier in the trial, "far from it."[60] As he brought his four-hour speech to a close, he was full of compassion for Theresa. "For him, I tell you, I care but little—for the unhappy lady to whom he has united himself I cannot but feel the deepest commiseration." He did not want to justify Yelverton's iniquitous actions, and he had "endeavored from the beginning to the end, not to say one word to wound the feelings of the lady." But, he reminded them, he had a "duty to perform," as did the members of the jury, "and that duty [was] to elicit truth in reference to these two marriages" and the woman who claimed their validity.[61]

CHAPTER FIVE

Vindication

Ah! Woman still
Must veil the shrine,
Where feeling feeds the fire divine,
Not sing at will,
Untaught by art
The music prison'd in her heart!

—Frances Sargent Osgood "Ah, Woman Still"

Spectators filed in for the sixth day of proceedings just as they had for the previous five. They peeled off their gloves, draped their jackets over the banisters; there was scarcely room to move from one end of the gallery to the other. Those who came too late to claim a seat hovered in the hall, hoping to catch a glimpse of the wronged woman and her nefarious seducer as they entered the court. On this day, the man who had become the villain would take the stand, and when he entered the courtroom it was amid a chorus of taunting voices. Dark-haired and sleek, Yelverton dressed the part of the dashing dandy. But no matter how carefree he might have wished to appear, a Sisyphean task stood before him. A stubborn cloud of scorn hung about the rafters of the Four Courts; it was up to him to clear it.

If he failed, Yelverton would suffer the consequences of his youthful flirtation for the rest of his life. As he probably saw it, his real life had just begun, and now he stood to lose his wife, Emily, and his son, the foundations of a respectable domestic existence. If the jury determined that his marriage to Theresa was valid, not only would he give up these things; he would be tied to a woman he did not love—a woman who had grown tedious and demanding over the years and who would undoubtedly worsen with age. Other men dallied in their youth and evaded the consequences. He just had to prove he was like these men and hope that his honesty would mitigate his sins.

"I am the defendant," Yelverton began; "I am a captain in the artillery and a brevet major in the army."[1] He was an upstanding member of society, he said, not someone who was inclined to accept invitations from strangers. But when Theresa invited him to her aunt's house after their first meeting—to change his clothes, he reminded his audience—he did not feel that he could decline the invitation. Nothing improper had taken place, but she had kept him there for two hours, idling over tea. And Theresa was the one who had issued the invitation for their second meeting. With her incessant complaints about isolation and loneliness, she had practically implored him to scale the convent walls.

In Istanbul she indulged his attraction. Despite the sweltering heat, and despite the fact that she had not officially taken the vows, Theresa wore the typical Soeurs de Charité attire—a black gown with a white collar—a forbidding costume that, Yelverton admitted, only made her more desirable. She had tantalized him from afar with her letters; now she teased with her veiled body. They sat on the divan in her private room, and the temptation was too much. He kissed her; she pushed him away. "I made some love," he admitted to the chief justice, "I cannot put it into other words."[2] If Theresa had been the one to initiate and propagate the first stages of their relationship, Yelverton conceded that he now took the reins. When Theresa departed the Crimea after her stay with the Straubenzees, Yelverton again made his desire known. Theresa did not rebuke him. He had accompanied Major Straubenzee to see her off, and on the deck of her departing ship, he pulled her to him "to take possession of her," he admitted to the chief justice.

When Yelverton reached this point in his story, the chief justice was faced with a dilemma. Allowing Yelverton to tell his lascivious stories in front of a crowded courtroom populated in large part by women compounded the violation of innocence—the most poignant of the transgressions that had taken place in this saga. "If ladies wish to remain in court during this examination I cannot help them," the chief justice announced. If they "choose to remain they must expose themselves to a very unpleasant scene."[3] After a few minutes, all but two or three of the women withdrew. The justice made himself clearer: "Any who choose to remain will expose themselves to be considered in a very unpleasant light."[4] The remaining women left, and Yelverton continued.

Such entreaties for the sanctity of innocence persisted throughout the trial. Sergeant Armstrong—another of Yelverton's lawyers—extensively apologized for the lewdness of the letters he was forced to read. On the last day of the trial a juror wrote an anonymous note to the chief justice, worried that the expressions used in a certain letter were such as "could scarcely be repeated before a crowded court where ladies chose to attend."[5] One of the court reporters curtailed his coverage when he deemed the material "unfit for publication," concerned that his transcription would expose an innocent reader to depravity she would not have conceived of on her own.[6] The descriptive omission, of course, left his audience free to imagine that much racier events had taken place.

To a certain extent, the same concerns affected considerations of Theresa's character. Like the women watching the trial, she possessed a dangerously healthy curiosity. Brewster had argued that Theresa's initial exposure to depraved French literature was not her fault, but he had also implied that her failure to curb its influence illustrated a moral shortcoming. The women in the courtroom should not be blamed for hearing the beginning of Yelverton's story, but they were culpable if they lingered. An innocent woman who was exposed to temptation, and then enjoyed the entertainment it provided, was perhaps not so innocent.

These concerns also echoed wider apprehensions about female courtroom observers. Sensational trials often attracted a large number of women to the galleys, and their ostensibly wanton curiosity was not happily tolerated. One novelist complained that "women of family and position, women who have been brought up in refined society, women who pride themselves upon the delicacy of their sensibilities . . . such women can sit for hours listening to the details of a cold-blooded murder."[7] At the 1857 trial of Madeline Smith, who stood accused of poisoning her shipping clerk lover, female spectators were chastised for dishonoring their sex by "eagerly drinking in that filthy correspondence" between Smith and her lover.[8] (The male observers of the trial escaped this admonition.) *Thelwall* presented another correspondence with potentially unclean content, and the women in the courtroom were fascinated.

But the women in the Four Courts probably felt a more substantive interest in the case. Beyond its vicarious thrills, the trial demonstrated the plight of the "unplucked flower," or "redundant" unmarried woman; the double standards to which men and women were held; and the dearth of opportunities for ambitious young women. Theresa had charted an unconventional path through these irritations and obstacles and was now fighting for respect and recognition. If she succeeded, maybe they could too. Their curiosity may have had less to do with titillation than with a sense of possibility.

These issues, however, were unspoken, and increasingly suppressed as the trial progressed. By ushering the women from the courtroom, the judge preempted any assessment of their interest, and allowed the simplified narrative that was coming to dominate the trial to blossom; women were innocent until corrupted; men were corrupt until corrected. Dissatisfaction with the limitations imposed on women did not factor into the equation. The jury's duty, the judge reminded, was not merely to punish Yelverton's deeds but to ensure that this type of misadventure, propagated by the base instincts of men, did not repeat itself. The trial was the first testing ground of this moral imperative to protect innocence, and so they could not allow the retelling of the story to cause an immediate affront. As Theresa's identity became narrower—reduced to her chastity and sacrifice—the symbolic terms of the trial became larger. The judge and jury had been called upon to protect not only Theresa's virtue but the virtue of all women.

If the trial invoked stereotypical female susceptibility to explain Theresa's poor judgment, stereotypes of male weakness abounded as well, becoming particularly pronounced as Yelverton continued his testimony. By admitting to his transgressions, Yelverton hoped to position himself as the victim of his passions—a common trope in Victorian culture. A popular nineteenth-century translation of Aristotle's "Words of Warning" cautioned that "rules which we approve and to which we adhere in our calmer moments are utterly violated under the influence of passion."[9] If Yelverton thought that admitting this flaw would gain him sympathy, Theresa's lawyers soon showed him his error. A man who planned a seduction, who gave in to these forces knowing of their consequences, was entirely different from a man who unwillingly suffered under their sway. Crimes of passion were forgivable; those designed by intellect were not. Sullivan tossed aside Yelverton's claims that the correspondence began without dishonorable objectives and argued that Yelverton's misdeeds were produced by cool, calm calculation.

Yelverton had admitted that he had "formed the desire" for Theresa at the convent. Was Yelverton sure that he had formed "the 'desire' and not the 'design?'" Sullivan asked.

"'Design' is a strong word," Yelverton responded, sensing that Sullivan was greasing a slippery slope beneath his feet.

"And desire is a weak one, is it?"[10] Sullivan shot back. How exactly had Yelverton conducted himself at the Straubenzees', where he had been frequently invited to dine? Was desire or design at work in his dealings there? Was he "plotting to make Theresa Longworth [his] mistress all the time?" asked Sullivan.

"Plotting is a very hard word," Yelverton responded.

"I do not care; you will swallow it before the case is over. Were you plotting to make her your mistress?"

"It is a hard word."

"Hard or soft, you will answer it?"

"Carried away by my feelings—"

"Carried away by your feelings, you were plotting?"

"Plotting is a hard word. Planning."[11] But "plan" was only mildly better since his "plan" included no promise to make Theresa his wife; nor did it seek to protect her from a sad and sordid fate.

"Did you speak of Theresa Longworth as 'a person,' as if you had picked her up in the street[?]" asked Sullivan.

"I recollect some expression of that sort," Yelverton responded after a long pause.[12] The exchange continued, with Yelverton fending off the most damning of Sullivan's accusations and, in the process, admitting to still dubious behavior. He had been reduced to a player on the stage, and his role as the devious villain—the engineer behind Theresa's misfortune, rather than a victim of mutual passion gone awry—had been cast.

At some point, Yelverton realized that he could do little to avoid this designation, and even more openly acknowledged his indecent instincts. When Sullivan returned to the "second steamer scene"—Theresa's departure from the Crimea—Yelverton now admitted that he had "exposed his person" on the ship. The formerly bashful reporter had no trouble recording *this* speech; the crossfire, it seems, was too tantalizing. His actions, Yelverton conceded, were as dark as the circumstances in which they had taken place; he "could not have done it"—exposed himself—"if it was light." When Sullivan pressed him, he abandoned all precaution.

"I went on board that vessel to see her and talk to her, but I was led away afterwards by my feeling," Yelverton admitted.

"Is that what you swear?" Sullivan asked.

"By my passion."

Sullivan was shocked at Yelverton's calm delivery. "You appear to me very cool," he said.

"Not in bed," Yelverton responded as the sound of hissing swelled.[13] Yelverton's lawyer Armstrong jumped up, attempting to defuse Yelverton's unexpected boast of sexual prowess.

"He says; 'Not in that,'" Armstrong insisted.

"He did not, Sergeant Armstrong," Sullivan retorted. "He said, 'not in bed.'"

The chief justice ended the debate: "There is no mistake about it."[14]

As the trial continued, Yelverton amplified his sexuality. He admitted to having sex in Mrs. Gemble's sitting room. When he couldn't recollect the exact day that intercourse had first occurred, Sullivan asked Yelverton if "the frequency of these events cause[s] them to be less impressed on your mind."[15] Yelverton dodged the accusation, but his casual recollection suggested that he had not given much weight to the encounters. And when he admitted that he was "anxious to have possession of her person," that, in Sullivan's words, "the idea [was] constantly before" him, he seemed entirely without compunction.

"Would you have stopped at anything to realize it?" Sullivan asked.

"I would not have committed a rape to do it," Yelverton said. The crime that had simmered just below the surface of the proceedings had finally arisen. Although Yelverton denied his culpability, he had introduced the possibility of the transgression—the most extreme violation of virtue. His lies and lesser crimes grew more sinister in the shadow of this aspersion.

Yet another criminal act lurked in the background. What had Yelverton suggested, Sullivan asked, when he had learned that Theresa was pregnant? Yelverton waited a moment, then mumbled something about the dangers of childbirth and means to avoid them. Sullivan pressed him, asking four times how the birth of a child was to be avoided. It could be avoided, Yelverton finally answered, by preventing it from "coming to maturity."

"Procuring an abortion, in fact?" asked the chief justice.

"No," Yelverton responded.

"What else do [you] mean?"

Yelverton was silent.

"How could the birth be avoided?" the chief justice pressed. "What do you mean, Sir?"

Yelverton responded slowly: "I understood that if a woman was in great danger from childbirth that the doctor would manage—would manage to get the child born alive without letting it go to its full time."[16] If he had not actually procured an abortion for Theresa, his painfully slow response did not make his motives less suspicious.

Sullivan continued: What exactly did Yelverton mean by calling Theresa his "mistress"?

"It was not in the ordinary case of a paid mistress," Yelverton hedged, "it was not for money," as though this qualification diminished the taint of the title. There was love in their relationship, Yelverton explained, and this love created bonds that transcended ties produced by mere monetary exchange.

So, this relationship created responsibilities and obligations, Sullivan surmised. What were "the duties of a mistress to her keeper?"

"To be honest and true to him," Yelverton responded, to keep "faith with [him]" and to sacrifice whatever he deemed necessary to protect the secrecy of their arrangement.[17] "There was no sacrifice which she was not to make for me," Yelverton bragged. If he shared a sense of obligation, it was only that he intended to take care of her in some vague way, although he did not think that she needed it. "Theresa Longworth, at that time and at her age, was capable of making her own position, and she accepted that position with me."[18] Her choices did not extenuate his conduct, but she had entered into a relationship with him of her own will. She did not deserve sympathy simply because he had broken a promise that was never even formalized. He said that he never proposed a Scotch marriage, had never read the marriage ceremony with his hand on the Book of Common Prayer, and had not pronounced them man and wife—all of which Theresa had claimed in her testimony. In Ireland, he reported, he had only appeared before Reverend Mooney and gone through a portion of the marriage ceremony for the "lady's conscience sake," believing that, as a Protestant, the ceremony had no meaning.[19]

The union that *had* been sanctified, Yelverton reminded the courtroom, was his marriage to Emily Forbes. Throughout the trial, Yelverton insisted that Emily be referred to as his wife. She was a spectral presence, completely avoiding the witness stand. Still, Armstrong invoked her and her two children in Yelverton's defense. Was it likely, Armstrong asked, that Yelverton would have entered into a marriage with Emily Forbes if he had been fully committed to another woman? Whiteside objected, claiming "it is nothing to this case whether this gentleman has as many children as King Priam." But Armstrong insisted it was relevant, asking "his learned friends [to] say on what grounds they think it is not evidence." The crowd jeered, and the chief justice had to plead with them: do not "turn my court into a bear garden."[20]

In the midst of the commotion, Yelverton became, or affected to become, distraught. He placed his hands over his face and wept. Perhaps the thought of tainting his wife and children with his cavalier, possibly criminal, and certainly callous past upset Yelverton. It is unlikely that his tears did him much good. Tears were the province of women, acceptable for men only in cases of extreme grief. As the novelist and poet Charles Kingsley had written, "Men must work and women must weep."[21] Like so many of his other statements, this one backfired, an attempted show of sensitivity adding effeminacy to his mounting defects.

Yelverton's advantages were disappearing fast. His "gentle blood" had been connected to a snobbish disregard for the well-being of other people, his devotion to Emily a disproportionate compensation for the wrong he had done to another woman, and his display of emotion a sign of weakness. His depiction of Theresa—seductive, confident, assertive—did not match the weakened woman who had appeared before the courtroom on previous days, and the disjunction made his claims suspect. For the remainder of the seventh day and into the eighth, Armstrong desperately attempted to restore the case to its modest dimensions. All Yelverton's admissions of misbehavior and his unseemly display meant nothing. Unless the jury believed that the Scottish marriage was in fact a marriage, or that Yelverton was a Catholic, he was innocent. The desire to abrade misconduct could not make a marriage. Armstrong brought forth witness after witness—a captain in the army, an archdeacon who resided near Yelverton's family home, a man who lived near the Avonmore estate and who reported on Yelverton's church attendance at Protestant holy places—to try to prove these points.[22]

Hotel owners and employees from the various places that Yelverton and Theresa had visited were also summoned. Armstrong prompted them to speak about the rooms the couple had occupied, how many beds were made and unmade, how the pair had registered—the inquisition designed to further weaken Theresa's virtue. Most of the witnesses remembered the couple or kept records of their stay, but few were willing to describe Theresa and Yelverton's sleeping arrangements; nor was Whiteside willing to permit the admission of such evidence without contest. When Armstrong asked one employee if Theresa and Yelverton had lived in the sitting room as man and wife, Whiteside objected, saying it was as relevant as asking "who brought in the eggs and dinner."[23]

The succession of matter-of-fact testimonies about hotel rooms and unmade beds still occasionally invoked the Manichaean moral matters at stake. "What was the color of the handkerchief?" Armstrong asked a hotel employee in reference to an item that Theresa had left in one of the rooms.

"White," the employee answered.

"Emblematic of purity," Sullivan interjected.

"There is very little purity in the case from the beginning," responded Armstrong.

"On your side certainly," Sullivan said.[24] By the end of the trial, Sullivan's narrative dominated the Four Courts. Yelverton's sexuality and his disregard for Theresa's well-being had made him the villain.

Even if the favorites were apparent, the question of what constituted a marriage was still, in the final days of the trial, unclear. George II Patterson—"more than twenty-six years a member of the Scotch bar"—was called forth to clarify the meaning of irregular marriage on the eighth day of the trial. He stated that a marriage in Scotland occurred when there was "interchange of mutual consent, freely, unequivocally, seriously, and deliberately given with a genuine purpose of immediately becoming husband and wife, without reference to any further ceremony, and so expressed and evidenced as will be recognized by the law." Between two people, it could be contracted by "mutual writings accepting each other as husband and wife, or mutual declarations or acknowledgements of marriage—or by a series of letters passing between them, which from their own contents, as well as from the mode in which the parties address each other and subscribe themselves will create a clear and unequivocal recognition of a marriage."[25] In other words, a man and a woman who declared themselves married in Scotland were considered bound in matrimony; a clear, serious, and mutual recognition of the union was all it took.

"I wonder you are not all married," the chief justice exclaimed at the end of Patterson's lengthy explanation. The multiple forms of consent and contract were a boon to Theresa. There had been planning—Yelverton had admitted as much by using that exact word—and promises. Although Theresa and her lawyers were at pains to prove that it had not taken place before it was appropriate, there had also been sex. When Patterson articulated the third mode in which a marriage could be consecrated, "promise followed by *copula*," there seemed little room for doubt.

Whiteside further diminished the uncertainty by quoting from past cases that had determined that "it is not necessary to prove the contract [of marriage] itself." The implication, either in public behavior or in private writings, that Theresa and Yelverton were man and wife meant that a contractual agreement had taken place.[26] If reputation did not establish a union, secret commitments could. He mentioned another case in which a man posthumously acknowledged his secret marriage in his will. He had lived as a single man, but the House of Lords had decided that a valid marriage had taken place, thus protecting the rights and reputation of his longtime female companion. Irregular marriage, in Whiteside's examples, did not weaken the bonds of marriage. It protected women by preventing men from escaping their responsibilities.

In his closing address, delivered on the eighth and ninth day of the trial, Armstrong made one last appeal to the male spectators' baser natures. The men in the courtroom, he argued, could understand Yelverton's mistakes. "If any man in this crowded court were driven to review his own past life—his early life, when passions were strong, and the influence of youth and warm blood predominated, perhaps he might, if called to cast a stone at this gentleman, find [himself] more disposed to slink out of court."[27] All men had been like Yelverton at some point. An irresistible situation had presented itself; Yelverton was merely a victim of the "instincts of our common nature."[28]

Had Armstrong met this seductive "syren," and then received a letter from her—a "suggestive" and "burning" letter—"he did not know what he might not have done."[29] Armstrong would not guess how Theresa had behaved outside genteel company, but she was a girl who "wrote in . . . indelicate terms, who evinced . . . a want of maiden modesty." Once, she had even seemed repulsed by the idea of marriage, calling it "so formidable an affair." Yelverton was right to consider their relationship a casual one. It was natural "that a man who had been received into the embraces of a woman should have intercourse with her afterwards, and yet that was denounced as the most atrocious conduct."[30]

Abandoning Brewster's technique of indirect assault, Armstrong went straight to Theresa's vulnerabilities. The *really* egregious event was Theresa's seduction of Yelverton, not Yelverton's succumbing to it. Theresa's social ambition, her foreign education, and the ends to which she applied her many talents impugned her modesty. She could sing and draw, and a woman who excelled in the arts also supposedly excelled in artifice. Theresa was a "consummate performer," a "matchless player," a woman whose beauty and accomplishment—of a certain superficial type—gave her incomparable influence.[31] Armstrong had "seen the greatest actors of his time . . . but the lady in this case was superior to any he ever saw."[32] Like an actress, she told falsehoods and stretched the confines of acceptable behavior, taking advantage of an opportunity for independence, fame, and fortune.

The theatrics of the courtroom, according to Armstrong, had muddled judicial clarity. But "the jury were men of the world . . . They were not to be deluded with stage tricks like these."[33] To assert that Theresa and Yelverton's relationship was "an honest marriage, or a marriage at all, would be a blow to virtue, to the security of families, to the peace, and honor, and tranquility of married life greater than ever had been inflicted upon that sacred connection. God forbid that such a transaction, even if it had occurred, would receive the stamp of approbation from an honest jury."[34]

Despite the clear favoritism the crowd had developed for Theresa, audience members could not help but applaud Armstrong's rousing closing speech.

> We live in a world where immorality is rampant, crime common, seduction, unhappily, too frequent. This is not a case of seduction; I deny it. If there was seduction, it was in the artifices of this woman herself. Read the letters. Good Heaven, was any young and ardent man ever in this world subjected to such temptation, and was there a man [who] could do more than he did to avoid and escape from this syren? Did he not struggle against the temptress to the last, but in vain? Did she not endeavor to carry with her the public voice by deluding the public eye and ear, and did she not labour to excite that sympathy, which, if it were to continue . . . would, I believe, inflict a deadly blow upon the public morality and virtue of this country.[35]

No matter how chaste Theresa claimed to be, her story was filled with too many seductive unveilings—the slip of a shawl, the folded-back French bonnet, the dropped handkerchief—to deem them all accidental. They should remember these facts, and not be carried away by emotional impulses. Sympathy for Theresa was akin to sympathy for sexual liberty, indulgence, decadence, and seduction. It threatened to undermine the foundations upon which their society stood.

When Whiteside took the stand for his closing argument on the ninth day of the trial, he asserted that the story that stood to do *real* damage had been spun by nefarious lawyers. Rarely was such a wealth of unfiltered evidence at a lawyer's disposal, and yet Yelverton's lawyers had twisted Theresa's letters into deformed variations of their original selves. "Pick out a line here and there—leave out the context—put a color upon what you read—misconstrue the English tongue—don't read what goes before—don't read what follows," the technique was perverse enough to make the Bible an atheist tract.[36] Whiteside had his own reading: the authentic Theresa was a motherless child who "listened to the lessons of holy women, and endeavored to repeat them with the lisping accents of childhood" before she even understood what they meant.[37] She was a young woman who stood by her father on his deathbed, tortured by her inability to share with him the consolation her religion provided her. Her hand was the hand of a gentlewoman; her face—although now besmirched by suffering—had won her suitor after suitor; and her education placed her among the most refined women of their day. Armstrong had asked why the son of a lord should fall in love with a commoner like Theresa. The answer was simple: "The woman with whom he did fall in love was every way worthy of a higher and better man."[38]

If there was any doubt as to her valor, her forbearance under interrogation had proved it. She had been expected to recount her every move from the moment she met Yelverton up to the present. She had been asked to disclose the contents of her confession. She had been called a courtesan and suffered under the implications of worse accusations. The onslaught was a blatant attempt "to assail the virtue and asperse the honor of the witness." But it was to no avail; "she has come out unscathed from the inquiry—clear she is of every imputation."[39] Why should the jury now "rob her of her honour, all that is left her, upon the rotten testimony that has been concocted against her"?[40]

Theresa was not the only one who stood to suffer from the misrepresentation of her life and character. Whiteside told the jury that they owed it to Yelverton to reject the argument of his counsel that "he was her deliberate, skillful, scientific, and unconscionable seducer."

Yelverton had been goaded into admitting to "hypocrisy, profanity, deception, and blasphemy" by claiming he was not her wedded husband. "Save him from the consequences of that argument," Whiteside implored; "do not brand him as his counsel do, as a scientific, deliberate, unprincipled seducer."[41] If the jury forced Yelverton to accept Theresa as his wife, they would not be punishing him; they would be giving him the opportunity to reform and improve himself—to embrace the spirit of the age.

"Her crime," Whiteside concluded, "is she loved him too dearly, and too well. Had she possessed millions, she would have flung them at his feet. Had she a throne to bestow, she would have placed him on that throne. She gave him the kingdom of her heart, and made him sovereign of her affection. There he reigned with undisputed sway." The jury could not "restore her to the husband she adored or to the happiness she enjoyed; you cannot give colour to that faded cheek, or luster to that eye that has been dimmed by many a tear. You cannot relieve the sorrows of her bursting heart, but you may restore her to her place in society." He hoped that she would find "an advocate in you . . . in the respected judge on the bench . . . in every heart that beats within this court and in every honest man throughout the country."[42] At the conclusion of his speech, the halls of the Four Courts echoed with applause.

On the tenth and final day of the trial, the justice addressed the courtroom. Never, in the course of his career, had he witnessed a case such as this one, "one that requires the greatest effort of a man's mind to divest himself of feelings that ought not to be entertained on the judicial bench." He felt compelled to remind the jury that their inquiry was straightforward: to determine the validity of the alleged marriages. It was not their responsibility to parse the consequences of their decision. They were not expected to protect either this one woman or the myriad values her story evoked. Despite his admonitions, at the end of his speech, even the judge could not resist straying from legalese. Was the flame that burned within Theresa "an honest, virtuous flame, or an unholy one?" he wondered.[43]

At quarter past five, the jurors were released to deliberate. A little more than an hour later, they reemerged. The air inside the stuffy courtroom was electric with excitement and anxiety. The room was silent but for the rustling of dresses, a brief uncontainable cough.

"How say you, gentlemen. Was there a Scotch marriage?" asked the chief justice.

"Yes, my lord," responded the foreman.

"And was there an Irish marriage?"

"Yes, my lord."

"Then, you find the defendant was a Roman Catholic at the time of the marriage?"

"So we believe, my lord."[44] By this last statement the foreman could hardly be heard. Cheers filled the courtroom. The news spread from the courtroom to the hall, and then to the streets, where a massive crowd had convened to hear the verdict. Between fifty and one hundred thousand people, it was said, had gathered to watch Theresa as she traveled down Sackville Street.[45] Not satisfied by mere auditory adulation, the crowd carried Theresa the final stretch of her journey from the courthouse to her hotel in a makeshift chariot. Her horses were released from their tethers and tied to a post while her carriage was lifted by the men in the crowd.

Raised to this height, Theresa was transformed from an individual into an icon, not just an icon of feminine virtue, bravery, and conviction, but also a symbol, unpredictably, for Ireland. Although Yelverton was Irish and Theresa was English, aristocratic, Protestant Yelverton had more in common—it seemed—with oppressive Anglo-Irish landlords than with the Dublin crowds. Unprivileged, Catholic Theresa had been the victim of an unfortunate union and now seemed a true native of Ireland. In a speech delivered from the balcony of the Gresham Hotel, where she settled after her victory and would reside for several months, Theresa intuited the scope of her appeal. "My noble-hearted friends," she said, "you have made me this day an Irishwoman by the verdict that I am the wife of an Irishman. I glory to belong to such a noble-hearted nation."[46]

A ballad written only a few days after the trial celebrated the Irish laws that had vindicated Theresa: "Long live the judge and jury, who this lady did befriend, / According to the Irish laws they brought the verdict home, / And they proved the marriage lawful of the holy Church of Rome." Theresa, said the song, was "the talk of Ireland, and the pride of Dublin town." If Yelverton was so unlucky that the "Dublin females could catch him by surprise, / They'd make him curse and rue the day he ever had two wives."[47] In homes throughout Ireland the verdict would "be hailed with as much joy as if it restored the right and honour of some dear member of the fireside circle," wrote one reporter.[48] Theresa, who wanted to assume her rightful, domestic place, secured her reputation in homes across the country.

A demure, deferential costume had become Theresa's standard garb over the course of the ten-day trial, and it had served her well. Whether or not she was eager to embrace conventionality, Theresa had known that her options were limited. She was damned if she accepted her abandonment, since the standards of female virtue were assumed to be absolute: "Every woman who yields to her passions and loses her virtue," declared an authority, "is a prostitute."[49] But she was also damned if she made a fuss in the wrong form or forum. Victorian women—especially wives and mothers—did not air their troubles before inquisitive masses. Theresa and her lawyers were careful to cultivate a particular tone in the trial, putting just enough private information before the public to gain Theresa supporters, but not so much as to make her look suspicious.

The trial was remarkable not only because it determined the fate—damnation or salvation—of a woman, probed at society's understanding of love and marriage, and contained some of the most dramatic rhetoric ever to appear in a Victorian courtroom, but also because of the contradictions it contained. Despite the overwhelming narrative of conventional female virtue that dominated the tenor of the trial, there remained the fact that a Victorian woman had publicly exhibited her dissatisfaction and had successfully demanded compensation. At the end of the Dublin proceedings, a lengthier trial began: how long could Theresa tolerate the role she had assumed? After all, this supposedly meek and grateful woman had once written that her whole life was a protest against conformity.

CHAPTER SIX

Appeal

She had taken all the first steps in the purest confidence,
and then she had suddenly found the infinite vista
of a multiplied life to be a dark, narrow alley
with a dead wall at the end.

—Henry James, preface to *The Portrait of a Lady* (1907)

W hen Theresa and Yelverton left Dublin, their whereabouts and occupations become less clear. Theresa, it seems, moved to London, where she settled in Maida Vale, a northwest section of the city. The stomping grounds of writers, journalists, artists, and continental Europeans who had fled from their countries in the wake of the revolutions of 1848, the neighborhood, together with St. John's Wood, had developed a reputation for bourgeois vice. "The queens of St. John's Wood in their unblushing honesty" were setting a bad example for girls in the rest of London, wrote the essayist Eliza Lynn Linton.[1] For a woman who was hoping to remove any taint from her reputation, Maida Vale was an odd place to live. But the area had its advantages. Room and board were free since Theresa lived with a relative, and Theresa's financial resources were dwindling. From the grand house on Randolph Road, Theresa was just a few steps away from Regent's Canal, an elegant sliver of water lined with willows. Her neighbor Robert Browning, who had moved to Maida Vale from Italy after Elizabeth Barrett Browning's death, called the streets that lined the canals "Little Venice," and the name stuck. Here, Theresa's artistic inclinations would not be held against her since everyone surrounding her was cultivating similar talents. The St. John's Wood Clique was busy satirizing (and imitating) the Pre-Raphaelite Brotherhood. George Eliot and George Henry Lewes were tucked away in their house on North Bank working on novels and articles in the morning and strolling through the zoo in the afternoon. Among the quiet streets, Theresa began her own first novel, a book that would emanate the heat of Naples, the stench of gore in the Crimea, the silky air of Edinburgh—all the sensations that had been stifled in the courtroom.

Theresa produced the first volume of her autobiographical novel *Martyrs to Circumstance* in April 1861, just a few months after the end of the Dublin trial. In *Martyrs*, Thierna Saxelhurst, a young Englishwoman—described as "neither handsome, lovely, sweet, nor grand-looking; yet at times [all] these"—joins a monastic order so that she can help soldiers wounded in the Crimean War. The narrator, Thierna's elderly female friend (seemingly based on Mrs. Straubenzee), recounts the romance that develops between Thierna and Captain Cyril Etherington of the Royal Cannoniers, a man who "wore the stamp of power,—of manly, undaunted, fearless, bearing."[2] The novel moves between the Crimea, Thierna's uncle's castle, and the narrator's apartment in "Athenboro," where Cyril carries out an irregular marriage despite Thierna's hesitation. Thierna eventually finds an unappealing but acceptable reverend, Bartholomew O'Looney—with a smile that resembles "the contortions of a codfish"—to consecrate their union.[3] Faced with the disapproval of Cyril's family, the pair is forced to keep their marriage a secret and Cyril eventually marries a rich widow to ease his financial distress. The betrayal, however, is presented less as a crime than as a misunderstanding. When he is arrested, Thierna refuses to participate in the prosecution of the man she believes to be her husband, and de-

The cover of *Martyrs to Circumstance*.

spite his marriage to the wealthy woman, Cyril's love for Thierna lasts until his death. The lovers, separated by circumstance for most of their lives, die in each other's arms.

Theresa's wishful rendering of her past is purple and overwrought, but it is not pure melodrama or sensation literature, lacking the hallmarks of the genres: a leering sinister villain or domesticated iniquity. The novel is instead an old-fashioned romance of undying devotion. Thierna resolves never to "lose sight of her husband," to bar his way whenever he nears "the verge of a precipice," and she happily stands by him when criminal accusations are made.[4] "If they dare make a felon of him," she says, "I will be a felon's wife . . . his shame shall be my shame, and his sorrow my care; his home shall be my home, and where he goes I too will go."[5]

Despite the self-abnegating protagonist, *Martyrs* questioned the extent to which devotion and duty governed expectations for women. Is a woman really meant "to have no duty, no work to do in the world" and to depend entirely on her husband? Thierna wonders. "Is her husband to possess every virtue and talent in order that her faculties may lie dormant?"[6] In her youth, Thierna complains, she "was banned and barred in every way." Thierna's friend Eulalie finds an outlet in philanthropic activity. But she pushes herself to extremes, compelled "by a false idea of virtue, to make a sacrifice she was physically incapable of completing." Eulalie dies because of her unflagging determination to help her suffering fellow beings, but Thierna sees no virtue in the sacrifice: "Her self-martyrdom was unavailing; no one was benefited by her implicit obedience."[7] Had there been a more moderate way for Eulalie to participate in the wider world, she might not have died so tragically.

If *Martyrs* was part of Theresa's campaign to preserve her virtue by associating herself with wifely sacrifice, such resentment would seem counterproductive. And, as the literal author of her own defense, her naïveté began to seem less genuine. A writer for the weekly literary review the *Athenaeum* pointed out that while most of the novel closely followed Theresa's life, the trial scenes deviated on a few tactical matters that augmented the martyrdom of the heroine: "The purely fictitious portions of the concluding pages raise a suspicion that Mrs. Yelverton is ill satisfied with the part she has taken in the legal proceedings against her quondam husband."[8] Perhaps, the review implied, she manipulated the truth not to atone, but to bypass the hardships that such unwavering devotion would require. By refusing to testify against her husband, Thierna resigns herself to social ignominy, receiving her validation only in death. Theresa was not so patient.

Few contemporary critics, however, picked up on the subversive or manipulative content of her novel. They found other reasons to find it distasteful. Although female authors had been tolerated and sometimes even celebrated, they were still seen by some as a threat, women who perverted the natural order by diverting their energies from their innate role. George Henry Lewes reminded women that their "grand function" was motherhood and that the demands of raising children could not possibly leave time for "the intense and unremitting studies" required to develop literary prowess.[9]

Not only did writing distract from motherhood; it provided a backdoor entry to the squalid world of commerce and exchange. To the most disapproving minds, female writers and menial laborers were one and the same when they entered the workforce; both sweated unbecomingly for little profit. "The unfortunate authoress," *Tait's Edinburgh Magazine* reported, "steeps her fingers in ink up to the second joint, and then hawks her manuscripts from publisher to publisher," working harder "than the wretched drab at eight pounds per annum who cleans the parlour."[10] Forays into this arena contaminated not only the authors but also their work, giving it an overtly commercial taint. The sensation novel—a form often associated with female authors—wrote the critic H. L. Mansel, was "redolent of the manufactory and the shop."[11]

If reviewers overlooked the subtle subversions in *Martyrs*, they invoked this thread of criticism to attack Theresa's writing. They claimed that Theresa's performance in the Dublin courtroom had anticipated her crass intentions to profit indecently from her fame. She had teased the audience with confidences that were "either too lavish or too prudish," wrote one critic in the *Saturday Review*, readying her readers for additional sentimental and lustful exploitations. Knowing she already had a readership, "it did not much matter what she wrote," and so Theresa had produced a cheap, disposable work.[12] "We are sorry to see," wrote a reviewer in the *London Review*, "this lady's name advertised in connection with the 'blood-and-thunder' halfpenny sheets of 'Romance and Crime.'" He wondered if this was "the only method open to the lady of obtaining a livelihood," because no real lady would readily accept such an occupation.[13] The criticism was a powerful indictment of her modesty and placed the novel among those that were ostensibly corrupting the nation. The public, said Anthony Trollope, consumed salacious novels "as men eat pastry after dinner,—not without some inward conviction that the taste is vain if not vicious," and *Martyrs*, it seemed to critics, sated just the type of appetite it was unhealthy to indulge.[14]

Women, said critics, were the most susceptible to such temptations, and *Martyrs* provided alluring bait. Theresa's story had seduced innocent ladies into lingering in the galleries and the courtrooms halls, regaling them with tales of dissolution until they were forcibly removed by the judge. Too many ladies had already spoken "with delicious freedom on the most delicate questions of social immorality" because of the case, complained the *Athenaeum*. (When a woman spoke "as glibly as a man," wrote Eliza Lynn Linton, she "by preference [led] conversation in doubtful subjects.")[15] Don't waste your money on this novel, the *Athenaeum* implored its female readers; it was a "silly, dull and coarse" book, a book that any common "female of unenviable celebrity could be expected to write."[16] If female readers did not want to acquire similar notoriety, they should stay away.

The dark air surrounding Theresa's literary motives made subsequent legal obstacles additionally daunting. While the Dublin case had settled the question of marriage in Ireland, it did not resolve the issue in Scotland or England. As the judge who had dismissed Theresa's 1859 petition to the Court for Divorce and Matrimonial Causes had remarked, "for the purpose of this question of jurisdiction Ireland and Scotland are to be deemed foreign countries equally with France and Spain."[17] In Scotland and England, the matter of the marriage was still unresolved. After Theresa's initial accusation of bigamy in Edinburgh in 1858, Yelverton had filed a request to "put to silence" Theresa's assertions that she was his wife. Theresa had countered with a "declarator of marriage" in order to assert the validity of her claim. A Scottish court had combined the cases into a single case centered on the legality of the marriage. At the start of 1862, a little less than a year after the close of the Dublin trial, the combined case would finally have its turn before the Scottish court. The second trial of the now famous Yelverton case began in the Outer House of Scotland's supreme civil court, the Court of Sessions, in Edinburgh in January.

The Court of Sessions was part of Parliament House, the former seat of the Scottish government, and stood next to St. Giles Cathedral. Just off the busy Royal Mile, the building's sandy-gray stone facade was pillared and grand, with a spacious cobblestone courtyard out front. In the one-hundred-foot-long main hall, statues of robed men were nestled in bays, casting stony stares at the visitors. Girded by oak beams, the cathedral-like ceiling arched high overhead. Gowned and wigged advocates walked back and forth, the clipped sound of their footsteps on the marble floor filling the otherwise hushed space. The

PARLIAMENT HOUSE IN THE PRESENT DAY.

The Court of Sessions, Edinburgh.

actual courtroom for the Outer House was much smaller; lined with wood panels and filled with pews of wooden seats, the whole room resembled the inside of a cedar-lined trunk. Despite its modest size, it was still less crowded than the Dublin courtroom; fewer people were following Theresa's story this time.

The case was tried without a jury, by a panel of judges who worked from a collection of evidence—mostly a repetition of testimony from the Dublin trial—gathered by commissioners.[18] Neither Theresa nor Yelverton was permitted to testify. Their letters, even more than in the Dublin trial, were made to speak for them. Theresa ("the pursuer," as she was referred to in this case), the more prolific and expressive of the two correspondents, was, unsurprisingly, again at the center of the debate. Her letters, according to Lord Ardmillan, the lord ordinary, did not inspire much confidence. They were not, as he phrased it, "such as a lady of very correct and delicate feeling would have written."[19] She wrote with "talent" and "dexterity," he said (echoing the insults of Abraham Brewster, Yelverton's lawyer in the Dublin Trial), and she mercilessly marketed herself for marriage— "eagerly, adroitly, perseveringly, gathering from every field the materials for charming, and the elements of her power."[20] Marriage was the appropriate goal for a young woman, but that assumption did not justify a graceless hunt, especially when the pursued was "frequently cautious, and even cold."[21]

It was lust that motivated women who prostrated themselves in unrequited flirtations; "she actually did yield her person," Ardmillan stated, "without any marriage or form of marriage, and even before applying for marriage to a priest of her own faith, or of any faith."[22] The only reason that Theresa and Yelverton traveled, Ardmillan argued, was so that they could "facilitate intercourse under colour or semblance of marriage."[23] He knew that it took two to engage in such behavior, but the onus fell on the woman to maintain moral standards. It was Theresa who had followed Yelverton; "he was not the seeker, the seducer, the betrayer or the pursuer." Theresa's "charms, her talent, her misfortune,—even the intense and persevering devotedness of the passion by which she was impelled,—must excite interest, pity and sympathy," Ardmillan admitted. "But she was no mere girl,—no simpleton,—no stranger to the ways of the world,—no victim to insidious arts. She was not deceived. She fell with her own consent."[24]

Although colored by palpable dislike for Theresa, Ardmillan's decision was founded on logic—a tool that the Dublin jury was not, in the end, required to employ when they delivered their opinion. Ardmillan assessed the various ways in which Theresa and Yelverton might have been married and found them all lacking in evidence. He even denied the validity of a marriage sealed by promise *subsequente copula*. Perhaps most important, he ignored the effect his decision might have on Theresa's future. Without the looming specter of her blighted prospects, and without the opportunity to speak for herself, Theresa could garner little sympathy. Six months after the Scottish trial began, Theresa's triumphant reign as the queen of courtroom drama came to an end. On July 3, 1862, Ardmillan declared that she and Yelverton were not married.

Statues of a laurel-crowned Mercy and Justice, both holding the royal arms of Scotland, had once graced the entryway to the main hall of the Court of Sessions. The former facade was well known, its image preserved in old books and on banknotes.[25] STANT HIS FELICIA REGNA (these virtues make kingdoms happy) was once inscribed below the figures' feet, and below the national arms, UNI UNIONUM (the union of unions) was carved in the stone.[26] Justice and Mercy had been carted off when renovations took place earlier in the century, and Theresa may have felt that they had abdicated their influence as well as their position. So much for the solemnity of unions—the court had just dismantled her most meaningful relationship.

She was not dissuaded for long. On November 3, 1862, Theresa brought the case before the appeals court, the Inner House of the Edinburgh Court of Sessions. For two more months, the case lingered in the Court of Sessions. When the verdict for her appeal was delivered on December 19, 1862, two of the three lords presiding over the case—Lord Curriehill and Lord Deas—sided with Theresa. In their opinions, Theresa was again cast in the rosy glow of innocence. Lord Deas was particularly vocal in his admiration. Theresa was a well-educated Englishwoman "of respectable birth, of fascinating manners," one who "possessed abilities and accomplishments which might have graced the rank of any society."[27] Her courtship had been an honorable one. He could not accept that her letters showed "that sensual passion had usurped the place of virtuous love."[28] Her heart was genuine, and there was "no grossness" in her metaphors.[29] Was it likely that such a respectable woman would "yield her virtue with the prospect of a life of degradation and shame"?[30]

But the dissenting lord, Lord President Duncan M'Neill, was troubled by the nature of the evidence.

The correspondence, on which much has rested, is so mystical—so vague and figurative—that the real meaning and intention of the

writers is left in obscurity and uncertainty. Instead of plain matters being stated in ordinary language, we are asked to extract
marriage and promise of marriage from metaphors, riddles, dreams,
imaginary dialogues, and vague allusions to unexplained occurrences. Instead of treading on solid ground, we are launched upon
a sea of conjectures.[31]

In the Yelverton case, "metaphors, riddles, dreams, imaginary dialogues, and vague allusions to unexplained occurrences" had all been
taken as, or twisted into, hard evidence. The trials had proceeded as
though there was a definitive truth to the matter of the marriage,
when it was becoming increasingly clear that no such clarity could be
obtained.

However many witnesses were brought forth to describe the interactions between Theresa and Yelverton, the validity of their union
boiled down to an event that only the two of them had witnessed. All
that was completely certain was that Theresa believed she was married and Yelverton did not. Although Theresa was successful in her
Edinburgh appeal, it was becoming clear that the law leaned toward
Yelverton. "I have been unable to overcome the difficulties, in fact
and in law that appear to me to have beset the pursuer's case," M'Neill
concluded.[32] Theresa won this battle, but nagging concerns about the
evidence would continue to hinder attempts to fully reclaim her respectability.

For an entire year, rather than ten dramatic days, the public was
aware of the Yelverton case. Although the Edinburgh trials did not
generate the minutely detailed coverage of the Dublin trial, they occupied their share of newspaper inches for a wearying length of time.
In the *Manchester Guardian* alone, thirty-three articles were written
during 1862.[33] Critical voices emerged, now attacking not only
Theresa's writing but also her behavior. An editorial published in the
Times near the end of 1862 accused Theresa of attempting "to con-
vert the position of mistress into that of wife at the expense of a rival
[Emily Forbes Yelverton] against whom society had no reproach."
She had corrupted the courtroom by bringing cheap theatrics into a

sacred forum, and the consequences were severe: "Life or property or character can never be safe in a country where the mob undertakes to decide private lawsuits, and where children can be bastardized amid a popular howl."[34] Theresa's old enemies continued to rear their heads: she was not the rightful wife, and even if she was, who was she to expose her suffering so publicly?

By May, Theresa had left Edinburgh and was again living with the Thelwalls in the northeastern port town of Hull. She was surrounded by the hustle of shipbuilders, whalers, and sailors, but she was idle, unsure of her position despite her Edinburgh victory. When it rained in Hull, the flagstones reflected shimmering pools of yellow light from the gas lamps, and the people walking through the streets turned into shadow figures veiled by the mist. Just two years earlier, in Dublin, she had been a local celebrity. Here she moved among the crowds with anonymity.

In defiance or desperation or out of sheer financial necessity, Theresa did not recede from the public's view for long. She gave concerts and readings, wrote articles and essays, and petitioned members of Parliament for her cause. In May 1863, she contacted A. H. Layard, an archaeologist, Liberal politician, and a friend of Alcide's. She asked him to support the 1863 Irish Marriage Bill, which would allow for the civil registration of marriage between people who had been united in a Roman Catholic ceremony.[35] As she understood it, the bill was founded "entirely upon [her] unhappy case," and she was certain that if "the hardships of the case [were] known, the House would listen."[36] Ignoring the fact that Yelverton was not really a Catholic, Theresa asked why, if they were going to formally recognize Catholic unions, the decision could not retroactively apply to her.[37]

In August, she wrote again to Layard to remind him of her personal prerogative: "There can be little doubt that my [lawsuit has] brought the imperfect state of the law to heights and it is so very hard that I should not derive any benefit from the tardy justice."[38] She softened the argument with a maternal angle: surely "the innocent Mothers" should receive "the same considerations as their offspring," she wrote to another prominent figure. Although her "child did not live, that is no reason why [Theresa] should be deprived of the advantages."[39] She waged her campaigns on a small scale, but using her personal plight for a political appeal was risky. With each letter she penned, the galleys of self-appointed judges expanded, armed with new examples of her indiscretion.

Her motherly invocations probably did not win her any new supporters since Yelverton's "other" wife, Emily, was the only woman directly involved in the triangle who was actually a mother. Unlike Theresa, and despite her headstrong reputation, Emily Forbes Yelverton had remained mute throughout the trials, effectively disabling critics from attacking her. Her well-timed reticence allowed her to avoid having to explain, for example, why Barry Nugent Yelverton, her first son, was born only seven months after her marriage to Yelverton, how she had become acquainted with an officer, or whether a respectable period of time had passed between her first husband's death and the beginning of her flirtation with the second.

Because of her insulation from the scandal, Emily came to represent a type of private femininity that Theresa had relinquished. Emily's defenders objected to any insinuation that she had entered the forums of debate, as though a mere brush with publicity would contaminate her. A friend wrote to the *Times* "to give authoritative contradiction" to the "absurd rumour" that "Mrs. (Forbes) Yelverton was present" in the Edinburgh courtroom. "[I was in] constant communication with her solicitor," he said, "and I can assure you that she was not there, and that she is quite incapable of appearing there."[40] Theresa no longer provoked this type of solicitous concern; she freely circulated in public view. In the years since the first accusations, Emily had stayed quiet and produced several children. Theresa had become increasingly vocal and had produced a novel. One wife resembled the domestic stereotype; the other was beginning to look like a women's rights campaigner. Ironically, Theresa thought that if she kept writing, her case might improve.

In 1863, Theresa published her own version of the letters she had exchanged with Yelverton with additional correspondence from various people. Most of the correspondence had already been printed and distributed to the judge and jury during the Dublin trial, but Theresa disagreed with the ordering of the letters and her lawyer in the Edinburgh trial had already publicly complained in the *Times* that "the scraps of quotation" did not "represent anything like a fair representation of the letters or evidence in the case."[41] Theresa was frustrated that people were making up their minds about her before reading what she had to say. Now she published the letters for all to see, confident that they would not "justify the opinion that had been formed of them."[42] She didn't want her fate decided by journalists and three old men sitting in a room in Edinburgh. She wanted the public to judge for itself, just as it had in the Dublin trial, with cheers and jeers and broadsides and ballads. But she did not leave it *all* up to interpretation; she knew that strategy could backfire, as it had with her novel. If readers saw smut in the letters, it was a reflection of their own corruption, she wrote in her introduction to them; "the purer the mind of the reader the less evil will be found in them."[43]

Conscious that the attention might do more to damage than to repair her reputation, she took additional precautions to deflect criticism. "These letters were written in blissful ignorance of law proceedings," she wrote. She did not wish to further desecrate "that sacred confidence which should exist between correspondents," but the violation had already taken place, and there was no harm in reminding her audience of the greater violation of Yelverton's actions.[44] The letters would present her as she had been before lawyers and journalists twisted her story, and would restore her to a state of grace. Making her misery public was a risky tactic; as a public commodity, her story was ammunition for detractors and supporters alike. Unlike the publication of *Martyrs*, however, the *Correspondence* caused little stir. People, it seemed, were losing interest.

Yelverton was most likely encouraged by this fading of his ignominious star. Like Emily, he had adopted an approach opposite to Theresa's in handling the whole ordeal, avoiding publicity as much as possible, and hiding from his former lover. He had entered a notice of petition to the court of last resort, the House of Lords, in January of 1863, but since then had been scarce.[45] In February of 1864, John

The interior of the House of Lords, photographed around
the time Theresa's case appeared.

Thelwall—still laboring on Theresa's behalf—fleetingly located
Yelverton in Paris before he disappeared again.

On April 6, 1864, in the faux Gothic buildings next to the River
Thames, the lords took up the case that had been in and out of the
courts for more than three years. At this point it was clear that Theresa
was never going to lead a conventional married life no matter what the
courts decided. Even after Theresa had been declared Yelverton's wife
by the Dublin court and then the appeals court in Edinburgh, she had
not spent a single night with him. But the lords felt that the ambiguity
surrounding her position—and marriage law in general—still war-
ranted their attention.

Hoping to establish her status immediately, Theresa submitted a
petition asking that Yelverton pay five hundred pounds in order "to
defend her interest." As her husband (according to the Scottish Court
of Sessions), he was responsible for her expenses. The lord chancellor
was doubtful of the legitimacy of this maneuver, but precedent in-

structed that Yelverton should pay something toward her legal fees. The lord chancellor and Yelverton's lawyers settled on £150. Theresa's momentum would not last. On July 28, 1864, three of the five law lords who had listened to the case ruled against her.

In his decision, Lord Chelmsford complained that the proceedings—in previous trials and in the current one—had strayed from their proper course. Narrative had overtaken reason. "It appears to me," he said, "that there was a great deal of preliminary matter dwelt upon at considerable length in the course of the argument . . . which is not very material to the question being decided."[46] Both parties had indulged in a dangerous degree of sentiment. Chelmsford also thought that the evidence was mystical and vague: "The enigmatical character of the correspondence, which might be intelligible to the parties themselves, renders it extremely difficult for a third person to be certain that he had put a correct interpretation upon it."[47] This was the basis of his decision; the writings were too circuitous and indirect to establish that there had been a promise of marriage.

The majority of the law lords were more concerned over Emily's fate than Theresa's. To allow a man to escape his second marriage without consequence would be "adducing a new peril to our law of marriage," not to mention the damage it might do to the second wife.[48] Only one lord saw it differently: "Mrs. Forbes can have no right to say that it is injustice to her that the law should give Miss Longworth her legal rights."[49] For this dissenting lord, the decision set a dangerous precedent; any man who married a woman in private, then married another, might escape his obligations to the first wife by claiming that the second wife stood to suffer. He could not concur in such reasoning. "I see neither law nor justice in it," he wrote.[50] The *Times* printed the full decision the next day as well as two editorials.[51]

Theresa attempted an encore but met with little success. She submitted a note to the Scottish Court of Sessions asking that new evidence be considered. The evidence came from Sarah Mallins, a nurse who had attended Frederick Yelverton, Yelverton's brother, on his deathbed. Now deceased herself, Mallins had confessed to her priest that Yelverton had told Frederick of his marriage to Theresa. Two

years after Mallin's death, the priest sent a letter to Theresa inform-
ing her of this confidence that the brothers had exchanged.[52] Not
surprisingly, the lords were not swayed by this dilute evidence, and
they denied its admission.

In 1867, the case for the consideration of new evidence was taken
to the House of Lords. During the proceedings, Theresa proposed
that the whole outcome of the case rest on an oath. If Yelverton could
swear to the lords, Theresa, and the world that he had never married
her, Theresa would accept his declaration. No matter what other evidence had been presented, the involved parties would take the oath as
the final, unimpeachable truth. When this ultimate test was applied,
Theresa hoped that Yelverton would admit to and accept his responsibilities. On the day that the law lords gathered to listen to her petition, Theresa's lawyer was late, held up in a trial in Edinburgh. They
waited as long as they could, and were about to postpone the hearing
when Theresa stopped them. Dressed in a light gray suit with a black
shawl around her shoulders, she stood up to speak for herself.

> I am not pleading for something as yet unheard of . . . What I am
> pleading for is a law which, as admitted by the judges, is one of the
> oldest and most firmly established in Scotland. The facts I am
> seeking to bring to light have already been sworn to. Yes, my
> lords, sworn to by the respondent himself, and are on record, not
> in these volumes unfortunately, but in the Irish Court, and in
> every journal in that country. This is no vague dream of an ex-
> cited fancy wrought of frenzy by its sufferings. I appeal to every
> honest heart in Great Britain, and ask if Major Yelverton did not
> marry Theresa Longworth.[53]

But the question had mutated over the course of its long journey
through the courts and was no longer so simple. It was no longer only
a matter of resolving past disputes—a £260 bill or a quarrel between
lovers. The question evoked the disadvantaged position of young
unmarried women and unhappily married women, the tangled skein
of marriage law, and the incapacity of the courts to deal with certain

types of evidence and stories. The request for the oath was denied and the House of Lords dismissed the case.

Despite the fact that the highest court in the land had ruled on this case, it continued to serve as a primary example of the muddle of British marriage law. "On this side of St. George's Channel, the widow of Professor Forbes is Lord Avonmore's wife; in Ireland, Miss Longworth is his wife—and his English and Scottish wife has neither titles nor *status*," wrote *Freeman's Journal and Daily Commercial Advertiser*.[54] The reputation for inconsistency spread farther afield as well. "The Yelverton case showed the strange jumble into which the marriage laws of the United Kingdom had fallen," wrote the *Albany Law Journal*. "Such a loose doctrine doubtless held out a bounty upon immoral living."[55] When Yelverton's father died, and the case was again in the news, the *New York Times* noted that the death was likely "to call attention once more to the absurd and cruel condition in which the marriage laws of Great Britain have been left."[56]

Theresa perpetuated her case's reputation as well. Having exhausted all opportunities before the courts, Theresa tried once more to make her argument by pointing out the logical flaws of marriage law in writing. At this stage, she adopted a more articulate role, foregoing her male exponents—her lawyers and friends—and abandoning the shield of fiction through which she had previously expressed her more controversial leanings. The motion to "put to silence" (the legal mechanism that Yelverton had used in the Scottish court to stop her from saying they were married) was a "barefaced barbarism . . . only serviceable to protect a man from the consequences of bigamy." Men could mistreat women, while women were forced to stay quiet or suffer accusations of promiscuity. If a man has "committed a felonious act himself, he can . . . get rid of it by striking at the very roots of his first wife's honest fame."[57] A woman, on the other hand, immediately faced suspicion when there was conflict between her and her husband. If she did not want to "lie down and die" under false accusations, she must defend herself.[58]

Before the courts, Theresa had argued for her prerogatives along conservative lines of logic; she had not been justly compensated with male protection for the sacrifices she had made, and she deserved retribution. But her independence had implicitly undermined the argument of defenselessness. Now, when she related the events of her life, middle-class values and the rhetoric of melodrama were no longer appropriate. She would never be an angel in the house; no knight would free her from the Soeurs keeping her captive or rescue her from an evil landlord. Instead of relying on the stories that she had previously summoned for sympathy, she argued for reform. New laws might help her, but she stated that the issue was larger than her own concerns. If the messy system was allowed to persist in its current state, Theresa wrote, all women would suffer.

> When we come to consider the amount of domestic misery occasioned by this patchwork marriage law—falling chiefly on the weaker portion of society, women and children; when we see the wear and tear, the gnawing and corroding effect of litigation for honor, virtue, and social status; when we see the broken hearts of wives, deserted in the first marriage, and dishonored of the second, the weary mother claiming legitimacy for her offspring, the down-trodden, shame-branded children vainly claiming the honorable heritage of their parents—all these things filling the land with wretchedness and sorrow . . . [we] have no hesitation in saying that there needs a thorough and radical reform in the marriage laws of Great Britain.[59]

Theresa still traded in images of destitution—broken hearts and weary mothers—but her ability to formulate a complex argument, combined with the industrious and public way in which she had recently lived her life, belied the claim that women were defeated and disabled by mistreatment at the hands of villainous men. If Theresa no longer epitomized the stereotypes of the "weaker portion of society"—the "deserted" and the "dishonored"—she would be their spokeswoman. Theresa held herself apart from contemporary feminists, but her stubborn detachment from their movement derived more from her disagreement with their priorities than with their underlying desires. "The ardent supporters of 'Woman's Rights' can find abundant employment for their energies long before they reach that of voting," she wrote. They would do better by going after the "patchwork marriage law" of Great Britain than pursuing a goal that they were far from attaining.[60]

After six years of romance and six years of litigation, neither love nor law nor literature nor logic secured Theresa's position as Yelverton's wife. The conviction behind her cause had been squeezed out by the *Jarndyce*-like proceedings, vilification in the press, the discrediting of her letters as indecipherable effusions, and the collapse of the tropes that had established her victimhood. Friends had drifted away; Theresa's funds had been exhausted. She had no child or companion to keep her company. A shadowy, uncertain life unfolded before her. But there was a dim light. Her tragedy—her failure to secure a husband—left her unfettered, able to escape the society that was unwilling to accept her.

CHAPTER SEVEN

The Lady Traveler

How womankind, who are confined to the house still more than men,
stand it I do not know; but I have grown to suspect that most of them
do not stand it at all.

—Henry David Thoreau, "Walking" (1851)

The ink sloshed over the edge of the bottle and formed a kidney-shaped splotch at the edge of Theresa's writing pad. She raised her umbrella and hit the roof of the stagecoach. Her secretary, schooled in the signs of her displeasure and riding on the seat beside the driver, communicated her discomfort. She was trying to write—was almost successfully ignoring the odor emanating from the propped-up feet of the so-called gentleman beside her—and she had just managed to achieve a degree of concentration. Since she had arrived in America in September 1867—only a few months after losing her last appeal before the House of Lords—peace and quiet had been hard to come by.

Throughout the nineteenth century, British women like Theresa traversed the North American continent, scribbling down their observations as their carriages bumped over dusty roads. They bemoaned the lack of privacy in hotels and the hurried habits forced upon them by dining in railway cars, but they continued to make reservations and purchase tickets, encouraged by a proliferation of guidebooks that advised on matters ranging from sandwiches to steamships, manners to mountain climbing. America was the perfect place for the curious lady traveler who did not want to stray too far from home. It was wild around the edges and in vast swaths of the interior, but with certain familiar comforts—tea trays and timetables—relatively nearby.

By the mid-nineteenth century, the ranks of female travelers had grown so large—or, at least, their reputation had reached such sizable proportions—that they evoked acute ire from men and women who thought that their behavior was an affront to female decorum. The supposedly most traveled man in the British cabinet, Lord Curzon, referred to this "genus of female globetrotters" as "one of the horrors of the latter end of the nineteenth century."[1] *Punch* echoed the disdain.

> *A Lady an explorer? A traveler in skirts?*
> *The notion's just a trifle too seraphic.*
> *Let them stay at home and mind the babies,*
> *Or hem our ragged shirts;*
> *But they musn't, can't and shan't be geographic.*[2]

If the traveling woman had any domestic duties, she neglected them, leaving herself free to partake of all kinds of unladylike activities. "Travelers are privileged to do the most improper things with perfect propriety," wrote the Victorian traveler Isabella Bird; "that is one charm of traveling."[3] Bird celebrated this impropriety by sewing pant legs under her skirts to make riding more comfortable.

While lady travelers neglected the minding of their babies, and altered the patterns of their mending to suit their new endeavors, their written accounts further removed them from traditional female duties. Travel writing was not yet an explicit genre, but it still had sentinels who wanted to guard its masculine prerogatives. The "inexperienced novice," the "superficial coxcomb," and the "romantic female" were debasing the standards of travel writing, complained

Tourists viewing Niagara Falls.

one critic in the British periodical *Blackwood's Edinburgh Magazine*. They viewed "everything through the medium of poetical fiction."[4] Though sentimentality and melodrama did infiltrate some of these women's writings, more often, their supposedly fanciful descriptions followed a practical and well-trodden route through America's social oddities (the peculiar institution of the South, the widespread social vulgarities) and natural splendors (the crashing waters of Niagara Falls, the expanse of wilderness). But the objectors were right that even these fail-safe subjects gave female travelers a chance to test their boundaries.

Frances Trollope (Anthony's mother) became the founding mother of this genre when she documented her travels in *Domestic Manners of the Americans*. "I could not but ask myself," Trollope wrote, "if virtue was a plant, thriving under one form in one country, and flourishing under a different one in another."[5] If the cultivation of morals lagged in America, a wilder life—and wildlife—flourished.

"We might have thought ourselves the first of the human race who had ever penetrated into this territory of bears and alligators," Trollope wrote of one of her family's grass-thrashing excursions through the swamps.[6]

Harriet Martineau came later in the 1830s, prepared to admire rather than scorn Americans. But if her aims were different from Mrs. Trollope's, the two women shared the sense of liberation resulting from their excursions. Martineau's travels forced her "to work hard and usefully . . . to think and learn, and to speak out with absolute freedom what [she had] thought and learned." They gave her a life that she "had truly lived instead of vegetated."[7] Isabella Bird was plagued by back problems throughout her life but felt no pain while traveling across the Rockies on horseback, rising at dawn, clearing snow, and fighting a constant battle against the wind in a drafty cabin. Her ailments only flared up when she returned to her sedentary life at home.

No matter how severe or soft a Victorian woman's attitude toward American society, continent-spanning treks were a dramatic escape from the restrictions and expectations of everyday life back home. Life on the road or life on the frontier not only necessitated an adaptation of everyday responsibilities and standards of decorum, but offered spiritual and philosophical expansion. Possibility pulsed through the untainted, undeveloped landscape—unmarked by the ruins of antiquity. Even the most windswept moor in Britain was studded with traces of the deep-seated past: stone circles, moss-covered gravestones, crumbling country churches. In America, such remnants were few and far between. If America was closer to its immature origins, this did not condemn it to chaos but perhaps positioned it closer to paradise.

"We have it in our power to begin the world over again," the British transplant Thomas Paine had once suggested. A century later, the sentiment resonated for a new, female population seeking a different type of renewal. It wasn't very often that a British woman was the first to bend back branches, clear a path, and forge forward into unknown territory. These women were aware that their footprints would not leave a lasting impression of their travels, so they pushed their pens across the page to document their voyages. British law denied most women property, but by writing about America— particularly the areas beyond the well-trod circles of East Coast society—they established a claim to this new land. "Estes Park is mine," wrote Bird. "It is unsurveyed, 'no man's land,' and mine by right to live, appropriation, and appreciation."[8] Theresa claimed she was the first white woman to scale the Little Yosemite Valley and that by plunging her walking stick into the ground she had "claim to several hundred acres of land."[9]

In 1867, long before she reached the Yosemite Valley, Theresa joined this tribe of female travelers when she sailed from Liverpool on the *City of Washington*.[10] She wrote throughout her journey and later published her collected writing as *Teresina in America*. In topic and trajectory she followed the experts, starting with domestic matters and moving from East Coast cities to the South. She did not abandon the bread-and-butter material of the fed-up female traveler—insisting on the superiorities of British society and showcasing the amusing hodgepodge of American eccentricities—but she also wanted to examine the dizzying diversity of the United States, and to find something to admire in this panoply of peoples.

No matter how benign her intentions, Theresa most likely knew she was going to have to be careful; Americans did not take external examination lightly. Because of his satiric portraits, Dickens had faced a harsh backlash from formerly adoring American readers when *American Notes* was published in 1842. But such defensiveness, Theresa thought, was misguided, an outgrowth of each American's belief "that nothing can be called American that differs from his own individual knowledge and experience of men and things."[11] The regional disparities of American character had by this time become a recurring trope in British literature, but Theresa's intent to approach all shades of life with an open attitude was reinforced by her experience. She knew all too well the paralyzing perils of narrow conceptions of propriety. That was precisely what she, and other lady travelers before her, had come to America to escape.

After a brief tour of Boston and the surrounding area, Theresa arrived in New York—a city unlike any she had seen. The grandest thoroughfare of late-nineteenth-century New York began at Battery Park and stretched north for about four miles, eventually petering out into a country road. Along its busiest stretches, Broadway was crowded with carriages, hackney cabs, omnibuses, and pedestrians, a surging river of color and commotion. Twirling their parasols and swinging their shopping bags, silk-clad women teetered down the sidewalks in pointed boots. Squawking street urchins waved gray sheets of newsprint like dirty sails and darted between rickety carts transporting sweating hunks of ice. Young men with turned-down collars smoothed their lapels and made their way to Wall Street. A few blocks away, on the Bowery, carts selling cheap hunks of cooked meat emanated gusts of heat. The clattering noise of loaded wagons replaced the sound of clinking carriages. At the notorious slum of Five Points, porcelain countenances were replaced by faces scarred by disease and swollen with drink. Pigs dug their noses into decaying debris lying in the gutter. Behind broken windows, in the depths of dark corners, those too weak to venture outside lay wrapped in rags.

As the carriage whisked her to her hotel, Theresa would have glimpsed both the radiant and the wretched. She had lived between splendor and shabbiness before, but the slivers of squalor nestled between the teetering tenements were new to her. Having left her family and friends behind, and with notoriety rather than acclaim announcing her arrival, her position in New York society was tenuous. Yelverton, the lodestar that had guided her movements throughout her adult life, could no longer direct her. Would she float in the sunlit stream of Broadway or drift into darker, more obscure regions?

When she reached her hotel, a letter scrawled in an indecipherable hand was waiting for her. The messenger explained that it was from Horace Greeley, editor of the *New York Tribune* and onetime presidential candidate. It requested to meet the lady who had given his colleagues across the Atlantic so much to write about. With its ambiguous slashes and careless loops, Theresa's handwriting had never been her best attribute, and so perhaps Greeley's poor penmanship endeared him to her. Once she met him, she deemed him delightful. Greeley, she wrote later, had only been defeated in his run for the presidency because of "the fearfully villainous machinations, deceits, egotism, peculation, frauds, briberies, &c., which the elections periodically bring forth." His intellect was "one of the finest ... the country can boast of," and he possessed a "great, glowing heart!"[12]

If Theresa saw a genuine life force in Greeley, she was ultimately less impressed with New York as a whole. New York was a city of glittering facades—"lofty and imposing in their wealth of precious marble," the windows draped with silk and velvet. But these fronts were just that. "If you are a worshipper of gold," Theresa wrote, "fall down and do homage, for all these are the ensigns of the God of America. If you are a worshipper of solid worth, pause; for the buildings are only veneered; the wearers of silk will be penniless in a few years, perhaps a few months, and ere long will become common clay, forgotten by all the world, because they will have done nothing for it to remember, and have built nothing which will outlive themselves."[13]

Monuments to prosperity were fragile, and social conventions were similarly delicate. "Some of the more advanced spirits among the New Yorkers," Theresa wrote, "have really succeeded in persuading themselves that they are aristocrats."[14] Any man could jump from one social tier to another: "If a man is dissatisfied with the station he occupies in the world," Theresa wrote, "there is no place like America for changing it."[15] For women, respectability was similarly mutable. "Who *are* ladies in America?" Theresa asked. If "the wife of a grocer, a tailor, or a chandler keeps, probably, the handsomest equipage in the city, lives in the most expensive house, and dresses in the most costly style, she is, therefore, considered the highest and most important leader of town."[16] If a woman, Theresa wrote, could afford an appropriately elaborate dress, "she will consider herself the equal of whoever may be present."[17] One evening, startled by the informality of a servant, she asked why the servant didn't treat her mistress with greater respect. The girl replied: "There be no *rale* gintry in this country . . . just the same ladies as I'll be myself, when I git my new silk suit, and go to housekeeping, and keep a girl."[18]

Theresa's derision toward America's relative social fluidity was at least partly tongue-in-cheek. She, after all, wanted to persuade the world that she was an aristocrat by marriage and manner, if not by blood. Who was she to scorn people who had succeeded? But even when she defied the conventions of her native land, Theresa had probably never wanted to abandon completely the idea of respectability. Status had always been desirable and delineated by formal standards. In America, it seemed, eminence was open to all who trimmed their windows and their frocks with the appropriate material. The relative informality of society was both a relief and a terrible irony. She had lost the ten-year battle to preserve her reputation. Now she faced the possibility that her whole enterprise had been a waste of time.

But before she could dismiss her former foes she faced a new cadre. No matter that their social graces differed, American critics had sharp words for Theresa. When she delivered her final address to the House of Lords, the *New York Times* wrote that her speaking style foreboded "what we shall have in Congress when women's suffrage is fairly established," and it did not intend the assessment as a compliment. "The language is arabesque—the ideas are confused and ladylike. The point is to crowd as many poetical quotations and images into a given space as human ingenuity is capable of." Its sympathies lay with Emily Yelverton: "Nine points of the law are with her, and the tenth the beautiful oratress is in search of." If Theresa could not find the tenth, the *Times* coyly conceded, she "will at least be able to start afresh as a lecturer on the strength of her brilliant display in the House of Lords."[19]

The double-edged compliment perhaps spurred Theresa to entertain the idea of embarking on a new career. She had already given several readings, including one in Edinburgh in 1866 that had been deemed a great success. At that event, when she read from Tennyson's "Lady Clara Vere de Vere" and when she reached the line "Kind hearts are more than coronets, / And simple faith than *gentle blood*," she was met with a "storm of applause," according to one report.[20] (She had changed the actual line—"And simple faith than Norman blood"—but no one objected to her revision.) When she arrived in New York, she planned a series of readings.

Just before her first performance at Irving Hall she published a note in the New York newspapers stating that she did not intend to read from her letters to Yelverton. The correspondence had not been published in America, and both fans and enemies were eager to hear the words from her own lips. But to Theresa, the letters were "only relics of 'love's young dream.'" Now that her heart had been broken and Yelverton had become "a nameless wanderer," the missives were a "funereal urn which contain[s] the ashes of all that ever was, of all that ever can be." She conceded that the letters' innocence had already been defiled by judges, lawyers, and British newspapers, but that era of violation was past, and she had to "respect the green turf now growing over the grave."[21]

The hyperbole and sentimentality of this note irked the American press. Here was another European lecturing them about decorum and curiosity, when Europeans—with their endless editorials and crowds of courtroom vultures—were already guilty of the sin. "Mrs. Yelverton," wrote the *Round Table*, "knows better, and it is no very fair return for the courtesy and good feeling which Americans have shown her to insult their taste and intelligence with a letter which we do her the credit of believing she would not have dared to print in any English paper."[22] Theresa's pedagogy was most likely an effort to move in small steps away from her past. After fifteen years of chasing the same man, she wanted to prove she was capable of different pursuits.

When she gave the reading, a crowd assembled to hear her. Wearing a blue silk dress with a silver belt, she read Tennyson's "Locksley Hall" and the "May Queen," Thomas Buchanan Read's "Sheridan's Ride," Longfellow's "Excelsior," and selections from Richard Brinsley Sheridan's play *The School for Scandal*. Her nervousness showed, and she visibly shook as she stood onstage. The *Times* was guarded in its review: "Mrs. Yelverton has chosen a difficult task. She deserves credit for her courage, as well as sympathy for the misfortunes that compel her to seek public support." Her failing, according to the *Times*, lay in the limits of her theatrical ability: "To be a good reader she must be the greatest of actresses," and Theresa's reading "betrays the amateur." She was successful, however, "in enunciating passages from the books which are particularly applicable to feminine weakness, passion and remorse." She was too much of an actress in the courtroom, it seemed, and not quite sufficient on the stage, only succeeding when her real-life experience fleshed out her poetic interpretations. The audience was less cagey and more appreciative; "She was greatly applauded," said the *Times*.[23]

Reports from other readings were more enthusiastic, more closely mirroring the reaction of the audiences. Her performances were seen as acts of bravery—a woman making the best of her unfortunate situation. "How strange it is that so elegantly an accomplished woman, so wronged a wife and so popular a heroine, should be compelled to come before the public and give readings in order to support herself," wrote the tabloid *National Police Gazette*. "Mrs. Yelverton is among us. Let us treat her well, and remember her sufferings as a wife and as a woman."[24] One magazine forecast that in the winter of 1867–68 Theresa was "destined to be the bright particular star of the lyceum firmament."[25] Stepping on stage in St. Louis wearing a robe of blue antique silk, fringed at the top with gold lace, white satin shoes, and white silk stockings, she struck her audience as a figure of magnificent, if somewhat faded, splendor.[26]

But even endorsements were combined with accusations. The St. Louis newspaper that had begun its review of her performance by describing her majestic aura, also included a less demure description of her snowy bosom, exposed to the crowd when she curtsied. She was hailed for her honesty, but when theatrical artifice was required, her abilities were seen as insufficient. She was admired for her plucky fight against a British noble but scolded for talking down to Americans. Her motions toward modesty, in fact, immodestly stoked the scandal. The terrain of celebrity, it seemed, was as difficult to navigate in America as it had been in Britain.

Despite the mixed reactions she elicited, Theresa took pleasure in

her travels. When she had had enough of New York, she packed her
dresses in a coffin to prevent them from creasing and set sail from
New York for Charleston. As she neared the city, she probably sensed
that life here assumed a slower pace, closer to that of the Mediterranean climes where she had thrived. Waxy, broad-leafed magnolia
trees lined the river, their broad branches draped with a ghostly
silver-gray moss. Men sauntered through the streets without the
frenzied energy that had marked the northerners' gait; ladies sipped
tea from tall glasses. Along the fringes of the town, plantation culture died a slow death under the unstoppable growth of the natural
world; vines of passionflower, sweet pea, and rose crept over balcony railings while neglected porch fronts gathered dust and debris.
Clusters of unpicked wild strawberries speckled the ground with
splashes of red, and raspberry bushes grew into thorny barriers. A
pelican swooped across a pool of water, lord of an abandoned
land—a "miniature Roman galley proudly breasting the waves."[27]
Postwar Charleston was luxuriantly languid and grand in certain
corners, but also economically blighted and desolate, reminding
Theresa of a "beautiful cemetery" cast in a "sad, suffering, woebe-
gone look . . . that appealed to the heart, as well as to the sense of
poetic melancholy."[28]

   Although she did not wish to see the Charleston man "in all the
glory of a slave-owner . . . to behold him in the ruins of his former
power was very painful."[29] The sympathy generated by the formerly
rich man's poverty did not extend to freed slaves. "The negro children," she wrote, "are funny little round black things . . . They have
much the same sort of beauty as little pugs, or little pigs, lacking entirely that exquisite loveliness and angelic sweetness, which sur-
rounds the rosy form of a white infant."[30] As for the adults, they had
made a mess of their freedom, living in "idleness and filth."[31] The
northern triumph had turned "five million savage natives" loose
"upon civilized society," an event that "was very much like throwing
open the flood-gates of [hell]. That such an experiment did not result
in the production of five million demons was owing to the fact, that
more than four million of them were yet too imbued with the nature

of the lower animals to rise to that of the fallen angel, and participate in his capabilities for mischief."[32]

The prevalence of such beliefs at this historical juncture certainly does not excuse them. But Theresa was also not the only British citizen who did not condemn slavery or the mistreatment of black people upon arrival in America—even though Britain had banned the slave trade early in the nineteenth century. Frances Trollope came away from America with the opinion that the slave trade was "less injurious to the manners and morals of the people than the fallacious idea of equality."[33] (Trollope's book was published in 1832, when the rumble of reform in England might have weighed more heavily on her mind than the condition of slaves in America.) Although the explorer Frederick Marryat thought the freed black slaves of superior intellect to their bound brethren, he dispelled any notion that they would "ever attain to the same powers of intellect as the white man," for, as he put it, "I really believe that the race are not formed for it by the Almighty."[34] Although she was morally opposed to slavery, Harriet Martineau noted that slavery had helped to produce a class that was attentive to hospitality, manners, and other finer aspects of servitude without expressly noting an objection to this form of training.[35] Incisive criticism, for many of these writers, was often obstructed by studies of manners and mores.

Still, Theresa left ugly evidence of her prejudice—evidence that illustrates that even an independent, open-minded thinker sometimes adheres to pervasive inhumane beliefs. Theresa's racism, however, should not be considered a seminal aspect of her attitude toward America. No matter how virulent her prose, she quickly spewed her venom, then left it behind. The apparent ease with which she abandoned her prejudice suggests that she amplified her disgust for literary purposes. If her audience wanted a gothic cemetery of former glories, she would give them one haunted by ghouls and would-be demons. The fallen-glory, slightly scary fairy tale of the South was a common literary trope by the time Theresa arrived.[36]

Theresa had always embellished her autobiography with dramatic flourishes, and America, particularly the South, fed her taste for the

Bonaventure, Savannah, Georgia.

fantastic. When she arrived in Georgia she surveyed the dusty streets of Bainbridge from her hotel window. A one-armed man, his hat pulled low on his face, was riding his gray mare toward a lone figure in the street. As he leaned down in his saddle, the man in the street lashed out, swinging a heavy wooden stick at the rider. The horse bolted, and the one-armed man looked back at the assailant with angry surprise. Standing motionless, the man pulled a revolver from his pocket, raised it, and shot four times in the direction of the retreating rider. Theresa contemplated calling the police, but no one else seemed anxious to raise an alarm. The quarrel that had erupted between these two men was no business of hers, she decided; she might, as she put it, be seen as "the stranger who interferes between man and his wife" if she were to step in.[37] Determining that it was best to refrain from meddling, Theresa shut her balcony doors and prepared to meet a friend. But now there was a new commotion.

A riotous crowd of disgruntled soldiers had assembled in the courtyard of the hotel, their guns and bowie knives flashing in the sunlight. Her friend sent word; he could not possibly enter the riotous scrum to escort Theresa from the hotel. Unless she was prepared to make her own way through the crowd, they would have to cancel their appointment. Theresa steeled herself, Mrs. Trollope's words ringing in her head. Chivalry, Trollope had written, "is not to be looked for where [it] has never been."[38] Clenching her teeth, she walked through the clusters of swarthy men, ignoring their jeers. "It was a cruel thing to frighten a woman," she thought as she moved through them, propelled by her increasing indignation. But it was worse to give in to fear: "To recede before a danger is surely to be overtaken by it."[39] The next day the mayor arrived at her hotel to apologize for the soldiers' misbehavior (there was no mention of the shooting) and suggested that three of the most unruly men make a personal appeal for her forgiveness. Theresa waited for the men in a chair in the hotel lobby. One by one, six-foot-tall "haughty warriors"—"as handsome men as one could see in the highwayman style"—apologized on bended knee.[40] When the ceremony ended and her fearlessness had been commended, Theresa sipped mint juleps with the soldiers.

The longer Theresa stayed, the more adventurous she became. At dusk one evening, she rode into untended fields and found herself farther from her hotel than she had anticipated. She decided to take a shortcut through a swampy cornfield but was soon slowed by the sucking mud that clung to her horse's hooves. Corn stalks lashed at her legs as she rode through the field. Night was approaching, and her path was becoming increasingly dim. Theresa held fast to her horse; if she fell, the creature would plunge ahead, leaving her stranded and hidden within the towering stalks. If she did not see a road before darkness engulfed them, she would have to sit on her horse through the night, hoping that the snakes stayed in the nearby river. At last, "bruised and torn," she found the path home, just as total darkness descended. "Well," remarked her guide when she returned, "I guess you are the first lady ever took that ride."[41] The adventure had been unintended, but it gave Theresa another chance to test her mettle.

When Theresa left the South, she moved North again, visiting the mid-Atlantic cities she had skipped over on the way down: Philadelphia, Baltimore, Washington, and Richmond. The redbrick of Philadelphia's Independence Hall charmed her with its relative antiquity.

Such a facade was worth, she felt, a hundred "costly marble modern fronts" and inspired "all those feelings of affectionate veneration which one would feel for the old-time garments and white hairs of some aged general."[42] But the evocation of a noble past did not necessarily presage a dignified future, particularly when it came to the awkwardly evolving relations between men and women that were unfolding within. A crowd of hundreds had assembled inside to hear the contemporary campaigner Anna Dickinson hold forth on women's rights. "From the magnitude of her audience," Theresa observed, "it may be assumed that the sentiments to which she gave utterance had the sympathy, if not the actual support, of the American people." Very few, in fact, openly concurred with Dickinson, which indicated, Theresa guessed, "the continued prevalence of the dominion of the male over the female mind."[43]

As always, when matters arose that bore directly upon Theresa's public past, irony entered her writing. On the one hand, Theresa poked fun at the "women's rights sisterhood" as they marched gracelessly down the path to independence. They "preached and practiced simplicity in dress" to such an extent that they resembled men, insisting upon shearing "off the locks in which lurks woman's fascination."[44] On the other hand, Dickinson's speech gave Theresa an occasion to air her belief that women were more resourceful than they sometimes acted. "Before they marry," she wrote, girls "are too anxious to conciliate their admirers to throw out even a hint that they could possibly protect and help themselves." Married women perpetuated the farce of defenselessness—and the stereotype of female duplicity—by only asserting their ascendancy over their husbands "by covert and insidious means." Women *could* protect, help, and assert themselves, Theresa implied. She was a living example of these capabilities. It was only the "old-fashioned, the timid, and the enthusiastic, who really 'obey.' "[45] Strong-minded women such as Anna Dickinson might not yet find a chorus of like-minded acolytes—and Theresa certainly did not count herself among these few adherents. But they brought out the virtues that lay dormant within all women.

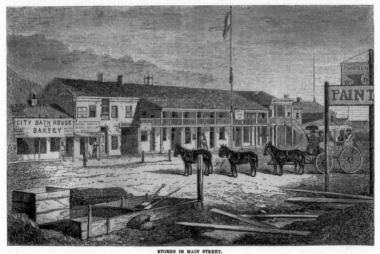

STORES IN MAIN STREET.

A Mormon town.

Her contemplation of women's abilities led her to the subject of marriage in general. In America, where "marriage is not the solemn affair that it is in Europe," wrote Theresa, it was especially important to cultivate self-reliant virtues. In certain cities, the bonds of marriage could be dissolved and re-formed almost instantaneously, it seemed. "All trains passing through Chicago," Theresa wrote, "stop for *twenty minutes* for divorces and for the performance of the marriage ceremony."[46] In Chicago, "wed*lock* is not a proper term," wrote Theresa; "there is no *lock* whatever to the *wedding*."[47] A second wife was added without a second thought; men committed bigamy with impunity. A woman could also "get more husbands than one knows what to do with" if she so desired.[48] If Chicago was a perilous city for marital integrity, the whole state of Indiana was governed by a mess of marital standards; it was the "Gretna Green of the West, and the goal of many runaway couples."[49] There was one striking counterpoint to all this hypocrisy, a community that owned up to its eccentricity: the new Mormon settlements in the West. When she felt that she had seen enough of the Northeast and the South, she boarded a train and headed to the West.

The train traveled through shady darkness, walled-in by firs and balsam pines, emerging amid meadows of swaying grass whose trembling tips shimmered in coordinated ripples. When the train stopped at night and sleepy passengers stumbled from their cars onto the plains, Theresa felt wide awake, breathing the thin and crystalline air and examining stars that seemed to hover just beyond arm's reach. The angels, she wrote, might be used to such stimuli, "but we frail mortals felt very giddy, and as though we had been swallowing ether."[50] She was entering a strange new landscape.

The first Mormons, whose followers' tents dotted the fields that Theresa was passing through, had arrived in the West in 1847. Twenty years earlier, Joseph Smith, then a twenty-five-year-old farmer, declared himself a prophet after—as he claimed—the angel Moroni showed him golden plates inscribed with writings in an ancient language. The writings became the Book of Mormon; acolytes soon flocked to Smith's side, and the Church of Latter-day Saints was officially called into being. Smith received a steady stream of revelations that solidified the doctrines of the faith, including, from 1852 on, a sanction of the practice of polygamy. The Mormons endured a precarious and nomadic existence, vilified in popular literature, hounded in daily life, and subject to surprise attacks. Throughout the 1830s and 1840s, they moved constantly—from New York to Ohio, from Ohio to Illinois, from Illinois to Missouri. In the winter of 1846, just over a thousand set out for Utah. They arrived the following spring, establishing the foundations of what would become a U.S. territory in 1850.

In the ninety communities established around Salt Lake City, an average of 20 percent of the population lived in polygamous arrangements.[51] Because of their intense proselytizing and the abnormality of their domestic arrangements, the Mormons were seen as a sinister threat, as well as a challenge to the limits of toleration and pluralism. An entire genre of anti-Mormon literature emerged from outsiders' visits. In *Roughing It*, Mark Twain saw Mormon country as a "fairy land . . . of enchantments, and goblins, and awful mystery," where "thrilling evening stories about assassinations of intractable Gentiles" were told for entertainment.[52]

Among British writers, however, there was something of a precedent for toleration—even after the practice of polygamy was officially acknowledged. In 1855, Charles Dickens boarded a ship of Mormons headed for New York prepared "to bear testimony against them if they deserved it."[53] But the industrious ship-bound community undermined stereotypes of the indolent polygamous lifestyle. When the explorer Richard Burton traveled to Salt Lake City he described it as a land of concrete features—walls of red sandstone, ornamental iron fences, wooden gates—not the threatening, semi-mystical place that Twain had described. He searched in vain for the so-called outhouse harems and discovered them to be "but one of a multitude of delusions."[54] Although about half of the eighty-five thousand Mormon converts who moved to the West in the middle decades of the nineteenth century were from the British Isles, British writers seemed willing to focus on the improvement in these emigrants' lives rather than what might have been perceived as their moral degradation.[55]

Most of Theresa's readers probably assumed that the polygamous arrangements in Salt Lake City embodied her worst nightmare. But Theresa surprised them, falling into line—at least initially—with the male writers from her country who had indirectly or directly endorsed the religion. The Mormon man, she wrote, was bound by the strictures of his society to take care of the wives he accumulated, a responsibility that Yelverton (in Theresa's view) had evaded. If you believed the testimonies of women who proclaimed their contentment with their polygamous position, the fate of the fourth or fifth or sixth wife was not a life of struggle, deprivation, and sadness, but one of exaltation and reverence. Whether Theresa believed these claims, she was willing to humor their arrangements. The tangle of British law, after all, had proved inadequate to protect a woman who believed she was married. At least there was some clarity in the Mormon household.

Marriage, she wrote, is "gradually assuming a new character in America," clear "of all the bugbears by which it is surrounded in Europe."[56] It was a new country, and, as one man put it, Americans "couldn't be cramped with all these old world notions," like the impractical ideal of monogamous romantic love.[57] Polygamy could even be given a women's rights slant. One Mormon woman wrote that the preoccupation with securing the perfect marriage for a young girl limited her potential: "Is there nothing worth living for, but to be petted, humored, and caressed, by a man?"[58] By distributing the duties of a wife among several women, a woman was left with more time to herself. "Would it not grieve you if you fancied that your husband loved your sister more than yourself?" Theresa asked one of her host's wives. The woman thought it over and agreed. But, she hedged, "it would be my duty to resist and conquer such feelings."[59]

As Theresa spent more time in Salt Lake City, and moved farther away from the conventions and concerns that had ruled her life, these arguments began to make a certain sense. "The most startling dropping off from my eyes of the cherished scales of prejudice occurred during my visit to the state of Utah!" she wrote. "Before I went to Utah, I did not know that I was prejudiced; though I thought I knew all about Mormons."[60] She "had lived in Wales, the hunting-ground of the Mormons, and whence they had carried off our best housemaids and cooks, and the prettiest girls of the village," and where, "consequently, the Mormons were regarded there much in the same light as men-eating tigers."[61] But rather than predatory animals or sexually voracious but luxuriously lethargic Easterners, the Mormons of Utah seemed like secluded but generally happy individuals living with their extended families.

Over the next few weeks, Theresa witnessed the ins and outs of Mormon domesticity, and it was familiar to her in a way that the rest of America was not. Hospitality reigned; a woman from Cheshire made a special cheese; come summertime, English flowers would bloom in the gardens. A ball she attended reminded her of country balls back home, with the "young people behaving with the most perfect modesty."[62] Waste was everywhere in America, but in Salt Lake the "labourers in the Lord's vineyard" could ill afford haphazard cultivation of the land and so they diligently toiled.[63] In the theater, a place where hidden desires and transgressions might exhibit themselves, Theresa found nothing inappropriate. "There was no vice, no drinking, no intrigue; all was as straightforward as the arrangements of an household."[64]

But domestic harmony came at a price. These Mormon wives, Theresa eventually realized, had become servants, their positions defined by their housework. The eleven wives of Theresa's host took on the positions of "cook, laundress, parlour-maid, housemaid and dairy-maid." When the husband needed a new servant, he just asked another girl to join the ranks. Or he "saved" one of the half-caste Red Indians from a life of sin and idolatry by bringing her into the fold. His "strikingly handsome" half-Indian wife was the most diligent of the bunch, "always working hard" at scrubbing and cleaning the floors, the most mundane and laborious tasks.[65] The fabled Mormons who carried off the best housemaids and cooks from Wales apparently knew what class of woman to target.

If supposedly worthy sacrifice validated polygamous life, the burden fell disproportionately upon the women, and Theresa had always struggled against the inequality of sacrifice between the sexes. A woman often feels compelled, she wrote in her first novel, "by a false idea of virtue, to make a sacrifice she [is] . . . incapable of completing . . . Self-martyrdom was unavailing; no one was benefited by . . . implicit obedience."[66] Her own experience justified the sentiment. Conceding to Yelverton's wishes had not secured her a husband and had left her a single woman with a tarnished reputation. Rarely did a man risk everything, lose everything, and then have to build a new life without the foundations of respectability when he attached himself to the wrong woman. As Thomas Hardy had pithily summarized the consequence of transgression in the title to one of the phases of *Tess of the D'Urbervilles*, "The Woman Pays." Theresa was one of the first female travelers to visit Salt Lake City, and thus uniquely privy to the apparent efficiency of the Mormon household, but she was also uniquely situated to understand that this productivity rested upon a subjugation that prevented the women from thinking for themselves. Although the Mormon wives professed satisfaction with their positions, they could not *explain* their contentment. "If you are astonished," said one, "you ought to have a talk with my father . . . he can make it all clear to you."[67] The responsibility for articulation fell to the fathers and husbands.

No Mormon woman was forced to marry, Theresa admitted at the end of her stay with the Mormons, but she imagined that entering into marriage in Salt Lake City "may be something like going into a convent: you are not compelled to stay; nevertheless, it is uncommonly difficult to get out."[68] Theresa understood the predicament of inadequate options. Rejecting convent life, and having been rejected by married life, she was now forced into itinerancy by a culture that was hostile to single women. The Mormons had an alternative to the "woman question"—the superfluity of unmarried women—but by the time Theresa left the community, she had reached a verdict as to its fairness: she was lucky to get away "without the matrimonial noose being cast over [her]."[69]

Theresa did not advertise her past, but she did not flee from her ghosts. She knew people would read her writing at least in part to check up on the so-called Viscountess Avonmore, to see what happened to a woman who was thrust under public scrutiny, exiled from respectability, and who reemerged in the "genus of female globe-trotters." She toyed with her readers, piquing their curiosities by visiting convents, moving in elite social circles where aristocracy carried no currency, staying in Mormon homes where multiple wives crowded the hearth, and, finally, by criticizing the bloodthirsty American press, a bulked-up version of a beast she knew well.

The press, she wrote, dug for stories in whatever squalid corner they happened upon, then fed them, ream by dirty ream, to the news-hungry public. British antipathy for the sensationalism of American newspapers was widespread by the time Theresa visited the United States. If you picked up an American newspaper, wrote one visitor, you "might suppose that the whole political machine was about to fall to pieces."[70] Dickens wrote that the newspapers dealt "in round abuse and blackguard names; pulling off the roofs of private houses . . . pimping and pandering for all degrees of vicious taste, and gorging with coined lies the most voracious maw; imputing to every man in public life the coarsest and the vilest motives."[71] A veneer of respectability kept these papers functioning despite their degraded incentives; they affected horror but remained "ready for the next plash of blood," Theresa wrote, and this was "sure to spurt across them ere long."[72]

If blood had not splattered across the newspapers that had reported her story back in Britain, it had flowed forcefully beneath the surface—in the young girl's veins, in the older man's desire. The exposure had briefly elevated Theresa to a public stage, but what was she left with now? A coffin in which to store her dresses, an inattentive secretary to keep her company, and her reputation. Nomadic life was not new to Theresa, but each time she boarded another train she was reminded that she now owed her membership to "the rolling stone tribe" as much to necessity as to her own volition. Her past followed her like a mongrel dog—with pride and shame swirled together in a muddy mix. It removed her from anonymity but trapped her in lingering scandal. She complained that unknown gentlemen claiming to be from the press constantly rapped on her hotel doors at inappropriate hours, wanting to take her photograph. Is this what the American ladies want, she wondered, when they "dress, and flirt, and give entertainments, solely that they may be noticed in the newspapers?"[73] Was such risk-ridden midnight entertaining necessary in order to remain in the glitz and glamour of society, rather than its obscure shadows?

In New Orleans, she stumbled upon an anonymous grave that made her think of her legacy. A single word, "'Malheureux' [sadness] . . . was alone carved in ugly letters on his mean and lowly resting-place." As long as the gravestone stood standing, she wrote, "'Malheureux!' uttered by every passer-by, will be the only word his lonely silent spirit will hear." How unfair it seemed that this supposedly disgraced soul should endure an eternity of pity and censure whispered by strangers. "If my penknife could have obliterated the vindictive stigma," she wrote, "it would not be there now."[74] She could not erase the carving, but she continued to defend herself—with a pen instead of a penknife—against her condemnation.

CHAPTER EIGHT

California

*I want to "live." I hate the artificial existence of London; I hate the life
of a vegetable in the country; I want a wild, roving, vagabond life. I am
young, strong, hardy, with good nerves; I like roughing it and I always want
to do something daring and spirited; you will certainly repent it, if you
keep me tied up.*

—Isabel Burton, *The Life of Captain Sir Richard F. Burton* (1893)

On May 23, 1870, the populace of San Francisco took a daylong
holiday to watch the demolition of Blossom Rock. The large reef
stretched across the bay, preventing deep-bottomed ships from nearing
the shore and frustrating the growing number of merchants who
wanted to transport their goods to the bustling new city. With picnic
baskets hanging from the crooks of their arms and binoculars dangling
from their necks, men and women hiked to the hilltops for a better
view. The most daring observers paddled into the bay and bobbed in
their small boats on the gentle waves. Earlier that afternoon engineers
had lowered twenty-one tons of explosive powder into hollowed-out
spaces drilled into the rock. When they lit the fuse, there was a mo-
mentary pause, then a column of water rose several hundred feet, forming a looming tower that stood magnificently frozen for a split second

as a monument to man's manipulation of nature, before crashing down. The city had been opened to the sea.[1]

By the 1870s, the Golden Era of San Francisco had lost its luster, and the Silver Age was growing tarnished. Trade was increasingly important, and the city was physically expanding beyond its ramshackle frontier settlements. Almost exactly one year before the explosion of Blossom Rock, the last length of the transcontinental railroad had been laid, uniting the Central Pacific and the Union Pacific lines and reducing the three-week overland journey from the East to the West by a significant margin. The "magician's rod" of railroad iron, as Ralph Waldo Emerson called it, sparked a boom in San Francisco.[2] In the same year, twelve hundred new houses were built and ten thousand people moved to the city, bringing the total population to just under 150,000.[3]

Less than thirty years before, in 1840, only one thousand people called San Francisco home. But by the start of the 1870s, the city was "unlike any other place in creation," said one of its early inhabitants; it was "not created in the ordinary way"—by slow accumulation and expansion—"but hatched like chickens by artificial heat."[4] It was an early example of what would later be recognized as a distinct phenomenon—an instant city, sprung from serendipity, fearlessness, and the momentum of a sense of possibility. Construction was fast and flimsy at first. The men who laid the city's foundations wanted rapid fortunes, not second homes. But they needed better accommodation as they remained out West, and so sturdier constructions began to cover the steep slopes.

Theresa arrived in San Francisco via the transcontinental railroad in the fall of 1869. She was not enchanted by the gleaming Silver Palace Sleeping Car or its famed speed: "The poetry of the route is gone . . . we get across the continent in less than a sixth of the time, but I doubt if there is now half the enjoyment in it," she wrote.[5] She had flown past the scenery, unable to experience it at a leisurely pace. Some days antelope galloped alongside the train, "as if in defiance of our power to outstrip them in speed." Occasionally, a wolf loped along beside them—"in a careless sort of run, with his long tail

San Francisco, at the corner of California and Montgomery Streets.

touching the ground"—as if warning the passengers of their intrusion in an untamed wilderness.[6]

If the journey took place too quickly, Theresa was pleased by the laid-back life that met her at her destination. After the cramped and rushed trip, San Francisco was full of sparkling light and sea air. Boys ran up and down the docks jutting into the bay, stopping to check on friends fishing through gaps in the boardwalk planks. Girls in frilly dresses bought bags of candy from the shouting vendors and waved lollipops like miniature batons, keeping time to the metallic jangle from a far-off brass band. Men and women strolled arm in arm, decked out to an extreme that Theresa had not witnessed since leaving New York. Gone were the days when practicality governed everyday attire. The city's nouveau riche wanted to show their affluence with fur-trimmed capes and satin scarves. Though the life of San Francisco pulsed through its avenues, the press of people was never overwhelming. Just like men's fortunes, the hilly streets rose and fell; lengthy vistas opened at each turn, and the air stayed cool. "Glorious" was the best word to describe the city as it transitioned from frontier outpost to cosmopolitan center, and it was on everyone's lips.

If social graces suffered as a result of instant affluence, financial

insecurity created an honest awareness of the ephemerality of eminence. "The sand-shoveler and the millionaire may change places
to-morrow, and they know it; so the former does not usually cringe
nor the other strut when they meet," wrote John S. Hittell, one of the
earliest historians to chronicle the rise of the region.[7] This surprisingly level social playing field was not to everyone's liking. Europeans, like Theresa, had recurrently criticized American society for the
sway of the almighty dollar, crass social proclivities, and the inadequacies of culture. Now, these accusations were regurgitated by both
Europeans and eastern Americans as white western society in California established its first social and cultural institutions. When Richard
Burton surveyed the artistic scene, he determined that "of artists they
have plenty, of Art nothing."[8]

Despite these dismissals, Californians took pride in their nascent
culture and sensed the riches of their native soil. It was impossible for
their eastern compatriots, let alone European visitors, to begin to
comprehend the natural splendor that daily stirred their artistic sensibilities. Natural beauty existed in hyperbolic proportions, wrote Bret
Harte, a founding father of the San Francisco literary scene. If one
faces a mountain, "it is something stupendous; if a valley, it is a perpendicular chasm of several thousand feet . . . Rains are deluges . . .
droughts are six months long." This landscape wasn't refined, but it
had integrity: "What she loses in delicacy she makes up in fibre," he
wrote.[9] Life in the West encouraged artistic opportunity rather than
discipline. "Almost everything in California is fresh and virgin for
the purposes of art," wrote one enraptured Yosemite pilgrim.[10]

The *Overland Monthly*—an *Atlantic Monthly* for the West—was
among the fresh, new cultural offerings. Theresa found her first
American literary home at this publication, which was founded in
1868 when the San Francisco bookseller, publisher, and failed miner
Anton Roman—a man who had never written a word himself—
published the first issue. Unlike other western magazines and journals, the *Overland* was to be a product of original and local talent. It
would not lift from other sources; it would pay its writers cash and
would pay them—if not lavishly—on time.[11] An engraving on the

title page showed a bear standing on train tracks, a snarl parting its thin lips. The frontier days were coming to a close, the drawing seemed to say, but not without a departing roar. With nine hundred dollars of guaranteed advertising money from flush California businessmen and a sketch by Mark Twain in the first issue, the *Overland* was poised for success—a last hurrah for pioneer culture and a welcome mat for impending development. Roman had convinced Bret Harte to be the magazine's editor by showing him a map of the two hemispheres and pointing out San Francisco's central position. By the mid-1870s, circulation was in the thousands.[12]

"The nervous, rocky West is intruding a new and continental element into the national mind," wrote Emerson, "and we shall yet have an American genius."[13] Despite Roman's pedestrian intentions for the magazine (he was inclined to focus on material development), the *Overland* became part of the widening parameters of national genius. The magazine headquarters became a literary fiefdom ruled by the "Golden Gate Trinity": the olive-skinned, dark-eyed poet Ina Coolbrith; the fair-haired, blue-eyed essayist Charles Warren Stoddard; and their ringleader, the mustached, opinionated Harte. Members of the trinity made the *Overland* office their second home, haunting its corridors at late hours, napping with their feet propped up on the desks, clustering in corners to stage intensely competitive limerick-writing contests. When things were slow, they would decamp to Coolbrith's airy apartment for tea. Their contemporaries clucked over their lack of orthodoxy. "Mr. Harte!" wrote the abolitionist and women's rights campaigner Anna Dickinson. "You are an iconoclast. Where did you find such ideas? Are you in polite society? And who is your pastor?"[14] Polite society, however, had never existed in San Francisco. Its first sons and daughters created their own parishes, worshipping in sanctuaries ringed by redwoods and guarded by mountains.

Theresa was invited into this scene by Stoddard, who had read *Martyrs to Circumstance* and followed her plight through the courts. In the 1860s, the foppish, friendly young man had made a reputation for himself as "the Boy Poet of San Francisco." His homosexuality was tolerated, or overlooked, even as he celebrated his thinly veiled

The *Overland Monthly* title page illustration (*left*), Ina Coolbrith (*right*).

dalliances in his *South Sea Idylls*. Of his time in the tropics, Stoddard recalled, "[I could] act as my nature prompts me." Even in San Francisco, "where men are tolerably bold," he complained that he could not exercise similar freedom.[15] Roaming the halls of the *Overland* office, he longed for warmer climes.

In the fall of 1869, Stoddard found a project to distract him. He had learned of Theresa's arrival and offered to show her the city. Theresa proposed a recital to introduce herself to the western public, thinking that the people of San Francisco "might like such a guarantee of [her] power of elocution"—the quality that, she claimed, had been much lauded by the British press.[16] When Stoddard met her in person it was not bravura but nervousness that struck him. She was "doubtless once possessed of an admirable physique, and must have been beautiful in her youth; but grief, disappointment, and distrust of the world had well-nigh wrecked her." Her eyes drooped at the corners, and her brows stretched straight across the lower portion of her forehead. Despite her melancholy aspect, she knew how to play up her remaining strengths. Her hair had darkened over the years, and

Charles Warren Stoddard (*left*), Bret Harte (*right*).

she wore it coiled in a thick bun atop her head, leaving her face open and her flashing eyes clear. She accentuated her ample bosom by drawing a sash around her waist. At thirty-six, she was past her youthful prime and had the appearance of a woman poised on the brink of a more matronly stage in her life. She was still "attractive in an uncommon way and to an uncommon degree," admitted Stoddard, but her appeal came from an air of experience.[17]

Stoddard and Theresa met and discussed the program for her debut at Platt's Hall. She would alternate Longfellow and Harte with Tennyson and Browning, mixing America's poetic offerings with her cultural roots. On the day of the recital, Theresa ate nothing but limes and oysters to preserve her voice. Stoddard had done his best to drum up interest, but it had been hard work. Just before the performance he paced, pockets full of unsold tickets, while Theresa prepared her outfit. She emerged, finally, wearing a delicate lattice of lace over an ivory satin gown, a string of opals round her neck. The theater was empty.

A few friends and admirers returned to Theresa's unfashionable but respectable hotel, where they indulged in "chagrin and champagne," as Stoddard put it. "That was the beginning and the end of her career as a public reader in California," Stoddard reported.[18]

He took Theresa on rambles through the hilly streets to lift her spirits, attempting to stir up a little excitement in her increasingly quiet life. "There was a touch of the Bohemian in her," wrote Stoddard, and he did his best to entertain it.[19] But even while exploring the city, Theresa was dissatisfied with the unproductive busyness of the traveler and craved more substantive activity. On one of their walks they came across a factory. "If I could but find work for my hands to do . . . my brain might stop thinking and rest in peace!" she said. "If I were only one of those happy human automatons over yonder," she said, referring to the factory workers, "I should feel content."[20]

Tired of circling around the city, she left San Francisco and retired to Sausalito on the north shore of the bay, where the ocean air and the sound of the waves outside her window revived her spirits. At that time, the town was mostly inhabited by Italian fishermen, and she claimed that she too could catch fish by leaning over her balcony railing and dropping her line into the water. They were "bright, silver little creatures, all dripping with pearls," she wrote to Stoddard.[21] She brought her pencil and papers into the hills and wrote letters, holding "communion on the mountainside" with her far-off friends.[22]

She urged Stoddard to visit. He needed a holiday, she said, but her own loneliness more likely motivated her insistence. She wrote frequently, and, like Yelverton, Stoddard could not keep up with her pace. Her handwriting slowed him down; it was hard to read, he explained. Theresa was indignant; no one could read her handwriting— not even the authoress herself—and if he objected to the torn scraps she used for stationery, that too was "irremediable"; because, she explained, "*disorder* is really at the root of my character."[23] Despite her gruffness, she did not want to scare him off. "She was lavish of her affection," wrote Stoddard, reflecting on their friendship years after her death. One would imagine that the deception she had suffered "would teach her to be very cautious in the selection of her intimates; but . . . she continued to interest herself in others at almost any cost"—even in those, like Stoddard, whose romantic proclivities were obviously directed elsewhere.[24]

In the midst of Theresa's retreat, the tranquillity was shattered. She was sitting in her room with Stoddard at her side when a bullet broke the glass of her window, passed over her head, and lodged in the ceiling above her. Theresa froze in terror. Stoddard leaped to the window, where he saw a hunter moving sheepishly and quickly into the distance. Nothing could convince Theresa that she had escaped an errant shot rather than an attempt on her life. The misdirected bullet fed a growing paranoia, and she began preparations for her departure. She wrote her last Sausalito letter to Stoddard on the back of a program from her fateful reading at Platt's Hall: "Dear Friend,—We have taken, I fear, the last of our pleasant rural strolls; for I find I shall have to leave my peaceful quarters next week . . . I do not as yet know where I shall go; I feel in a rather desolate and forlorn condition—as though there was no place for me in this great world."[25]

Theresa found a temporary home in the Yosemite Valley. In 1864, President Lincoln had bequeathed Yosemite to the state of California, and since then it had been venerated as America's Eden, a place where the contaminations of industrial society diffused in the clean, mountain air, where the trees were as said to be old as Christ, and annual renewal provided solace for mortality. When the photographer Carleton Watkins sent to New York his photographs of rough-faced cliffs towering above pools of water surrounded by whorls of vines and roots, they were met with rave reviews.[26] East Coast pilgrims flocked to the feet of the "Big Trees," mammoth redwoods that betrayed all sense of proportion. By the 1870s, Yosemite had become for San Franciscans their particular retreat. "Californians have only to go east a few miles to be happy," advised the founding father of American environmentalism, John Muir. "Toilers in the cities by the sea, whose lives are well-nigh choked by the weeds of care that have grown up and run to seed about them—leave all and go east."[27]

The first part of Theresa's retreat to the fabled land of restoration

Carleton Watkins, *Yosemite Falls, 1600 feet.*

did not go smoothly. She left San Francisco in a four-person carriage packed with nine people. When they stopped the carriage to finish the journey on horseback, Theresa took off, riding sidesaddle. Her female traveling companions rode astride, Theresa reported, "fully convinced that side-saddles were diabolical inventions of the tyrant man, to drag woman lop-sided through the world."[28] Theresa had no time for fads of clothing or thought.

When she arrived in Yosemite, memories of the unpleasant journey faded. "To live in the very midst of a forest, to make friends of the trees and the mountains, beyond the sight and sound of humanity, has always been the yearning of my heart," she wrote.[29] Her newfound refuge had granite walls that sparkled in the sunlight, and was guarded by ten-foot-wide trees. "There are moments in the lives of most men," she wrote, "when a sweet intangible communion seems to establish itself between us and a thing of nature, when some leaf, or flower, or blade of

Carleton Watkins, *Piwac, Vernal Falls, 300 feet, Yosemite.*

grass, brings in the same delight as the grasp of a friendly hand, or the touch of beloved lips. Thus it appeared to us upon making the acquaintance of these leviathan trees, and although we saw them frequently afterwards, the feeling of reverent affection never diminished."[30] Although Isabella Bird became famous as the first European woman to celebrate the "glorious sublimity, the majestic solitude, and the unspeakable awfulness" of the American West, Theresa made similarly reverent observations years earlier.[31] In the Yosemite Valley, "a man may worship in purity of heart and mind," she wrote. Hollow trunks formed organ pipes, and clarinet tones came "warbling through the dulcet throat of birds." For this music, she wrote, "the soul prostrates itself before its Maker, the great Omnipotent Author of all, and needs no other priest or presbyter."[32]

While she lived in the Yosemite Valley she lodged with James Mason Hutchings, an English-born failed miner, successful journalist, and newly minted hotel proprietor. Hutchings had gained a degree of fame in California by laying out miners' mantras. His "Miners' Ten Commandments" sold ninety-seven thousand copies when it was published in letter-sheet form in 1853 and included such assertions as: "thou shalt discover that all thou hadst in thy purse has quietly drifted away," and "thy patience will be like unto thy garments; and, as a last resort, thou shall hire thy body out to make thy board and save thy bacon."[33] He bought a failing hotel and transformed the flimsy two-story building into a hub for valley tourists. As guests streamed in, he needed to expand. Unable to face cutting down the 150-foot-tall cedar tree at the rear of the house (or, aware of its gimmicky potential), he built around it, and the new sitting room was christened the "Big Tree Room." Theresa spent, according to Hutchings's guidebook, the "happiest months of [her] life in this glorious valley."[34] She had planned to stay three weeks. Instead, she stayed several months.

Theresa got along with Hutchings's wife and was fond of their two daughters, black-eyed Florence—reportedly the first white child born in the Yosemite—and the younger Gertrude. After a breakfast of poached eggs and bacon rashers, she would sit on the porch with the girls in her lap and pick tangles out of their sun-streaked hair. When new visitors arrived, Theresa would entertain with songs and stories. If prompted, she would lead them to a lake and recite Tennyson into the surrounding hills, pausing at the end of each line so that a silvery echo returned to her awestruck audience. One visitor, the writer Mary Viola Lawrence, was so taken with Theresa that she wrote an adulatory profile—"Summer with a Countess"—for the *Overland*. "For her my admiration was unbounded, being, without exception, the most interesting woman I ever knew," she wrote. "Others think likewise; so this is not only the impression of enthusiasm or partiality."[35]

In Lawrence, Theresa found a rapt attendant, and she again retold her history, embellishing it with details that had not yet been woven into the mosaic of letters, court documents, novels, and articles that formed her biography. She told Lawrence that everyone had opposed sending a young fragile thing into the war-torn Crimea, but she had used her connections to gain an audience with the pope, hoping that his blessing would smooth a temporary entry into the Soeurs. Impressed with her tenacity, the pope referred her to the empress Eugénie, who was contemplating a trip to the front. Eugénie was charmed by Theresa and offered her a place as a maid of honor. For months, reported Lawrence in the *Overland*, Theresa "dwelt, in her new and delightful position," while the empress stalled on her plans to visit the Crimea.[36] Had Theresa actually lived in the empress's palace, it seems likely that the story would have already emerged. Theresa knew that amplifying her aristocratic connections would increase her novelty in America, and, with an adoring audience before her, she felt little need to preserve the exact dimensions of her supposed relationship with the empress.

When news of the death of the old viscount—Yelverton's father—arrived at the Hutchings's Hotel, Theresa already reigned unchallenged as the in-house aristocrat. But she prepared to leave, to attempt, once more, to assert her status as the wife of the *new* viscount. (Yelverton's brother, ahead of him in the succession, had passed away while the trials were still taking place.) After kissing the Hutchings girls good-bye, she saddled her horse and set out to cover the 150 miles or so back to San Francisco. As she led her horse over the rocky path, her saddle kept slipping, and she decided to return to camp to fix it. She urged her guide and his companions—a visiting English nobleman and his followers—to continue; she would catch up with them. As she rode back, a November snow began to fall, lightly at first—wispy flakes against a stone gray sky—then heavier, until Theresa could hardly see the mountain ahead of her. Her horse stumbled, sending her to the ground. She decided to walk. Pulling the reluctant horse along beside her, she pressed forward with only a vague sense that she was heading in the right direction.

No one was waiting for her at the cluster of cedars where she had planned to meet up with the others. The peak that had been guiding her had disappeared, engulfed by the swirling mass of snow. "To continue was simply to invite a fall," she later wrote, "and to rush into the jaws of death."[37] She remembered a hollow tree that she had passed earlier and returned to it. She spent the night huddled next to her horse in the hollowed-out tree, warming her hands by capturing his cloudy exhaled breaths. In the morning, a noise startled her from her half-starved, half-frozen stupor. She rushed outside and found a bear standing only a few feet from the tree. The bear regarded her with calm disinterest, almost sympathy. Like the trees that had offered unique communion, this creature seemed to understand her plight. The bear retreated, and Theresa, gathering the reins of her tired horse, trudged on. Her will withering and her body weak, she placed one foot in front of the other until she could go no farther, and collapsed in a wet, worn, and wind-whipped heap.[38]

When she awoke, the snow had stopped falling. The sun was high in the azure sky, and the ice coating the branches was cracking as it melted. She was found later that day and taken back to the Hutchings's Hotel. Florence and Gertrude hovered outside her room, peeking in at her as she sweated and swore beneath a mound of blankets. When her limbs had thawed and her head had healed, she set out again. When Theresa finally reached San Francisco, where she intended to attempt, once more, to begin the process that would legitimate her assumed title, a fever set in that kept her bedridden for days. There was little she could have done anyway as Yelverton was nowhere to be found. Having disappeared somewhere on the European continent, he showed no interest in surfacing to claim the title that Theresa so desperately wanted.

Lawrence learned of Theresa's ordeal in the blizzard and came to hear the story from the convalescing survivor. When she was alone inside the hollowed-out tree, Theresa confessed to her visitor, her mind had wandered. The memory of her last meeting with her husband came back to her: Before she left England, Yelverton had confronted her as she waited in an idle railroad car, demanding the marriage certificate. Stooped but looming over her in the low-ceilinged compartment, he cursed her, wishing her to "know every sorrow and misery so long as she lived, and, finally, die an awful

The Big-Tree Room at the Barnard Hotel.

death, away and alone, with no human being to relieve her agony, or close her eyes, or listen to her dying words."[39] Lawrence tried to comfort her, but it was of little use. Her close call had given her a glimpse of a terrifyingly solitary and anonymous demise. Nature could comfort and inspire, but it could also leave you alone and defenseless, without human communion in your final hours. If she had perished in the snow, she could not even hope for the ignominious tribute of a gravestone marked "Malhereaux."

Before she left the valley, she had been involved in a relationship that was perhaps her last real hope for enduring companionship. The man was John Muir, then a fortuneless, nomadic, unattached, and unknown rambler. Theresa most likely met Muir at the Hutchings's Hotel, where he lived and worked, but she romanticized their meeting in *Teresina in America*, saying that they met on her overland journey. He had entered her train compartment swathed in fur and had dropped himself into the seat opposite her. When they shook hands, she placed hers in his "large paw"—as she described it—"where it disappeared for ever so long." Muir knew her story and was a staunch defender of her innocence. She had been wronged, Muir assured her. She would have done "better married to a *bear* than a nobleman," he told her.[40] Theresa smiled; in this new world, the bears were apparently the gentlemen.

Wherever they actually met, Theresa and Muir became friends in the Yosemite Valley. Muir had not yet published the books that would make him famous—the very incarnation of romance in the West—but the delay was due to an overabundance of material rather than a lack of inspiration. "These mountain fires that glow in one's blood are free to all," he wrote to his patron Jeanne Carr, the wife of a former professor; "but I cannot find the chemistry that may press them unimpaired into bookseller's bricks."[41] In the meantime, he wrote letters, kept capacious diaries, and sent occasional articles to his friends, who placed them in the *Overland* and other western publications. Theresa, too, kept copious notes, inspired by all that she encountered.

A union—brief but nonetheless portentous—emerged between a woman, done in by imperial Britain, and a man who would do more than almost anyone else to create the West as a place of rebirth, a place where disparate parts coalesced and yet retained their distinctiveness. "In streams of ice, of water, of minerals, of plants, of animals, the tendency is to unification," Muir wrote.

> We at once find ourselves among eternities, infinitudes, and scarce know whether to be happy in the sublime simplicity of radical causes and origins or whether to be sorry on losing the beautiful fragments which we thought perfect and primary absolute units; but as we study and mingle with nature more, the pain caused by the melting of all beauties into one First Beauty disappears, because, after their first baptismal submergence in fountain God, they go again washed and clean into their individualisms, more clearly defined than ever, unified yet separate.[42]

While social forces beyond her control had left her defeated, in Yosemite, Theresa was content in the sublimely simple world that placed her at the mercy of storms and seasons. The uncontrollable wash of nature revived and restored her distinctiveness.

At the Hutchings's estate Muir lived in a cabin he had built for himself and slept in a leaf-lined bed suspended from its rafters.[43] For Theresa, who would use him as the basis for a fictional character named

Theresa Yelverton in Yosemite (*left*), John Muir (*right*).

Kenmuir in her second novel, *Zanita*, he epitomized the ever-appealing "chivalrous savage." His clothes "had the tatterdemalion style of a Mad Tom. The waist of his trousers was eked out with a grass band; a long flowing sedge rush stuck in the solitary button-hole of his shirt, the sleeves of which were ragged and forlorn, and his shoes appeared to have known hard and troublous times." Moral sophistication and true learning lay beneath his roughshod exterior: "His refinement was innate, his education collegiate."[44] Theresa hiked up and down the mountains by Muir's side and passed on any botanical observations that she made on solitary excursions. Muir needled the holes in her increasingly ornate autobiography, yet his touch was light. Her adopted stateliness, Muir pointed out, paled in comparison to the grandeur of nature. He jokingly called her a duchess "and was struck with the grand bow with which she bade [him] good-bye."[45] He humored her dogged claims and even appreciated her outsized gestures for the sake of their friendship.

Not only did Muir embody Theresa's masculine ideal—the chivalrous savage she had thought she had found in Yelverton—he echoed sensations Theresa had felt her whole life. Her soul, she thought, had always been trapped in her "casket" of a body.[46] "Soul and body receive separate nourishment and separate exercise," wrote Muir, and "living artificially," with "our torpid souls . . . hopelessly entangled with our torpid bodies," we hardly see our real selves.[47] Theresa had always thought that some magnetic, fluid force guided the world, and that it only took a willingness to loosen the ties of reality to perceive it. "If my soul could get away from this so-called prison," wrote Muir in one of his early journals, "I should hover about the beauty of our own good star" and study "nature's laws in all their crossing and unions; I should follow magnetic streams to their source and follow the shores of our magnetic oceans."[48] Thousands of miles from the waters where Theresa had first found a like-minded companion, her mind converged with another's.

When Muir went off on his treks and failed to write to Theresa, the same petulance that characterized her previous infatuation crept into her letters to him. "What do you mean by not writing to me?" she wrote. "Here are all the ferns turned golden, and the oaks and maple every shade of yellow . . . everything is doing its duty but you." She informed him that his character was beginning to take shape in her new novel: "I do my duty by you better than you by me." But her chastisement was lighthearted, and her friendliness reciprocated. He wanted to know when she would leave the valley, presumably so that he would not miss her ultimate departure. "When do I leave the Valley?" she responded to his query, "I don't know, and never shall, until I am out."[49] While Theresa found a sympathetic soul in Muir, their connection never took on the all-consuming dimensions that her relationship with Yelverton had assumed almost from the beginning. She was older than when she met Yelverton, and her affection did not now refract into a single, intense, misguided ray. Instead it radiated in multiple directions, striking the silver-flecked mountains, the placid water, the Hutchings girls, and her new woodchopping friend.

Muir's romantic attachments at this stage in his life are unclear; he seems to have had some sort of affair with James Hutchings's wife, Elvira, and his letters betray a deep-seated attachment to his patron Jeanne Carr.[50] But when Muir learned of Theresa's travail in the snowstorm, which had been widely publicized in American newspapers, he expressed genuine regret that he had not been able to prevent it. Theresa had asked Muir to guide her out of the valley, but when the news arrived that the old viscount had died, Muir was not available, having left the valley on one of his solitary trips. "It seems strange to me that I should not have known or felt her anguish in that terrible night, even at this distance," he wrote to Carr. "She told me that I ought to wait & guide her out. I feel a kind of guiltiness in not doing so."[51]

Over the next few years, Theresa and Muir sporadically communicated. Muir relied on Carr, his most regular correspondent, to keep abreast of Theresa's whereabouts, and often asked Carr to convey short messages to Theresa. Over a year passed without much direct communication between them, and then, almost two years after her departure from the Yosemite Valley, Theresa wrote to Muir from Hong Kong, where she had arrived after a stopover in Hawaii—the first leg of the worldwide jaunt that would consume most of her remaining years. "My dear Kenmuir," the newly minted world traveler wrote, calling him by the fictional name she had assigned to him in *Zanita*, "how I have wished for you, and sometimes longed for you . . . I never see a beautiful flower, or a fine combination in nature without thinking of you and wishing you were there to appreciate it." The flora and fauna of Asia left her breathless, but her company lacked the honest humility and appreciativeness she had found in her California companion. The expatriate community was all "money getting men and drawing room ladies who can not imagine I can have any other object in travelling fourteen thousand miles to Hong Kong than to lounge on a sofa." As had so often been the case, her intrepidness created social vulnerability. "It is strange that at first wherever I go people are greatly delighted to know me," she wrote, "but then the very qualities which have brought me out here . . . are the very ones they dislike."[52]

Zanita—her novel based on her time in Yosemite—had been published in her absence, and she wondered if Muir had encountered any of the reviews. She feared that her editors had changed much of it, and she had been informed that one critic had called her portrait of Muir "bosh"—a figment of her imagination. "I should like to tell him that you had an existence in my heart as well!" she wrote. Despite the distance that now separated them, Theresa's warm feelings for Muir persisted alongside the memories of their idyllic retreat. "If you will make a discovery of a new valley as beautiful as the Yosemite I will surely come and see it and pitch my tent for a time."[53]

The lasting literary product of Theresa's time in Yosemite, *Zanita: A Tale of the Yo-Semite*, was a thinly veiled portrait of the people and places Theresa encountered in California. The story was narrated by Sylvia Brown, the wife of a geology professor and herself an amateur botanist. The profile conforms most closely to Jeanne Carr, but despite the obvious similarities, Theresa saw herself, rather than Carr, as the narrator, signing her letters to Muir, "Mrs. Brown." Carr, or her fictional incarnation in "Mrs. Brown," moved easily between Oakland's intellectual circles and the Yosemite wilderness, was respected but uninhibited—the type of woman Theresa still aspired to be.

The plot of *Zanita* centers on Mrs. Brown's friends Oswald and Placida Naunton (inspired by the Hutchings), who have created an isolated paradise for themselves and their two daughters, Rosie and Zanita. Just as the Hutchings's Hotel formed the hub of Yosemite Valley activity, the events in *Zanita* circle around the Nauntons' home. When Mrs. Naunton falls gravely ill, Kenmuir, the trusty all-purpose handyman, is sent to Oakland to recruit Mrs. Brown as a surrogate mother for the wild, unmannered Zanita. Despite their best efforts, Mrs. Brown and her husband cannot control Zanita. They send her to an Ursuline convent, hoping that the nuns will tame her.

While Zanita is away, a man named Mr. Egremont joins the narrator and her husband as his secretary. Upon Zanita's return, a strange, uncontrollable attraction emerges between her and the new secretary. Mr. Egremont then departs for the valley, where he falls in love with the now-grown and lovely Rosie. Intensely resentful of the mutual attachment, Zanita lures Egremont away from the valley camp. They are found sometime later, Egremont's body dashed upon the rocks at the bottom of a cliff, Zanita's floating in a lake. The characters disagree over the cause of their deaths, and in the midst of the disagreement they find a letter implying that Mr. Egremont may have already been married—and worse, a noble. To escape the turmoil, the narrator and her husband take a trip to Europe, where they encounter Rosie and Kenmuir on their honeymoon.

Although the novel was threaded with strands from Theresa's past life (the Ursuline convent, the magnetic forces of destructive love, a deceptive bigamist), *Zanita* was also a record—albeit messy and melodramatic—of the effect that her more recent life in America had on her. While many European travelers before her had noted the North-South regional diversity of America, few had moved from the glittering northeastern cities to the untouched landscape of the West and chronicled it in fiction. The novel was part of the growing body of environmentally oriented American literature, and perhaps the only work in that genre written by a European woman. Many travelers had descended upon the various utopian and communitarian experiments attempting to establish an alternate way of life in America, but few had embraced the entire West as a certain type of social experiment, with instant cities and isolated retreats, a place where nature and society sometimes harmonized and sometimes clashed.

Zanita displayed Theresa's unique and new perspective, but it also revealed certain deep-seated personal desires. It showed her longing for a peaceful retreat where she could fill her days with useful, stimulating activity and ignore the wider world. "We built up a fantastic fairy tale of our own lives," says Placida Naunton, "and dwelt in it, until it became part of ourselves and our real existence. The commonplace outer world . . . receded from our view, and we felt as though an eternal separation had taken place."[54] But the novel also showed that Theresa was still hesitant to commit to such a sequestered life. She knew that those who moved between an isolated fantasy and the reality of the wider world had to deal with the complications that the latter imposed.

In less equivocal terms than ever before, the novel showed Theresa's sense that women possessed the same capabilities as men. Physiology does not prove, she wrote, "that woman, though more graceful and beautiful than man, is so much more fragile, as we are accustomed to think. The Indian women . . . are quite as strong as the men . . . they can walk as far, and ford rivers with the same ease."

The fact that a woman was more equal in "the primitive state than in the position in which civilization has placed her" was "a very strong argument for woman's rights."[55] Mrs. Brown, though married, is fiercely independent: "My husband," she states, "never exercised any authority over me in his life, and never opposed any project in which I even imagined I had a good object in view."[56]

Zanita also showed that Theresa's feelings toward American children were not as dismissive as the attitude she publicly advertised in *Teresina in America*, where she wrote that "a child with its rosy cheeks and bright joyous laugh, its docile obedience and simplicity, its healthful play and its disciplined work, is a being almost unknown in America."[57] The tender depictions of Rosie, the affectionate concern for Zanita, and the narrator's immediate willingness to step in as the girls' mother show a more sentimental side, perhaps borne of the realization that she was likely never to have children of her own.

Like so many of Theresa's desires, the underlying longings in the novel were seemingly contradictory. She wanted to withdraw from conventional society, to change its customs, and to adopt a role in keeping with its traditions. From a historical perspective, the novel evokes contemporary debates—nature versus civilization and women's rights. In its day, however, it was difficult to categorize, and Theresa found it hard to find a publisher. "My ex-secretary called to-day," she wrote to Stoddard after she had finished the manuscript. The secretary had informed her that "even if [the novel] were well written [she] should not get one hundred dollars for it; that there have been as many as seventy works on the Yosemite Valley already."[58]

But she turned her bleak prospects into encouragement for her friend: "Now don't you see how much fairer your lot is than mine? You have a publisher and friends to encourage you and sympathize with you."[59] Early on, Theresa had become a sort of mentor to Stoddard: "I am going to work out your destiny for you," she wrote, "or rather make you accomplish it for yourself . . . Despair has no foothold in your case; you only need more effort to accomplish your desires."[60] As a spinster whose one love had escaped her, she had not achieved her greatest desire, but she lived by the principle that effort had brought her very close.

As she waited for a publisher to accept her novel, Theresa toyed with an entirely different career. "The Hon. Mrs. Yelverton (Lady Avonmore) has purchased a farm in Missouri, and intends to remain there," reported the *Reformed Church Messenger* of Philadelphia in February of 1871.[61] Throughout the spring, one-line updates of her progress appeared in various newspapers. "Mrs. Yelverton expects to make the farm she has purchased in Missouri a model one," wrote the *Atlanta Constitution*. "She intends to devote herself, it is said, to raising stock, and is to import cattle from England for that purpose."[62] The occasional updates, without mention of the events that had first made her famous, showed that Theresa had transcended minor-celebrity status; she was familiar enough to be gently ridiculed without additional explication. "It is reported that Mrs. Yelverton has become a farmer in Missouri," said *A Journal of Choice Reading*. "We hope her husbandry will be successful *this* time."[63] But Theresa did not stick with her scheme for long. She was more of a writer than a farmer and spent her time in Missouri translating chapters of *Martyrs to Circumstance* into magazine pieces for the *Overland* and dreaming of her next trip.[64]

In the fall of 1871, after just a few months on the Missouri farm, Theresa bought a ticket to Hawaii, then called the Sandwich Islands. The islands would provide a brief break on the way to Hong Kong, where she would write dispatches for the *Overland* and the *San Francisco Bulletin* and, she declared, "run the gauntlet over every feeling and sensation"—as though her experience until then had been lacking.[65] She wrote her last letters to Stoddard and Muir from Hong Kong. Muir, it seems, made no further attempt to reach her, but Stoddard, whenever he was in England, checked with her publisher to ascertain her whereabouts. More often than not, the publisher had no knowledge of her location. One day, however, Stoddard encountered a young autograph collector who obtained his treasures by scavenging abandoned notes in the pigeonholes and wastebaskets of publishers. Among the letters he had found was an allegory written by Theresa.

> The wind, blowing softly west, caught up a waif from her island home, and wafted her across the tumultuous ocean, ever rolling west until frowned down by the rocks of a western continent. But the wind, heedless of the rocks, and still blowing west, carried the waif over plains and forests and snow-peaked mountains, always west, until she seemed to reach the very flush where the sun takes his evening rest. The waif thought she had got to the end of creation, and wondered why. But not for long. Another wind, blowing from the opposite quarter, brought up another waif; and they danced together, round and round, cheerily, and made merry, as only waifs can, when suddenly brought together. The two winds, contending, gave them but a few short moments to laugh and love and kiss and part. They made a perfect whirlwind between them; then tore them asunder, and carried them around the world again, and will carry them until they meet in the island home, where they will plant themselves and take root, for such is the destiny, even of waifs.[66]

Like the waif, circumstance had lifted Theresa from one continent to another, had brought her to the far reaches of that new continent. There she found like-minded souls and danced in their company. The interlude of companionable happiness with her new friends was brief, and then she was off again. In leaving America, Theresa abandoned the prospect of a settled life. She might have advertised her adherence to "the rolling-stone tribe," but she now had few alternatives to perpetual motion. She was as light as a waif borne by the winds, she reflected with self-indulgent whimsy. But she also knew that only the truly rootless were so easily lifted by a passing breeze, and wondered if she would ever find a place to plant herself.

CHAPTER NINE

The World

The only true travelers are those who leave
For leaving's sake.

—Charles Baudelaire, "Le Voyage" (1861)

It took Theresa eleven weeks to get from San Francisco to the Hong Kong harbor, where old European clippers, paddle steamers, and fishing junks with bamboo-ribbed sails bobbed on the glassy water. When Theresa's ship stopped in Hawaii, she had found herself delayed, according to her own telling. King Kamehameha V—the last Hawaiian king, only a few months from his death—had tried to persuade her to stay, promising her a thousand acres if she remained on the island. She was flattered but had no desire to take over a Hawaiian estate. She had spent almost five years in America—was even tempted to plant real roots at the farm in Missouri. But she turned down the offer from the king. It had never been in her nature to settle down. The rolling stones, she always said, "have the best time."[1]

When she arrived in Hong Kong, she was stunned by the beauty of the harbor and again reassured of the rewards of an itinerant life. Even after her diverse American experience, striking new scenery still took her aback. "Comparisons of beauty are always invidious," she wrote; "but I should say that the Hong Kong Bay is . . . startlingly beautiful, like a brunette who dazzles with the flash of her brilliant eyes; while San Francisco has the placid beauty of a blonde whose soft sweetness wins your love." Onshore, the contest ended; "the dark belle carries away the prize."[2] Theresa's hair had darkened over the years; few would immediately associate her with the blond ingenue who had taken the stand in Dublin. Intrigue and elegance comprised her charms as she sailed into port, and here was a city to match them.

What had once been thought of as a barren and unpromising island had become a busy hub for Asian trade by the 1870s. Its prosperity was reflected in the gleaming white waterfront architecture— Venetian-style buildings with multiple levels of arched windows and columned balconies—the racetrack and cricket grounds; British gardens, where imported bushes and fragrant herbs spilled from large clay urns, and elegant villas with facades covered in creepers that spread like veils of lace. Along the main thoroughfare of the fledgling city of Victoria, bookbinders, watchmakers, and high-end importers set up shops in rows that imitated the London arcades, shaded by banyan trees instead of stone arches. Well-to-do Chinese ladies sailed through the streets in curtained sedan chairs, showing only narrow slices of their faces through shaded windows before returning to their high-walled homes. The rest of the traffic swirled around a clock tower that had been donated by a wealthy trader. Rickshaw coolies walked with merchandise slung from poles balanced across their bony shoulders, while street hawkers screeched for pedestrians' attention, their impromptu markets creating knots of congestion in the already crowded streets. Farther west, bandbox houses nestled among the banana, date palm, and pomegranate trees. In the hills behind, terraced roads and narrow staircases wound between huts built on red and gray granite.

On the day of Theresa's arrival, the streets were filled with commotion. She was testing the mattress of her hotel bed when she heard a swell of noise outside: chanting, singing, cymbal clashing. When she looked down at the street from the veranda of her hotel room,

Theresa saw women sitting cross-legged on trays, carried above the crowd. Their faces were painted with a thick coat of red and white face paint, and they clutched tin cases of the makeup, surreptitiously reapplying it when drops of sweat caused the colors to bleed. The mirrors sewn into their clothing caught the sun and sent flashes of light slicing through the sky. Platters of cake and sliced fruits were arranged at the side of the road, ringed by red candles and incense. Finally, a gold dragon appeared, looking like "the centipede of some champagne-supper dream," Theresa wrote.[3] Its gills glistened, and it contracted and expanded, accordion-like, above the heads of the men who carried it.

At night, Theresa followed the crowds to the temple where the culminating ceremony would take place. The temple shimmered silver in the moonlight; its bamboo rods were so delicate that they seemed likely to blow away, and yet the structure withstood the thousands of buzzing revelers that packed within. The celebration was flamboyant and theatrical, but when she wrote about it later, Theresa did not want to poke fun at the display. Each culture had its own "perambulating celebration," she carefully stated; their relative absurdity depended on perspective. If an American were to compare a festival in London and the Chinese Golden Dragon parade, "he will say that he guesses a good deal of barbarism still exists amongst the English." In "the very newest of worlds, California, and the oldest of worlds, China," she witnessed "instances of this same peculiar feature of humanity, the same allegorical procession, the same barbaric pageant."[4] Theresa had little desire to create a hierarchy among various ceremonies and celebrations of life. There was nothing necessarily superior about the values that determined the accepted form of revelry in her own culture.

As she began her travels through Asia, Theresa quickly learned to be wary of so-called European friends transplanted to the East who wanted "to colour your ideas with the right tint, to spare you the trouble of opening your eyes or ears."[5] Foreigners who had settled in exotic places were the worst, relentlessly endeavoring "to prevent your seeing anything, even when you have traveled hundreds of

miles to see a particular object."[6] They ignored the axiom that traveling benefitted mind and body, or at least thought it irrelevant advice
for a woman. It was "strongly urged upon every traveler," she
wrote, "never to look to the right or to the left—to journey upon
established companies' roads . . . never to diverge from the well-
established lines—and to see no more of Nature's wild and freakish
moods."[7] Theresa intensely desired to witness nature's wild moods
and to experience foreign traditions—particularly marriage, the
tradition whose regulation still plagued her own land, and whose
globe-trotting examiner she had become.

As Theresa understood it, Chinese marriage was decidedly less
formal and less restricting than Western marriage, and more honest
because of it. There was no official ceremony, "no actual acceptance
of the relative positions of husband and wife; no formula such as, 'I,
Mary Gold, take you, John Quill, to be my wedded husband,'" Theresa wrote. Upon the union of a man and a woman, "the families and
the medium have settled the marriage, and the parties are supposed
to agree"; there was a three-day feast, and then the event concluded
without anything like "a ritual marriage ceremony."[8] She met groups
of Chinese women, like the Mormons, who did not seem to mind that
their husbands married multiple wives. Because there was no shame
attached to polygamy, there was no need to hide it. Men in Western
society had the same urges, she wrote, only theirs were considered "a
terrible disaster and crime," forcing them to "practice it *sub-rosa*."[9] In
Chinese marriage, there was no expectation of monogamous loyalty.
Sexual instincts, she implied (in less direct language), were not re-
pressed, and so this society avoided the damaging and unpredictable
consequences of their resurgence.

The newfound wealth and prosperity of America had shown Theresa that respectability was more nebulous in the New World than in
the Old. Now, as she moved into an old world that was new to her,
the foundations upon which status supposedly rested—especially for
women—became increasingly ambiguous. In America, this made
her uncomfortable. She squirmed among the ladies who dressed up
to match their social aspirations, and she was forced to reevaluate the

campaign that had consumed her twenties. But in China, and most of Asia, she really began to question the virtues of her civilization's social institutions: "Can any one who has studied the various marriage laws in the various civilized countries say that civilization has done anything for us in this state, which sums up the vital interest of our whole lives?" she wrote.[10] People in Western society "invent . . . troubles and sorrows, and then weep [their] heart out over them, while there was an entire civilization that thrived without concerning themselves with petty emotions."[11]

A strange world existed when "one investigate[d] the outside ring of our own tether," Theresa concluded, but its curiosity did not eliminate its intrinsic worth. In recent years, Theresa had made a living by criticizing foreign cultures, but as she traveled through Asia, her judgments became less focused, upending assumptions more than asserting predominance. Perhaps the answer to the marriage-law mess was not to reform marriage but to reinvent the concept, she seemed to suggest. If she was willing to humor a state of law several steps beyond what her countrymen would even consider, she at least set a precedent that expanded the debate.

When Theresa visited Sri Lanka (then called Ceylon), she appeared to abandon any prejudices her native country might have instilled in her with respect to monogamous marital integrity. The island was paradisiacal—one of the places, it was said, where the Garden of Eden might have been located, and she could understand why it had acquired this reputation. In Point de Galle, a southwestern port town with an elegant and sprawling Dutch fort butting up against the ocean, cinnamon peelers sat crossed-legged in the streets, curled and fragrant shavings scattered around them like brown pigeon feathers. Merchants measured tea on brass scales, forming careful cones of dried leaves and standing with their backs to the gentle breezes to protect their piles. Women walked through the streets with umbrellas to guard against the sun, the peacock feathers sewn into their clothing flashing iridescent, while the less wealthy, wrapped in coarser cloth, balanced baskets on their heads. High in the trees, fan-shaped leaves shaded ripe fruit, and along the hills, where the

A Kandyan chief and his family in Sri Lanka.

land had not been cleared for coffee plantations, "glowing-eyed sun-flowers" turned "their heads with vesper hymns to the setting orb of day," wrote Theresa.[12] When the sun dropped into the ocean, it streaked the sky with bloody red and amber hues. The hills and white buildings reflected the light in a softer tone, blushing in the face of such violent natural display.

Beyond its sensory charms, the island held additional appeal: among certain populations, a *woman* could marry more than one man. "This, in truth, was a paradise; men and women . . . were beautiful—and here the latter had their full rights until that horrid British Government, having got possession of the island, enacted a law only five years ago making it a punishable offence to have more than one husband," she wrote. "There is masculine tyranny for you!" she said, with some seriousness. "There is the march of civilization!" she said, with a large dose of irony. She described a Singhalese queen who married seven men, and "when they chanced to annoy her, or not fulfill some promise made under the holy halo of love's sacred fane, she very properly poisoned them, to teach them their duty (or rather their successors) not to break their paroles d'honneur to ladies."[13] Theresa was amused by a case in which a "lady applied to be permitted to take a second husband, she having had enough of the first after three weeks of the honey-moon."[14]

Polyandry, Theresa reported, had a long history in this part of the world, although the British had done their best to suppress it in recent years. Half joking, half serious, Theresa proposed that they welcome the "queen-bee institution" into European society. It would "surely commend itself to Western woman-rights." It was better than polyg-amy, which was gaining such a devoted following in America. "Mor-monism should be destroyed, cut away root and branch, and polyandry gracefully planted in its place!"[15] The imposition of British regulations in Sri Lanka was a regression, depriving Singhalese women of not only their sexual liberty but their everyday freedoms. "What a come-down of women's rights," Theresa wrote. "Are nine-teenth century women only to sew on shirt buttons, darn stocking, and make puddings, while their less fair sisters . . . have been holding sway" for hundreds of years?[16]

Playfully suggesting the positive sides of polyandry inverted the analyses of most contemporaneous European ethnologists and arm-chair anthropologists. For these men, modern European marriage was an indication that civilization had reached its pinnacle. Though they disagreed among themselves about whether or not polygamy and polyandry were "normal" or "exceptional" phenomena, by the 1870s they concurred that "savage" populations found in Asia and Africa who still maintained polygamous marital arrangements repre-sented early stages of sociocultural development. John Ferguson McLennan wrote that polyandry was a phenomenon "most likely to occur at—the earlier stage of the progress of any race of men."[17] The president of the Anthropological Institute of Great Britain, John Lubbock, wrote that marriage could be "traced-up" through its dif-ferent stages of development. "Nothing," he wrote, "gives a more instructive insight into the true condition of savages than their ideas on the subject of relationships and marriage; nor can the great ad-vantages of civilization be more conclusively proved than by the im-provement which it has effected in the relation between the two sexes."[18] Polyandry and matrilineal relations were relics of barbarism;

"savage" civilizations, these men agreed, were a means of studying one's own extinct ancestors.[19]

Theresa accepted that certain civilizations could be classified along an evolutionary scale as superior or inferior, and when her comments are most strongly inflected with this sensibility, they echo her thoughts about black Americans. In bad weather, she reported, whole families of Chinese fishermen stowed themselves in the hold of their boats. "The reason they are not all suffocated," she wrote, "can only be explained on the hypothesis that they have an unsuspected amphibious nature. Darwin should have investigated this point."[20] But her quasi-serious suggestions that the women of Sri Lanka were better off than their British counterparts slyly reversed the assumed evolutionary trajectory of "civilization." Into a debate dominated by strict delineations of progress, she introduced relativism.

Her endorsements of polyandry, however, were not practical propositions. For Theresa, Sri Lanka was a metaphorical and mystical playground—a fantasy land that stood outside normal time, one that reminded her of Eden, but also of Circe's island. Her lyrical prose made little gesture toward serious reportage; she merely wanted to evoke the experiences that had readjusted her own expectations for her readers, to push people beyond the tether of their own knowledge so that they would question the fundamentals of their everyday life. One day, for instance, she described how she had picked a belladonna flower—an opiate—that had induced a state of delirium. She fell asleep and awoke wondering if she had bathed and then spent an hour deliberating which shoe to put on first, finally realizing she was already wearing both. As her fingers slipped through her hair, lifting a strand, letting it fall, the objects in her room rose from the surfaces on which they rested and vibrated in the air.

Sensory disorientation was a powerful force and could adjust an entire worldview. In India, she sailed down a river so placid that she could see every leaf and twig of the trees above her reflected in the water below. It was such a bewitching effect, that she thought "it might be a matter of doubt which was the right side up of the world, and if, after all, we were not living topsy-turvy."[21] As she paddled

Queens Road, Hong Kong.

through Cambodia, the charms of this "topsy-turvy" world became almost impossible to resist. "I had to tear myself away from this enchanted ground, for I had a feeling creeping over me day by day and hour by hour that it might be well to rest there during the remainder of my sojourn on this planet, and hold my soul in peace," she wrote. She looked back "to the modern European world, thousands of miles away, with a half-bewildered, half-yearning desire" and yet felt uncertain which world and culture she would "embrace as [her] own."[22]

Theresa traveled through Cambodia, Borneo, Singapore, Malaysia, and India in the three-odd years she spent in Asia. She became accustomed to the glaring morning light that had first burned her eyes and to the outrageous sunsets. In British-ruled areas, in the homes of local magistrates, she would start her days with champagne breakfasts and end them with tea and roast beef; where the empire had not penetrated, she awoke in makeshift tents and ate fire-grilled meat with fern salad in the evenings for her supper. Some of her hosts were friendly and curious; some communicated their disapproval of her intrusion and unfeminine expeditions. Neither reaction encouraged or deterred her; she had more than enough self-generated volition.

Anamese river huts, Vietnam.

On the way to Borneo from Singapore, she rode on the deck of the ship. Although she felt almost suffocated by the oily fumes of the steamer, she wanted to scan the maps and charts belonging to the Scottish ship engineer and probe him for information on the local mercury mines. Her only fellow passengers, a Chinese couple who mostly kept to their cabin, looked at her curiously when they emerged on deck. The steamer sailed into the harbor at Sarawak and docked in the shadow of a huge mountainous rock that projected out over the water. The rajah of Borneo met her there and lent Theresa a yacht that she then took up the coast, traveling into the interior of the country when she happened upon the outlet of a river. Houses lined these rivers, raised above the swamp on poles, like boxy insects with extra-long legs.

She was invited into one boxlike construction and had to climb a tree by sticking her pointed boots into carved-out notches in order to enter. Once inside, she stepped warily over the matted floor, afraid it might fall in and send her tumbling to the tangle of roots and the muddy earth below. The large common living space was divided up into distinct dominions, where individual Malay women held sway. They were fascinated by the lace on her clothing, reached out to

A Manchu bride, Beijing.

touch it with their fingertips, and she, in turn, was captivated by the swaths of silk they wore wrapped around their bodies, tied in knots that looked like roses at the tops of their chests.

They took her to a house where the silk was woven. The seated weavers passed the shuttle back and forth with henna-dipped fingers, working until a sheet of shining fabric spread across their laps. Her hosts were eager to show off their other valued possessions: jars of earthenware and dried heads. Both were highly valued, the former for its economic significance, the latter for its spiritual power. Theresa was disgusted by the collecting and cooking of human heads but admitted that "the ambition to rule in this world and the next is comprehensible."[23] In the weeks spent among the Dyaks, the Malay people, "[I] met with more kindness and true politeness than I have often encountered in more civilized places. Excepting that uncomfortable national institution of 'head hunting,' I think the Dyaks a very pleasant and interesting people."[24] As she sailed inland on the Ranjang River, the landscape became more startlingly beautiful, and "the tribes also became more unsettled and savage," she wrote. Here, the indigenous population stopped paying tribute to their imperial administrator, and the administrators did not attempt to collect it. She moved

Des Voeux Road, Hong Kong.

beyond the telegraph cables and mail-boat lines, the fragile threads that linked her to her native civilization.

After several weeks on the boat, Theresa decided her body needed more strenuous activity than her on-deck pacing. There was a bungalow that belonged to the rajah at the top of a mountain, and she decided to hike to the top and spend a few days there. The path was perilous and steep. Every hundred feet or so, she was forced to cross a bridge made of two ropes, one high and one low, tied to trees on opposite banks. She shuffled across with her arms above her, her hands clinging to the cord and her toes curling inside her boots. A dog had started to follow Theresa, and he leaped onto these rope bridges each time they approached one, only to tumble into the stream below and battle the current to shore. Theresa started out with her guides at nine in the morning; by noon they had not yet reached the halfway point, and it was over one hundred degrees. They stopped in a village and drank coconut milk.

When they reached the bungalow, however, she found that the retreat met her criteria: secluded, wild, solitary. She sent her guides back down the mountain and settled in with her only her aide, the bungalow caretaker, and his son for company, determined to stay for

A reception room in a Chinese house.

several days or maybe weeks. Time was becoming nebulous for Theresa. She was not even sure how long she had been traveling; "I take
no date / And I pay no rate / Under the forest trees," she recited to
herself.[25] Her watch had been broken for months. She spent as much
time outdoors as possible. The fresh-air "bathroom" at the bungalow
was her favorite spot. Behind a thicket of palms, a trickle of clear
water flowed over boulders streaked with silvery minerals, and
pooled in a dugout pit. The boulders formed the walls to her com-
mode, and a fern-covered bank gave her somewhere to sit as she
washed her hair.

   She was lingering in the pool one day when a bruiselike smear of
black and yellow spread rapidly across the sky. The birds fell silent,
and the leaves were immobile, as though the air had suddenly become
thick and gelatinous. She heard her aide calling and quickly gathered
her clothes. The darkness spread across the sky as she hurried to the
house. Just before she reached the veranda, a gust of wind caught her
from behind and threw her against the steps. Her aide pulled her inside, and the door slammed behind her. They stood silently in the
middle of the living room while the monkeys screamed and the limbs
of trees violently thrashed against the walls of the house. Pens and
paper and potted plants flew off the shelves, shattering on the floor.

The wind tore half the roof off the bungalow, and the rain streamed in, washing them with horizontal sheets of water before they could crawl under the table. The storm continued all night, the angry metallic gloom becoming a blanket of impenetrable darkness.

In the morning, when the rain finally slowed and then stopped, Theresa ventured outside. Broken pieces of furniture were scattered across the lawn; a tattered dress clung to the trunk of a tree. Gauzy mist drifted through the valley below the mountain. The wall of palms that had veiled the bathroom, her own private idyll atop the mountain, stood stripped of its leaves, like a row of broken matchsticks stuck haphazardly in the ground. She decided it was time to descend from the mountain and go home.

When Theresa finally left Asia, she returned via Gibraltar, intending to make her way north through Spain and France, even though Spain was in the middle of a civil war. Arriving on the shores of Europe, having supposedly left the barbarian cultures behind, she was immediately faced with violence and destruction: "Horrible stories were related to us of the terrible cruelties perpetrated up in the mountains . . . of the burning of atheists and socialists alive; of the flogging of women; of the destruction of the telegraph and the railroads."[26] Was she still in the "uncivilized" regions of the world, or had the manners and machines of civilization collapsed in her absence? The rest of her traveling party decided to make their way to England by water, but Theresa was determined to stick to her original route. She disliked the choppy Bay of Biscay and was curious to see a Spaniard in a Republican uniform, but mostly, she said, she was "averse to all retrograde movements" and had "an incapacity in realizing any danger yet unexperienced."[27]

While she waited for the necessary preparations to be carried out, she visited the Alhambra. The train broke down on the way to Granada, and she was forced to walk the final stretch, fending off sticky-fingered gamins with the pointed tip of her umbrella. When she finally reached the Moorish palace, the lacelike carvings, elegant white pillars, and terraced patios astounded her. She walked through the palace listening to the fountains, wandering into the cool chambers and then back into the bright sunlight. In the citrus grove, the oranges glowed against the dark leaves. If the country around her was thrown into a state of terror, here at least, in the ancient Islamic palace, civility was preserved.

Despite her professed enthusiasm for alternate modes of marriage, Theresa's sense of traditional romance had not entirely disappeared in her solitary years. "When we are thoroughly in love," she wrote, after walking through the corridors of the Alhambra, "we take all nature to our heart, so expansive does it become. Glorious sentiment, which turns the whole earth, sea, and sky into a boundless Elysium! Why is it so evanescent?"[28] Almost fifteen years after Yelverton had abandoned her, after she had given up her flirtations with Stoddard and Muir, the needling pain of solitude still afflicted her. The Moorish palace, she thought, was filled with the ghosts of whispering lovers.[29]

From Granada she headed north to Madrid, where a fretful and irritated English ambassador urged her to return to Gibraltar. He told her that she would have an easier time returning to England via the water than the war-torn roads that led to France. But Theresa would not be deterred. The countryside was filled with fighting Carlist and Republican factions that stopped her carriage at every crossing, waving their rifles in the air to command her driver's attention. When they peered in her carriage she duly repeated the catechism she had memorized in awkward Spanish: "I am an English lady traveling home from India," she said, smiling at the soldiers.[30] The mantra carried her safely through Spain, and she crossed into France near Irún.

Theresa crossed the Channel once more and arrived in England two decades after the fateful journey across the same body of water that had changed the course of her life. London, when she reached it, was mostly the same as she remembered: misty and cool even in the summer; coated with soot; a mixture of grandiosity, shabby splendor, and decay. But now, having reached her forties, she no longer saw it as her default destination, as it was for many women of her age and class. Her world was now much wider, and London itself had little to offer her—no family, no occupation, few friends.

She quickly set about to take care of business. In September of 1873 she signed a contract with the publisher Richard Bentley to transform her recent magazine pieces into a book. She worked fast, tying together her stories about Utah, Hong Kong, China, Cambodia, Macao, Saigon, Singapore, Sarawak, Johor, Sri Lanka, and Spain. She called her book *Teresina Peregrina or Fifty Thousand Miles of Travel Round the World*, playing with the Spanish word for pilgrim, *peregrino*. It was published the following year.

By the time *Teresina Peregrina* came out, Theresa had moved to Edinburgh and was organizing her writing about America into a book. Despite the city's distance from her sisters' homes in Wales and France, and her friends in Hull, Edinburgh had become her de facto home. As she walked along the gray stone streets in the shadow of the castle, through the pleasure grounds where she had once secretly met with Yelverton, she was not alone. Trailing a step or two behind her, his small brown hand in hers, was a young Singhalese boy—the aide who had followed her up the mountain in Borneo and back down when she had decided it was time to leave. He could not keep up with her brisk pace; the sculpted gargoyles with their twisted bodies and bared teeth—so different from the regal stone lions and fat, reclining Buddhas of his own country—distracted him with their menacing stares. His arms and legs must have felt stiff and confined in the suit Theresa had given him.

Curious eyes followed the couple as they walked down Chambers Street and rounded the corner near Greyfriars Kirk. Theresa was teaching the boy to read and write in English, reported the papers; he could already speak the language fluently.[31] She had obtained him—she did not like to say "purchased"—with "love and money." The love, she explained when asked about her companion, was "between the child and myself, and the money absorbed by the parents."[32] Theresa was unsure of what would greet her when she returned to Britain—what she would call her own in the country that was supposedly her native turf—and so she brought part of the enchanted Eastern lands back with her.

Reviews of *Teresina Peregrina* were marked by the same competing impulses that had shaped reactions to her public persona for years. She was commended for her unfeminine courage and criticized for her unfeminine style. The well-known Scottish magazine *Chambers's Journal*, which had chronicled politics and society for decades, called her a victim of the "disgraceful state of the marriage laws in the United Kingdom" and admired her writing for its "dash of the genius." But the journal also chastised her impetuosity: "Her wandering being dictated by fancy, she presents no regular narrative, either as regards dates or means of transit; but, like a butterfly zigzagging in its flight from flower to flower, she skips frolicsomely from scene to scene, just as the whim of the moment directs—her guiding principle, as far as we can see, being a determination to undertake journeys which, as fraught with personal danger, she was counseled by friends not to attempt."[33]

Theresa had probably assumed that readers would side with her in the face of the naysayers who had discouraged her more adventurous exploits. But back in England—having survived, even thrived, in the face of danger—she was scolded for taking risks. The fact that she had faced down perils that "even few men of nerve would care to encounter," as one reviewer put it, was a barbed compliment, yet another sign that she had moved beyond the pale of traditionally feminine conduct.[34] Her writing was "unfeminine," wrote the highbrow periodical the *Academy*, which solemnly advertised itself as "A Monthly Record of Literature, Learning, Science and Art." The magazine could not credit her claim that she—a woman who often dismissed her guides—had traveled as extensively as she claimed: "If the writer has really been to all the places of which she speaks, she has certainly performed a feat which, for a lady, is almost if not quite, without parallel."[35] Still, inclusion in the *Academy*'s pages was its own form of compliment. "The mention of New Books, Articles, etc., in our lists is intended as a guarantee of their importance," the editors stated on the front of each new issue.[36]

The more sharply disapproving portions of the reviews echoed the attacks of earlier years: Theresa was not who she seemed, and she would corrupt impressionable minds with her audacious and unusual behavior. "It is not . . . a work that we would place in the hands of unsophisticated youth of either sex, for the cool way in which the writer goes, with perfect calmness, into delicate matter which a man would hesitate to name or even hint at," wrote the *Academy*.[37] The reviewer at the conservative evening newspaper the *Pall Mall Gazette* repeated the concern. "Most women, if they had lingered in a crowd among frescoes that were obscenely gross, would have preferred silence on the subject," but this had not been Theresa's response; she had reveled in things she knew would shock her readers.[38] There was even something promiscuous about the prose itself; "the book leaves a general impression of being very much written *en peignoir*."[39] The *Athenaeum*, a weekly magazine slightly more inclined to society gossip, was the least equivocal: "We never read a more worthless book." Its episodes of violence and tropical decay were "disgusting."[40] More than a dozen years had passed since Theresa's first foray into public life, but the arguments against her had not changed.

When *Teresina in America*, a collection of her writings about America, was published in 1875, reviews were scarce, and Theresa seemed to have dropped off most people's radar. For the latter half of the 1870s, Theresa lived in relative obscurity, writing less, traveling more. She and her dark-skinned companion no longer cut a figure on the Edinburgh streets. Perhaps she thought that by avoiding the limelight she would be able to escape the ceaseless admonitions that had followed her during and after her travels. She returned to Sri Lanka and brought the boy home. The benefits of civilization came with restrictive prejudices, and he would avoid these in his native land.

CHAPTER TEN

Sunset

The voyage of the best ship is a zigzag line of a hundred tacks.

—Ralph Waldo Emerson, "Self-Reliance" (1841)

Getting to Pietermaritzburg, the capital of the South African British colony of Natal, was not an easy feat. After weeks on a steamship, several days spent idling in the Cape Town harbor, disembarking, reembarking, waiting until the tide was high enough to clear the sandbar surrounding the port of Durban, then waiting in Durban until supplies could be gathered—only *then* did the overland journey begin. A railroad cut through the bush for about thirty miles, but after that the only option was the rut-pocked road—marred by four-feet-deep watery pits in the rainy season and a honeycomb of holes in the dry season. Carcasses of oxen lay just to the side, flies circling lazily above. When it stormed, the sky darkened to an inky blackness, and the tips of the tall grass buzzed with electricity.

Near Pietermaritzburg—Maritzburg as it was and is commonly called—the road improved, shaded by a row of willows that grew alongside a river. The town itself was a relative oasis. Untrained rose vines spread like a carpet over the whitewashed houses. Rows of pineapple plants stood in a line outside verandas, while banana trees

South Africa.

dripped fruit from their branches. The small network of streets in the colony's capital had been laid out at perpendicular angles, but no street extended very far, tapering off in the open, grassy plain. Paths were wide; space was not lacking. A dozen oil lamps lined the roads, but when there was even a smattering of stars, they remained unlit. Few people ventured outside at night.

For travelers like Theresa, who made her way to Maritzburg in 1880, the destination was more pleasant than the journey, but life in a colonial outpost still required rapid adjustment to unforeseen conditions and unwelcome intruders. A steady stream of insects—moths, mosquitoes, dragonflies—flew into living rooms at night. To the north of Natal lurked the Zulu nation, a land, it seemed to the colonists, filled with unpredictable threats. At this edge of empire, Theresa's last home, penumbras of her past life—of love and war—surfaced.

On the coast near Port Elizabeth, visible from steamers passing between Cape Town and Durban, stood a short, squat sandstone pyramid,
a monument of love erected by a former governor as a memorial to
his wife. The Kafirs, as the indigenous people were indiscriminately
called, wore cast-off uniforms from European armies. Scarlet coats
from Inkerman or Sevastopol stalked the African plains. But despite
these shadows from her past, the colony of Natal—Vasco da Gama's
terra natalis, the land of nativity—might be a place for a final rebirth.

The British had colonized Natal in violent fits and starts, constrained
by conflicts between the Dutch settlers who founded the colony in
the seventeenth century, the British forces in the latter half of the
nineteenth century, and native populations struggling to maintain
control of their land. In the mid-nineteenth century, settlers of Dutch
descent—known as trekkers, Boers, and Afrikaners—and the more
recently arrived British colonists uneasily shared colonial authority
until the discovery of diamonds intensified competition. In 1875 the
colonial lord secretary of Britain, Lord Carnarvon, issued an invitation to the Boer authorities to discuss the confederation of the South
African colonies, supposedly to further the advance of civilization in
Africa, but really to expand his own empire.[1]
    As the British increased their hold on the South African colony,
they articulated their unique "civilizing" capabilities with growing
insistence. South Africa, many argued, was a region that desperately
needed social reform. The native was "unwilling to work, and unable to think; with a mind disengaged from every sort of care and
reflection, indulging to excess in the gratification of every sensual
appetite," according to early English settler John Barrow (later, the
secretary of the Admiralty).[2] The Boers, according to the British,
were peerless pioneers but lacked the impulse to build up towns, railroads, and a press. Not only did their development lag; their mode of
governing was debased. "Crime and outrage of all sorts are rife in the
land" controlled by Boers, wrote the *Cape Argus*. "There is not
merely a low standard of morals but no standard at all. Truth and

Zulu warriors with a shield and assegai.

honor and justice are unknown in practice, and religion . . . has all but died out amongst the people."[3]

In British-run Pietermaritzburg, on the other hand, there was "none of that evil talk of the 'damned nigger,'" wrote the Edinburgh-based *Blackwood's Magazine*, a popular publication among the colonial British population; "there is not a sign of cuffing or bullying; the natives are on the whole treated with the same justice and impartiality as the Europeans."[4] With their self-proclaimed tolerance, goodwill, and industry, the British were the natural champions of civilized society, and they were "chosen to rule south Africa," according to the English-language newspaper the *Natal Witness*.[5] Those who make the best use of the earth deserve to inherit it—or so went the official line of late imperialism's mission-driven mysticism. Social Darwinism further bolstered colonial justifications; if there was a scale of evolutionary ascent for societies, the undisciplined Boers were not far ahead of the native Africans.

In January of 1879, the British army invaded the Zulu kingdom, initiating a war intended to secure and expand the colony of Natal.[6] The British high commissioner in South Africa, Sir Henry Bartle Frere, believed the Zulu forces would quickly cave when confronted with British imperial might, and issued an ultimatum to the Zulu king. The Zulus, however, proved to be significant foes; at Isandl-wana Mountain, over thirteen hundred British troops and their African allies were killed. By mid-March, the British seemed better positioned, but their success was by no means secured. They cautiously advanced on the Zulu capital Ulundi, and in June reached it, forcing the Zulu king, Cetshwayo kaMpande, to flee. He was eventually caught and exiled to Cape Town. When the Zulu forces were defeated at their capital, the region was divvied up between thirteen pro-British chiefs.

When the Zulu war first began, thousands of miles away, a European prince rejoiced, and a chain of events began that would lead Theresa to Natal. The exiled French prince Louis Napoleon, the great-nephew of Napoleon I, the son of Napoleon III and the empress Eugénie, felt that this war was his chance to prove he had inherited the fearlessness of his forefathers. Since childhood, he had greeted passersby with a salute rather than wave, and his most-dreaded punishment as a boy was the removal of the make-believe epaulets that adorned his clothing. England had been his home since the Franco-Prussian War began, and he was eager to repay the hospitality. His friends and classmates from the Royal Academy at Woolwich had already departed for Africa, and he longed to join them. The life of an idle aristocrat—traveling aimlessly while invisible mechanisms arranged a marriage—was not for him.

The image of the French prince standing tall in his British uniform—the golden child of a diplomatic thaw—had symbolic appeal. But few on either the British or the French side encouraged him to go to South Africa. British authorities did not want to assume responsibility for the last hope of the waning Bonapartist contingent, or to put an emblem of the entente between Britain and France at risk. The prince's mother, Empress Eugénie, was also fearful, always aware of the dangers of belonging to a dynasty. When her fourteen-year-old son went to help his father fend off the Prussians, Eugénie wrote to her mother, "You are lucky only to have daughters, for at times I feel like a wild animal longing to take my little one far away into the desert and rend anyone who tried to seize him there." Fear, however, was followed by resignation;

Empress Eugénie.

she "would rather see him dead than dishonoured." With this attitude, she permitted the prince to go to South Africa.[7] The empress appealed to the queen, who agreed to support the prince's venture. "I did all I could to stop his going," said Prime Minister Benjamin Disraeli, when he looked back at the affair, "but what can you do when you have to deal with two obstinate women?"[8]

On February 27, 1879, Louis Napoleon set sail for South Africa, his proud and anxious mother watching him depart from the shore. The prince was sent as a visitor attached to the army rather than as a soldier, but as the responsibility for his safekeeping was passed from the higher ranks to the lower, directions grew diffuse. By the time the prince reached Zululand, *he* was giving orders. When he returned from a particularly dangerous excursion, his friend Evelyn Wood jokingly noted that the prince had not yet been pierced by an assegai, a Zulu spear. "No," replied the prince, laughing, "though I am in no hurry to be killed, I would prefer to fall under an assegai than from a bullet, for the first form of death would prove that I had met the enemy face to face."[9]

When he met the enemy "face to face," only a few months after he had arrived in South Africa, it *was* the Zulu spears that killed him. He

An illustration of the attack on Louis Napoleon, the Prince Imperial.

had been riding with a reconnaissance party through Zulu territory and had insisted that they stop near a river. The acting captain, Lieutenant Carey, was not comfortable resting there; in a valley, surrounded by high grass, they were an easy target for the Zulus. The prince insisted. Midafternoon, the prince acquiesced to Carey's concerns. As they were departing, dozens of Zulus emerged. Carey and the rest of the party mounted their horses and fled. The prince, attempting to alight his horse as it began to move away, fell to the ground. He fired his revolver and picked up a stray assegai, but he was outnumbered. He was stabbed seventeen times, including once through the eye.

The next day, the body was found stripped naked except for a gold chain with medallions, left by the Zulu warriors as a sign that the fallen soldier had fought bravely.[10] His clothes had vanished, but his spurs and a single sock, monogrammed with the letter "N," were found in the nearby bushes.[11] Soldiers who had not been at his side were struck by the tragic event. "When I think of the desperate struggle he must have endured while the helping power was disappearing," wrote his school-friend Captain Arthur Bigge, "I sorrow for his cruel death and think how different it *might* have been, indeed, *ought to* have been."[12] What *ought* to have been, according to the prince's designs, was a death with glory. "I should hate to be killed in some obscure skirmish," the prince had told a journalist from *Le Figaro*. "A big battle—yes: that would be Providence. But just a skirmish—no."[13]

For months the empress Eugénie had lived on tenterhooks; now, while she read her morning mail in her quiet, rented house in Chislehurst, news of the event she dreaded crawled into her life like a poisonous spider. "I am left alone," she wrote, "the sole remnant of a shipwreck; which proves how vain are the grandeurs of this world . . . I cannot even die; and God, in his infinite mercy, will give me a hundred years of life."[14] The prince's body arrived in England on July 9, 1879. The queen wanted to stage a full state funeral, but Disraeli refused. The private memorial service provided more than enough of an occasion for solemn spectacle. The path leading to the empress's home was lined with two hundred cadets. Louis's favorite horse, "Stag," was decked in white and silver and led by his grooms to the sound of muted drums. More than thirty-five thousand people came to pay their respects.[15]

In the months that followed, the empress sunk into a deep depression. She did not leave her house for twenty-three days. An invitation to Balmoral, the queen's Scottish castle, finally lured her north, and she took some comfort in walks through the Highlands, but her suffering was profound. "My grief is savage, unquiet, irascible . . . I don't want to be consoled, I want to be left in peace," she wrote to her mother.[16] More than ever, she felt like a foreigner, alone in an alien culture. She sensed that public sympathy was waning, and that her grief would soon be seen as excessive. But she could not escape the image of her son's death and decided that the only way to end her torturous imaginings was to visit the site of his slaying. She set out for South Africa in March of 1880, a few weeks before her fifty-fourth birthday, led by her son's friend and fellow soldier Evelyn Wood, and accompanied by an assortment of attendants and military officials, including Captain Bigge.[17] On April 16, the group arrived in Cape Town, where they spent a few nights before pressing on to Durban.

In Durban, a crowd gathered to watch the empress and her coterie arrive. This was the grandest occasion that the isolated settlers had ever hosted. A number of "half-mourning" bonnets—deemed appropriate for the situation—were shipped to local milliners. Florists stocked up on violets (the Napoleonic flower), and the liquor stores lined their shelves with Courvoisier (the supposed brandy of choice of Napoleon III).[18] But the empress was not willing to humor their curiosities or compliment their preparations. Two days after landing, she encouraged Wood to press on to Pietermaritzburg, where they would finish stocking the caravan. When they left Pietermaritzburg, the company was composed of seventy-eight people and two hundred animals. Wood followed the prince's path, taking the empress through the northern Transvaal town of Utrecht.

When they finally entered Zululand and neared the site of the prince's death, Wood became aware of another complication. They were being pursued by a "lady correspondent from an American newspaper," who had followed their path for weeks—a woman calling herself Theresa Yelverton, Viscountess Avonmore.[19] Theresa had learned of the empress's departure from England while she was in Sri Lanka, and quickly decided to head for Cape Town. She had not written for any magazine in years, but this story was too good to pass up. Despite the empress's express wish that the press leave her alone, Theresa followed the imperial party more than a hundred miles from Pietermaritzburg, persuading local authorities in the border town of Greytown to lend her troopers for an escort. As far as the Greytown officials knew, Theresa was exactly who she professed to be, an aristocrat attempting to join the empress. They were in no position to deny her the proper security.

In Theresa's telling, she had crossed the empress's path several times prior to this attempted South African meeting. Theresa had told her Californian friend Mary Viola Lawrence that she had stayed in the empress's palace in the years leading up to the Crimean War. Another story circulated that she approached the empress when Eugénie visited the troops fighting in the Crimea. She told the Greytown troopers who accompanied her through the veld that she was the prince's secret widow.[20] Later she would claim that she was writing the prince's biography.

If these connections were fabricated, Theresa's imagined association still makes sense. Eugénie, like Theresa, had been raised in convents and had risen from humble roots to celebrity. (Eugénie's grandfather was a Scottish merchant who made a living in Spain by importing and selling fruit and wine.) Their melodramatic temperaments were not dissimilar. In her youth, spurned by a lover, Eugénie swallowed a poisonous combination of ground-up matchstick heads and milk, and refused to take the antidote until her repentant (but unyielding) suitor was brought to her side.[21] After this episode, Eugénie and her mother flitted through Europe, until she caught the eye of Louis Napoleon, and, to everyone's surprise, secured the eventual title of empress by marrying him. Eugénie—a wild child who improbably rose to imperial prominence—was a more fitting royal idol for Theresa than staid Queen Victoria. Theresa had not managed to secure the glamour and security of rank that came with a successful social leap, but Eugénie had proved it possible.

If their paths had crossed, Eugénie had forgotten it by the time she reached South Africa. She did not want to be bothered by this annoyingly persistent lady journalist, so Wood asked the Zulus to prevent Theresa from approaching his charge. He quickly drew up a lease outlining the land within two miles of the spot where the prince had fallen and bestowed it on the local leader, briefly explaining the laws of trespass. The Zulus were to form a barricade if Theresa attempted to breach the two-mile marker. They seemed to understand their responsibility: "They formed a long line, and clasping hands danced away, showing how they would resist passively the approach of any one who endeavored to go on the property," wrote Wood.[22]

But Theresa was not deterred. As the empress waited near the river, anxiously passing the last few days until the one-year anniversary of her son's death, Theresa also waited. Finally, Bigge was sent to speak with her. "She affected to be greatly astonished at the request that she would refrain from coming to the place during the Empress' stay," wrote Bigge. She told him that she had traveled ten thousand miles in order to offer condolences. In his humble opinion, Bigge told her, "the best means of showing her sympathy and affection was by complying with the Empress' request."[23]

Theresa stayed put until Wood, flanked by Bigge and the empress's personal attendant, confronted her. In the face of military and imperial authority, Theresa still proved herself "quite equal to so formidable an attack," wrote Bigge in a letter relaying the events to Queen Victoria. Her devotion to the empress was her defense; she studiously ignored that Eugénie denied any connection. She displayed, wrote Bigge, "an extraordinary forgetfulness of facts" when it suited her.[24] Theresa finally relented and agreed to leave. But she did not depart immediately; she had not come all that way for a completely fruitless journey. On June 3, after the imperial party had gone, she approached the spot where the prince had died and made a sketch of the cross that had been erected to mark the site.

Despite the pomp surrounding the empress's journey, the untimely death of a powerless royal in an imperial backwater only held lasting interest for family members and news-deprived settlers. Back in England, a tepid debate ensued over a memorial to the prince. Queen Victoria wanted to clear a space in Westminster Abbey, but the new prime minister, William Gladstone, would not hear of it, and his view was closer to public sentiment; the memory of the brief war was fading rapidly. *Punch* proposed an inscription for the prince's tomb that reflected the diminishing interest.

Prince Eugene Louis Napoleon . . .
Brave, amiable and accomplished,
Who made many friends
And unfortunately lost his life
In a very doubtful quarrel,
Which in no way concerned him.
This monument is erected
By a small section of the British people
To exhibit to the world
Their slight respect

For the national feelings of France,
And their great regard
For the cause of Imperialism.[25]

If the death had disturbed the peaceful accord between two old European rivals, the effect was short-lived. The center readjusted, the peripheries faded, and the engine of imperialism pressed on, undeterred by the snuffing out of an antique dynasty in a distant scuffle.

Theresa had gambled on the story and had lost, but she decided to remain in South Africa nonetheless, renting rooms in Pietermaritzburg for two pounds a month. In January of 1881, a weekly column titled "Pen and Ink Sketches" began in the *Natal Witness*. Tone and timing suggest that Theresa was the author—one "Kate the Critic." A recurring interest in legal processes, and references to the overlooked ingenuity of women, further support the association. Offhand references to family gatherings and other personal details, however, imply that the author may have been someone else, or perhaps that Theresa embellished this new persona with domestic anecdotes that would endear her to her readers more than her spinsterhood.

"Kate" became a local—anonymous—celebrity. As the primary commentator on a secluded colonial society, she was both at its center and its sharpest critic. Spheres of influence were not readily apparent in the fledgling society, and so journalistic criticism was also an act of creation, defining credibility and determining relative importance. The columns were often intensely judgmental, but they were not just vitriolic attacks. Her array of ill-suited officials created an ambivalent portrait of the entire imperial project in Natal. If the officers of empire were its primary representatives, their shabby performances had more than just comedic significance; they signaled the decay of the standards that supposedly united the disconnected regions of the empire.

South Africa was not a place for British emigrant pioneers or laborers (those categories were dominated by other ethnicities), so it became a place for aspiring members of the middle classes. Though Theresa had represented her defeat in the courts as a vicious machination of "gentle blood" over an honest, middle-class woman, as "Kate" she had little sympathy for colonial social climbers. "Natal is a country of disappointments," she wrote, where unqualified people held prestigious positions.[26] Crass social mobility was most shockingly exemplified by the slovenly mayor. "There is something which at once puts on the stamp of a 'draper,'" she wrote; "one and eleven three-farthings is printed on that forehead to the close observer as if it were tattooed; the walk is eminently the salesman's . . . The *tout ensemble* gives one the idea of a shrewd tradesman." His commercial background was written on his body and inflected his voice, which had the "deep tinge of the North of England." Faced with such a countenance, Kate could scarcely believe she "was gazing upon so high an official."[27]

The individuals she profiled were elevated by their positions but revealed their inadequacies in their habits. Archdeacon Colley "[has] more the look of a prize fighter than a preacher."[28] John Shepstone, the secretary of native affairs, "is not at all a bad fellow when once you know him, but it is the getting to know him that is the worst part of the business."[29] Among the lesser lights of the colonial capital, there was no shortage of material: "The question," she wrote, "is with whom to commence!"[30] These men were obsessed with status, but status, in Natal, was no more substantive than punctuation. She instructed her printer to "not forget the etceteras" in one of her subject's titles: "For without them Mr. Ritchie's cognomen would be as incomplete as a picture of Jove without his thunderbolts, or Old Time minus that ridiculous-looking lock of hair overhanging his forehead."[31] Dandyish accoutrement was necessary to preserve importance in the murky realm of colonial distinction.

If Kate was in fact Theresa, why did she adopt such a scathing tone of superiority about the people among whom she had chosen to live? Her own background did not immediately raise her above her targets, and she had viewed social mobility in America with less express antagonism. Perhaps her spite emerged from the decrescendo of her recent life, the narrowing of her movements and her influence. Despite the charms that a rugged, unconstrained life might offer her independent spirit, her present location—away from people and events of significance—left much to be desired. She knew she was not that different from the people she chastised, and so she insulated herself with hyperbolic disapproval, perhaps hoping that her readers would not sense the similarity between the author and the aimless characters she disdained.

Or perhaps underneath the superficial nastiness lay a deeper critique. All her life, Theresa had fought to establish her respectability, and now she found herself surrounded by incompetent men who had risen through the colonial ranks to rule a colony. "Shakespeare says something about men clothed in a little brief authority, playing such fantastic tricks as makes even angels weep," Kate wrote, reviving an allusion that had been used during the Dublin trial.[32] From her current position, it seemed that the "fantastic tricks" of self-deluding men maintained an ill-formed empire built on ineptitude. Natal was not the well-mannered child of English society, spreading civilization to less-advanced populations; it was its unruly and ungainly offspring. Shadows of corruption, taint, and degeneration fell across the bright motives of the British Empire in these ostensibly lighthearted sketches. The "civilizing" mission could not be carried out by a society that alternately seemed a weakened dilution and a grotesque exaggeration of the civilization from which it sprang.

"Pen and Ink Sketches" was not *all* bile and spite. The music director of Natal, Charles Lascelles, was far more talented than his colonial compatriots. So why was he in Natal? "Is it because of any domestic troubles," Kate wondered, "or is it from personal disinclination to remain in a country where that freedom of action is not permitted which is allowed here?" Lascelles was "a true Bohemian, a thorough musician, an *artiste* to the very letter." His eyes were tinged with ink from the belladonna flower, his mustache was waxed, his hair long and shaggy, and his red cheeks "rather put one in mind of rouge."[33] With his blackened eyes and rosy complexion, perhaps his talents were better suited to a society where "freedom of action" was given liberal reign.

For Lascelles and, implicitly, for Theresa, the second-rate standards of colonial society were a necessary evil. Theresa's neighbors had been forced to make their careers in the colonies because they did not measure up in class and character. But there were certain individuals who had ended up in the colonies not because they lagged behind their compatriots but because they had leaped too far ahead. The mutability of colonial society allowed a talented, effeminate musician and an independent, opinionated spinster to find a niche in which to thrive. When an anonymous "Observer" wrote to the *Witness* that the authoress of "Pen and Ink Sketches" should mind her own business because her curiosity was unbecoming—a criticism he surely would not have leveled at a man—the newspaper came to her defense.[34] "Pen and Ink Sketches" was immensely popular, increasing the sales of the issues in which it appeared, and the paper would continue to support it.

Ever since the Dublin trial, Theresa had lived intimately with the press, courting, fleeing, and then requiring their attention and their paychecks. At the very end of her life, unwelcome publicity was no longer a concern; it was the weekly deadline that had become a burden, made worse by her failing health. "Whether for my sins or not I cannot say," she wrote, "but of late I have been racked with cruel pains in every limb until life has become anything but the halcyon affair it used to be in days gone by." Her doctors advised her not to excite herself with mental exertions, but if she wanted to survive, she had to keep writing: "The Press must wait for nothing, its voracious maw must be filled, and so once again I painfully struggle to trace on paper that which looks anything but what it is intended to be."[35] Theresa's handwriting had always been terrible. Now, as pain coursed through her inflamed fingers, its jagged loops tracked her physical decline.

Her livelihood had become her menace. But, in a way, this was merely a more explicit manifestation of an ongoing condition: that which sustained her also destroyed her. Writing was for her, as it was for so many women of her age and era, her most direct, most powerful way of expressing herself—of having some stake in the world around her. She wrote to persuade the love of her life to return her devotion, then to defend herself against accusations of ignominy. As her star faded, she wrote to assert the significance of her trajectory across the world, and then to dissect the motives of men who imposed their ideas of civilization in hostile lands. Her writing both gave rise to her sharpest critics and allowed her to subsist. A few months after she complained of her pains, Theresa finally stopped writing and stopped living.

Theresa Yelverton, née Longworth, Viscountess Avonmore, alternately known as Theresa Longworth, Thérèse Yelverton, or Kate the Critic, died on September 13, 1881, in Pietermaritzburg at the age of forty-eight. She had ten pounds to her name; her belongings—mainly jewelry—when sold by her landlord, fetched an additional forty pounds.[36] Her lack of possessions, at least, justified her boast that she had been "a rolling stone all [her] life" and had "gathered no moss"—no "papers, debts, cats, street-cars"—all of which she scorned.[37] She was buried the next day in the Church of England cemetery. Her death certificate marked her "married," and under "occupation" deemed her a gardener.[38]

Although she lived almost anonymously on the other side of the earth, some in her hometown still followed her affairs. A few days after her death, not having heard the news of her passing, the *Manchester Times* wrote that " 'Lady Avonmore,' the 'Hon. Mrs. Yelverton,' *née* Theresa Longworth is on her way home from Natal." The writer had come to this conclusion because "Kate the Critic" had ceased her column. The identity of "Kate" had been kept a secret to the inhabitants of Pietermaritzburg, but the reporter boasted, "[I have] reasons of my own for believing that 'Lady Avonmore' and 'Kate the Critic' are one."[39] The daughter of Theresa's landlord corresponded with friends in Manchester and most likely kept the Manchester journalist loosely apprised of Theresa's position. In the months after her death, interest in Theresa revived. A letter from Maritzburg was published in almost all the major newspapers in Brit-

ain, describing the "rather reduced circumstances" in which Theresa
had been forced to live in later years, her deepening depression
throughout recent months, and her lonely final hours. When death
finally came, Theresa did not resist it: "She died very peacefully, and
seem[ed] so glad to leave this world."[40] In moments of exasperation,
she had occasionally spoken of ending her life. While she never acted
on her threats, in the end, it seemed, she was unafraid of leaving life's
struggles behind.

The obituaries announcing Theresa's death were succinct, in no
way reflective of the short but wild ride of her life. "Lady Avonmore,
as she was known to her friends, or Miss Theresa Longworth, as her
enemies persisted in calling her, has just died at Pietermaritzburg, in
South Africa," reported the *New York Times*.[41] Stoddard learned of
her death by reading the announcement in *The Era Dramatic and Mu-
sical Almanac*. "Longworth—Miss Marie Theresa," the entry read,
"who claimed to be the Honorable Mrs. Yelverton and Lady Avonmore. Public reader and lecturer. Sept. 13."[42] The cause of death was
uncertain; some said it was dropsy—now called edema—others pa-
ralysis. Her fortunes of late, said the *New York Times*, had "been of a
somewhat uncertain character."[43]

Eighteen months later, William Charles Yelverton, who had quietly lived in exile while Theresa was traveling the world, died in Biar-
ritz, France. "Viscount Avonmore's Death Revives a Famous Episode
in High Life," said the headline in the *Chicago Tribune*; "The End of a
Noble Rake," announced the San Francisco *Daily Evening Bulletin*.[44]
But there was little to report about his later life, and so the obituaries
mainly rehashed the Dublin trial. Even that discussion was colored in
sepia tones to make up for a lack of substance; "Time has carried off
the famous lawyers who were present in that Court, and the dust is
piled thick on the record of the testimony."[45]

Yelverton's wife and two of his children survived him. He and
Emily had had four children, two of whom died soon after being
born. Barry Nugent, his first child with Emily, and Algernon William lived on past his death. Barry inherited the viscountcy in 1883,

and Algernon soon after, in 1885, when Barry died of enteric fever while stationed at Kirbekan in the Sudan. Algernon, now the sixth Viscount Avonmore, had one daughter, Evelyn Marianne Mabel Yelverton, who lived until 1956, but the title—the powerful but empty emblem of so many legal and emotional machinations—ended with the death of her father.[46]

Epilogue

As we look at the world, how absolutely, how inordinately, the Isabel Archer, and even such smaller female fry, insist on mattering. George Eliot has admirably noted it—"In these frail vessels is borne onward through the ages the treasure of human affection."

—Henry James, preface to *The Portrait of a Lady* (1907)

When the Yelverton trials began, marriage was considered—as it still is today—the central building block of society. It was "the fountain-head from which must flow the future population," wrote a contemporary author, the mold for "the moral nature of the people of the future."[1] Even sex, that sinister bogeyman, was not threatening when sanctioned by marriage. Celibacy, after all, did not aid productivity and progress, while marriage, "like the useful bee, builds a house and gathers sweetness from every flower, and labours and unites into societies and republics, and sends out colonies, and obeys kings, and keeps order, and exercises many virtues, and promotes the interests of mankind."[2] Marriage bore vitally on the perpetuation of the human race, the British Empire, and the social order. It was the tool that gave shape to a man's greatness and the tonic that fortified his constitution. And yet, as the Yelverton controversy made all too apparent, its parameters—what actually made a marriage a marriage—were unclear.

The Yelverton trials made the disparate marriage laws of the United Kingdom explicit. Ever since 1753, when Lord Hardwicke's Act declared that a legal marriage ceremony in England and Wales could only be conducted by a clergyman (an 1836 act recognized civil ceremonies), England and Scotland had different standards. The central and most controversial difference was that irregular marriage—the type that Theresa and Yelverton had supposedly undergone in Edinburgh—remained valid and staunchly defended in Scotland.

At a meeting of the Social Science Association in Edinburgh in 1864, John Campbell Smith (Theresa's lawyer in Scotland) argued that stringent standards for marriage sacrificed "justice on the altar of form." The Scottish system, he argued, had the merits of "simplicity and security; simplicity in the entering into it, and facility in proving and enforcing it."[3] Smith did not claim that it was necessary to protect women from the consequences of their misjudgments. But by narrowing the standards of marriage, the laws of England did not make it easy for women to avoid such missteps. Marriage should not be determined by bureaucracy and "cumbrous swaddling-bands," wrote Smith, and other Scots agreed.[4] A secret marriage was better than no marriage, wrote the lawyer and ethnologist John Ferguson McLennan; "wherever a secret marriage takes place, a union of a different nature would probably have been consummated, had marriage in secret been impossible."[5]

Before the Yelverton trials, novelists had already realized that the contradictions within British marriage law could provide them with compelling plotlines. When Lydia Bennet elopes with Wickham in *Pride and Prejudice* (1813), for example, her older sister Elizabeth fears that they have gone to the Scottish village of Gretna Green for a hasty marriage. After the first Yelverton trial, a host of marriage-law literature emerged. In 1861, the Irish novelist J. R. O'Flanagan published *Gentle Blood; or, The Secret Marriage.* "I preferred taking my hero and heroine from a recent trial in the Irish Court of Common Pleas," he wrote. The trial had "disclosed so many striking scenes, and stirring events, that even my unpractised pen could hardly make them unin-teresting."[6] The same year, the Lyceum Theatre in Edinburgh staged a play, *Woman; or, Love Against the World*, based upon an Irish law banning marriage between people of different faiths.[7] A few years later, in 1867, the journalist Cyrus Redding published the novel *A Wife and Not a Wife*, in which he berated "the sacrifice of a woman" in the courts.[8] A "heart crushed by misplaced affection," he wrote in his preface, was always an object of sympathy; "a recent case of this char-acter cannot fail to recur to the reader's mind."[9] The Yelverton case filtered into literature in more diffuse ways as well. Perhaps the most famous bigamy novel of the nineteenth century, Mary Elizabeth Brad-don's *Lady Audley's Secret*, began its serialization in July 1861, only a few months after newspaper headlines advertising "The Yelverton Bigamy Case" appeared. Subsequent years witnessed a veritable rash of bigamy novels. Out of the twenty-four books that the critic H. L. Mansel reviewed in 1863, about a third fell into this bigamy-based subgenre of sensation literature.[10]

These Yelverton-inspired works were intended to show that mar-riage law was a mess, but also to demonstrate that there were ways in which the law could not fully address the disorder. The suffering in-flicted by the mishmash of the law required literature. In Wilkie Col-lins's *No Name* (1862), two daughters are rendered illegitimate and penniless by the discovery that their late parents, Mr. and Mrs. Van-stone, were never married. Mrs. Vanstone, Collins wrote, had "re-solved to sacrifice her life to the man she loved . . . persuading herself . . . that she was 'his wife in the sight of Heaven.'"[11] Himself the father of three illegitimate children, Collins defended the irregular union between his characters by showing their committed relation-ship; they were married "for all intents and purposes (except that the marriage ceremony had not been read over them)."[12] He wanted his novel to show that love, devotion, and respect had flourished between these people, despite the informal nature of their arrangement.

Caroline Norton made a similar argument for the role of litera-ture in *Lost and Saved* (1863), which featured a secret marriage with disastrous results for the central female character, Beatrice. Norton downplayed the connection to the Yelverton trials but claimed that her story was still relevant as a representation of countless unfortunate young women. "I could find a parallel to Beatrice's easy credence in fifty out of a hundred girls," she wrote in a letter to the *Times*.[13] As a woman, it was easier for her to understand "the confusion that may exist in young and ignorant minds"; as a novelist, Norton wrote that she was more qualified to depict this confusion than the "educated and intelligent men to whom the law on these subjects seems clear."[14] Norton was no stranger to legalese; she was instrumental in the passing of the Custody of Infants Act of 1839 and the Matrimonial Causes Act of 1857. But even she felt there were certain experiences that required more expansive and empathetic storytelling.

For Norton, Collins, Theresa, and others, literature was necessary to tell the full story of the Yelverton case. Their plays and novels showed what the language of scientific rationalism could not: the emotion, passion, and individual suffering behind the tangle of the law. As Collins wrote in a later novel titled *Man and Wife* (1870)—also inspired by the Yelverton case—"the fact and the fiction shall never be separable from the other," and marriage law desperately needed fiction to dramatize its factual inadequacies.[15] "An uncertain marriage law," he wrote, "is a national calamity."[16] Even legitimate marriages disadvantaged unhappy women. "What can a married woman do for herself?" he asked. "She can make her misery public, provided it be of a certain kind—and can reckon single-handedly with Society when she has done it."[17] Advertising misery was risky for a woman, since she was likely to suffer the blame for her situation. Fiction had to step in to show the distress of those who could not do so for themselves. Although her goals were less explicit, in both *Martyrs to Circumstance* and *Zanita*, Theresa pursued a similar project.

The Yelverton-inspired literature shows the myriad social and legal problems made explicit by the trial; Theresa's biography shows the numerous historical forces reified in one woman's life. The problems with the law that these events illuminated and the literary inspiration they provided were significant, but the weight of the story cannot be boiled down to nuggets of legal or literary impact. Theresa's full, vivid story shows the ebb and flow of historical change, and how one woman navigated these shifts—specifically, how outdated mandates for women's lives linger, and how those ideas are subverted and overcome.

In many ways, Theresa was a harbinger of a new era. By the end of the century, the argument that Theresa had used to justify her trip to the Crimea—that an unemployed, unoccupied life was unproductive and unappealing—was widespread, stimulating both concern and enthusiasm. In his 1896 summary of the laws affecting women, Sir Arthur Rackham Cleveland somewhat begrudgingly wrote that women should not be expected to "remain passive and unemployed for the remainder of their lives."[18] By the 1890s, the stereotypical Girton-educated, bicycle-riding, cigarette-smoking, bloomer-wearing "New Woman" seemed to be everywhere in popular literature. Women were more openly articulating their abilities than ever before. "While on the one hand man has shrunk to his true proportions in our estimation," wrote the New Woman novelist Sarah Grand, "we come confidently forward to maintain . . . that there are in ourselves . . . possibilities hitherto suppressed or abused."[19]

Theresa publicly demonstrated these possibilities decades earlier. She disproved the fabled stability of Victorian marriage and did so using her own words and ingenuity. She manipulated the law so that she could testify against the man she claimed was her husband, defended herself before the House of Lords, and became a public advocate for marriage law reform. Though she wrote novels in a stereotypically feminine tradition of melodrama and romance, they were threaded with subversive claims that women were not compensated for their sacrifices or appreciated for their work. She had harsh words for women who labeled themselves women's rights advocates—disdaining their lack of feminine charm—but she became the type of figure these campaigners were likely to admire: a traveler who traversed the far reaches of the globe, supported herself financially, set up camp in rough-and-tumble terrain, and neglected all domestic responsibilities. "Killing the Angel in the House was part of the occupation of a woman writer," wrote Virginia Woolf, and perhaps this was truest for those women writers who left the house altogether.[20] Progressing from broadsheet darling to tabloid victim, Theresa eventually became perhaps the first woman to turn unwanted celebrity into a journalistic advantage, playing off her fame to develop an audience, then pursuing her stories with no-holds-barred determination. Her enterprising energy harkened a new era of journalism with fewer borders and increasingly investigative tendencies. She was part of, as William Thackeray put it, "the great engine" that "never sleeps"—the modern press—a vast organism with ambassadors in every quarter of the globe, and a "courier upon every road."[21]

Yet Theresa cannot be singularly perceived as a progressive catalyst of change. While Nightingale issued jeremiads to publicize her views about women's idleness, Theresa kept similar sentiments quiet, confining them to private correspondence. A cursory study of the Dublin trial might cast her as a champion of midcentury domestic values rather than someone who caused them to corrode. She had ambivalent feelings about women's voting rights, the democratization of culture, the destabilizing of social standards, and maintained prejudiced concepts of racial inferiority. And, of course, the greatest campaign of her life was aimed at securing a traditional and relatively subservient position in society.

Instead of as an icon or an iconoclast, perhaps Theresa should be thought of as someone who felt history shifting beneath her feet and had to stay supple in order to stay standing. At twenty-one, Theresa already anticipated the lack of control she would have over her fate with equanimity. "Did you ever watch the course of a stream running smoothly along," she wrote to Yelverton, "and notice that when impediment or interruption occurred . . . it blustered over and round them, but never resumed its former steady course? So I think it is with life."[22]

And yet, the most appealing thing about Theresa is that she did not let life's travails overwhelm, inhibit, or change her. She clung to her conceptions of independence, self-reliance, and, more than anything else, an idea of love that was not necessarily convenient or appropriate, but that was fervent and true. Passionate love did not disappear in the Victorian era, but such a tenacious belief in its importance was not standard among her contemporaries. She wrote to Yelverton of a "kindly-hearted worthy man," for example, who, despite "positively disapproving nearly every point in [her] character," still believed he should marry her, that after marriage "he could metamorphose [her] into a rather silly, very ignorant, amiable, *country-made* person. That was his *beau idéale*. He did not approve of women traveling, thought it spoiled them, etc." If she had given him a chance to test his plan, she wrote, he would have gone mad. "Now, don't you think it a great act of philanthropy on my part to have saved him from such a calamity?"[23]

To Theresa, love was something much grander than a practical arrangement; it was visionary in both senses of the word—ahead of its time, and made from the fabric of dreams. Relatively early on, she realized that Yelverton was almost a spiritual creation, something that was constantly just out of her reach. But despite this intangibility, she was willing to stake her life on him: "If we cannot enjoy reality we must be content with fiction. I think I can be happy in a dream."[24] In the early stages of their relationship, she did not commit herself to this apparent folly without encouragement. "Are you fairly ready for the land of dreams?" Yelverton wrote. "Have you got your passport? Yes. Very well then, I hope you will accept me as a traveling companion. May our impressions sympathise."[25]

With Yelverton ever retreating, the alacrity of her desire was to her detriment. But as a response to such a seductive invitation from her lover, it was supremely understandable, and even commendable. From the start, Theresa honored her instincts. Later, even when she understood the consequences of that honesty to her impulses, she was unwilling to relinquish the transient but exquisite rewards of love in the face of its acute pains. She comprehended that living through the torture of love was necessary to experience its sublimity. If, ultimately, her own era punished her for her tenacity and integrity, then perhaps she can be compensated, to a small extent, by the admiration that such qualities now command. She thought that her affair would appear as a "strange mythic incidence" when it retreated to "the shadowy past."[26] Mythic—yes. Strange—no. It is the emotional candor of this story that makes it so powerfully familiar, a vessel from a past age of the affections that persist in the present.

ACKNOWLEDGMENTS

I must thank Michael Carlisle, George Gibson, and Michele Lee Amundsen for believing in this story even before I had written it, and Michele Martinez for cultivating its seeds. I owe gratitude to the Gates Foundation for unknowingly supporting research that contributed to this book while I was getting a degree in something entirely different. I am fairly certain that I would not have thought myself capable of this project without the guidance of Leon Wieseltier. Thanks are also due to Cathryn Pyle for facilitating access to invaluable resources; to Charlotte Douglas, who kept me company in my Victorian obsessions; to Daniel Williams, who incisively edited later chapters; and to Isaac Chotiner for lending a kind eye and an ear to my concerns. A million thanks to the good-natured Gus, my family, and to Mike Pyle, who deserves my gratitude more than anyone, for his unending patience and love.

Preface

1. Walter Benjamin, "Theses on the Philosophy of History," in *Illuminations*, ed. Hannah Arendt, trans. Harry Zohn (New York: Schocken Books, 1969), 255.

2. Theresa Yelverton, *The Yelverton Correspondence: With an Introduction and Connecting Narrative* (Edinburgh: Thomas Laurie, 1863), 171. Henceforth referred to as *Correspondence*.

3. Thérèse Yelverton (Viscountess Avonmore), *Teresina Peregrina or Fifty Thousand Miles of Travel Round the World* (London: Richard Bentley and Son, 1874) 2:73. Henceforth referred to as *Teresina Peregrina*

Chapter One: Sunrise

1. Brian Roberts, *Ladies in the Veld* (London: John Murray, 1965), 29; Duncan Crow, *Theresa: The Story of the Yelverton Case* (London: Rupert Hart-Davis, 1966), 28.

2. *Full Report of the Important Trial Thelwall v. Yelverton (Marriage Case), Before Lord Chief Justice Monahan, in the Court of Common Pleas, Dublin* (Glasgow: William Syme, 1861), 47. Henceforth referred to as *Thelwall v. Yelverton*.

3. Ibid.

4. Herbert Sussman, "Industrialism," in *A Companion to Victorian Literature and Culture*, ed. Patrick Brantlinger and William B. Thesing (Oxford: Blackwell, 1999), 245.

5. Elizabeth Gaskell, *Mary Barton* (1848; New York: Penguin Books, 1996), 3.

6. Charlotte Brontë, *Shirley* (1849; New York: Oxford World Classics, 2000), 200.

7. "An Inquiry Into the State of Girls' Fashionable Schools," *Fraser's Magazine* 31 (1845): 704.

8. Quoted in Sara Delamont, "The Contradictions in Ladies' Education," in *The Nineteenth Century Woman: Her Cultural and Physical World*, ed. Sara Delamont and Lorna Duffin (New York: Barnes and Noble Books, 1978), 135.

9. Rebecca Rogers, *From the Salon to the Schoolroom: Educating Bourgeois Girls in Nineteenth-Century France* (University Park, PA: Penn State Press, 2005), 135–59.

10. George Sand, *My Convent Life*, trans. Maria Ellery McKay (Chicago: Cassandra Editions, 1978), 117.

11. Ibid., 96.

12. *Thelwall v. Yelverton*, 16.

13. Sand, *My Convent Life*, 122.

14. "A Woman's Thoughts About Women," *Chambers's Journal of Popular Literature, Science and Arts* 174 (May 1857): 2.

15. Ibid.

16. Quoted in Elaine Showalter, *A Jury of Her Peers: American Women Writers from Anne Bradstreet to Annie Proulx* (New York: Alfred A. Knopf, 2009), 173.

17. Ellen Bayuk Rosenman, *Unauthorized Pleasures: Accounts of Victorian Erotic Experience* (Ithaca, NY: Cornell University Press, 2003), 126.

18. Bracebridge Hemyng, "Prostitution in London," in *London Labour and the London Poor* (1851; New York: Penguin Classics, 1985), 486.

19. *Correspondence*, 14.

20. Ibid., 16.

21. James Kelly, "Yelverton, Barry, first Viscount Avonmore (1736–1805)," in *Oxford Dictionary of National Biography*, ed. H. C. G. Matthew and Brian Harrison (Oxford: Oxford University Press, 2004), http://www.oxforddnb.com/view/article/30212.

22. G. E. Cokayne, *The Complete Peerage of England, Scotland, Ireland, Great Britain and the United Kingdom, Extant, Extinct or Dormant* (London: G. Bell and Sons, 1887), 1:208–9; Leslie Gilbert Pine, *The New Extinct Peerage, 1884–1971: Containing Extinct, Abeyant, Dormant and Suspended Peerages with Genealogies and Arms* (London: Heraldry Today, 1972), 19.

23. Pine, *The New Extinct Peerage*, 20.

24. Michael Barthorp, *Heroes of the Crimea: The Battles of Balaclava and Inkerman* (London: Blanford, 1991), 17.

25. *Correspondence*, 18.

26. Ibid.

27. Ibid., 22.

28. Susan Nokes, "The Rhetoric of Travel: The French Romantic Myth of Naples," *Ethnohistory* 33 (Spring 1986): 144.

29. James Whiteside, *Italy in the Nineteenth Century* (London: Richard Bentley, 1848), 9.

30. Madame de Staël, *Corinne* (1807; New York: Oxford World Classics, 1998), 187.

31. Whiteside, *Italy in the Nineteenth Century*, 17.

32. *Correspondence*, 28.

33. Ibid., 29.

34. Ibid., 30.

35. *Correspondence*, 26.

36. Ibid., 28.

37. Ibid., 33.

38. Ibid.

39. Ibid., 41.

40. Ibid., 22.

41. Ibid., 34.

42. *Thelwall v. Yelverton*, 16.

43. *Correspondence*, 38.

44. Ibid., 34–36.

45. Ibid., 38.

46. Ibid., 43.

47. Ibid., 41.

48. Ibid., 43.

49. Ibid.

50. Ibid., 49.

51. Ibid., 43.

52. Ibid., 49.

53. Florence Nightingale, *Cassandra* (1852; New York: Feminist Press, 1979), 39.

54. Quoted in J. B. Conacher, *Britain and the Crimea* (New York: St. Martin's Press, 1987), 254.

55. Florence Nightingale, *I Have Done My Duty*, ed. Sue M. Goldie (Manchester: Manchester University Press, 1987), 17.

56. Florence Nightingale, *Collected Works of Florence Nightingale: Florence Nightingale's European Travels*, ed. Lyn McDonald (Waterloo, Canada: Wilfrid Laurier University Press, 2004), 750.

57. Ibid., 752.

58. *Correspondence*, 74.

59. Crow, *Theresa*, 55.

60. *Correspondence*, 82.

61. Mary Magdalen Taylor, *Eastern Hospitals and English Nurses; the Narrative of Twelve Months' Experience in the Hospitals of Koulali and Scutari: By a Lady Volunteer* (London: Hurst and Blackett, 1856), 1:328.

62.   Theresa Yelverton, *Martyrs to Circumstance* (London: Richard Bentley, 1861), 1:24–25. Henceforth referred to as *Martyrs*.

63.   Ibid., 1:62–63.

64.   *Correspondence*, 97.

65.   Ibid., 85.

66.   *Thelwall v. Yelverton*, 46.

67.   Ibid., 14.

68.   *Correspondence*, 91–92.

69.   Ibid., 92–93.

70.   *Correspondence*, 95–97.

71.   Ibid.

72.   Ibid.

73.   *Thelwall v. Yelverton*, 14.

74.   *Correspondence*, 106.

75.   Ibid., 79–80.

Chapter Two: Pursuit

1.   *Correspondence*, 118.

2.   Ibid., 107.

3.   Ibid., 108.

4.   W. H. Yelverton, letter to the editor, *Times*, January 17, 1863.

5.   *Correspondence*, 109.

6.   Ibid., 108.

7.   Ibid., 120.

8.   Ibid., 108–09.

9.   Mrs. Jameson, "Sisters of Charity and the Communion of Labour: Two Lectures on the Social Employment of Women," *Quarterly Review* 108, no. 216 (October 1860): 345.

10.   "Social Science," *Blackwood's Edinburgh Magazine* 88, no. 542 (December 1860): 713.

11.   Mary Hartman, *Victorian Murderesses* (New York: Schoken Books, 1976), 96.

12.   *Correspondence*, 133.

13.   Ibid., 116.

14.   Ibid., 120, 126, 128, 133.

15.   Ibid., 128.

16.   Ibid.

17.   Ibid., 105.

18.   Ibid., 129–130.

19.   Ibid., 129.

20.   Ibid., 134–35.

21. Ibid., 115.

22. Ibid., 130.

23. Ibid., 137.

24. Ibid.

25. Ibid., 138.

26. Ibid., 111.

27. Ibid., 141.

28. Ibid., 146–47.

29. Ibid., 148.

30. Ibid., 143.

31. Ibid., 146.

32. Ibid., 143.

33. *Thelwall v. Yelverton*, 32.

34. Miles Glendinning, Ranald MacInnes, and Aonghus MacKechnis, *A History of Scottish Architecture: From the Renaissance to the Present Day* (Edinburgh: Edinburgh University Press, 1996), 170.

35. Daniel Wilson, *Memorials to Edinburgh in the Olden Time* (Edinburgh and London: Adam and Charles Black, 1891), 2:207.

36. Robert Chambers, *Walks in Edinburgh* (Edinburgh: William Hunter, 1825), 203.

37. Ibid., 202.

38. *Correspondence*, 154.

39. Ibid.

40. Ibid., 156.

41. John Campbell Smith, *The Marriage Laws of England, Scotland and Ireland* (London: Simpkin, Marshall, 1864), 1–2.

42. *Thelwall v. Yelverton*, 28.

43. *Correspondence*, 157.

44. *Thelwall v. Yelverton*, 24.

45. *Correspondence*, 161.

46. Ibid., 164.

47. Ibid.

48. Hartman, *Victorian Murderesses*, 80.

49. *Correspondence*, 164.

50. Ibid.

51. Ibid., 171.

52. Ibid., 167.

53. Ibid., 178.

54. Emyr Estyn Evans, *Mourne Country: Landscape and Life in South Down* (Dundalk: Dundalgan Press, 1967), 181.

55. *Picturesque Handbook to Carlingford Bay: And the Watering Places in Its Vicinity* (Newry: Greer, 1846), 36.

56. *Longworth or Yelverton v. Yelverton and Yelverton v. Longworth: Cases Decided in the Court of Sessions: 19 December 1862* (Edinburgh: T. and T. Clarke and U. and R. Stevens Sons, 1863), 182. Henceforth referred to as *Longworth or Yelverton v. Yelverton*.

57. *Thelwall v. Yelverton*, 34.

58. *Correspondence*, 158.

Chapter Three: Betrayal

1. *Correspondence*, 180–81.

2. *Longworth or Yelverton v. Yelverton*, 86.

3. Malcolm Ferguson, *Rambles in Skye* (Glasgow: C. Murchland, 1885), quoted in Katharine Haldane Grenier, *Tourism and Identity in Scotland: Creating Caledonia, 1774–1914* (Aldershot: Ashgate, 2005), 178.

4. *Thelwall v. Yelverton*, 11.

5. Ibid.

6. R. Sauer, "Infanticide and Abortion in Nineteenth-Century Britain," *Population Studies* 32, no. 1 (March 1978): 88.

7. James Kingston and Anthony Whelan, *Abortion and the Law* (Dublin: Round Hall Sweet and Maxwell, 1997), 53.

8. Irvine Loudon, *Death in Childbirth: An International Study of Maternal Care and Maternal Mortality, 1800–1950* (Oxford: Oxford University Press, 1992), 109.

9. "Report from the Select Committee on Protection of Infant Life," *Parliamentary Papers* (1871), 149, quoted in Sauer, "Infanticide and Abortion," 86.

10. Patricia Branca, *Women in Europe Since 1750* (London: Taylor and Francis, 1978), 118–19.

11. Lionel Rose, *The Massacres of the Innocents: Infanticide in Britain, 1800–1939* (New York: Routledge, 1989), 23.

12. "Oxford Circuit," *Times*, July 13, 1853.

13. *Correspondence*, 184.

14. Ibid., 185.

15. Ibid., 185–86.

16. Ibid., 187.

17. Ibid., 187.

18. Ibid., 185.

19. Quoted in Charles Warren Stoddard, *In the Footprints of the Padres* (San Francisco: A. M. Robertson, 1902), 218.

20. Quoted in ibid., 219.

21.   Ibid., 190–91.

22.   *Correspondence*, 191.

23.   Ibid., 193.

24.   Ibid., 194.

25.   *Longworth or Yelverton v. Yelverton*, 86.

26.   Ibid.

27.   *Correspondence*, 196.

28.   Ibid., 195.

29.   Ibid., 197–99.

30.   *Longworth or Yelverton v. Yelverton*, 89.

31.   Ibid.

32.   George Wilson and Archibald Geike, *Memoir of Edward Forbes* (London: Macmillan, 1861), 438.

33.   Ibid., 444.

34.   Charles Darwin to J. D. Hooker, October 6, 1848, in *The Correspondence of Charles Darwin*, vol. 4, 1847–50, ed. Frederick Burkhardt and Sydney Smith (Cambridge: Cambridge University Press, 1989), 168.

35.   Wilson and Geike, *Memoir of Edward Forbes*, 459.

36.   Ibid., 447.

37.   Eric L. Mills, "Forbes, Edward (1815–1854)," in *Oxford Dictionary of National Biography*, ed. H. C. G. Matthew and Brian Harrison (Oxford: Oxford University Press, 2004), http://www.oxforddnb.com/view/article/9824.

38.   Charles Darwin to J. D. Hooker, August 10, 1858, *The Correspondence of Charles Darwin*, vol. 7, 1858–59, ed. Frederick Burkhardt and Sydney Smith (Cambridge: Cambridge University Press, 1992), 148.

39.   Emily M. Yelverton to Jessie Aitkin Wilson, January 27, 1860, Papers of Sir Archibald Geikie, correspondence concerning the compilation of *Memoir of Edward Forbes*, Edinburgh University Special Collections online records, http://www.nahste.ac.uk/cgi-bin/view_isad.pl?id=GB-0237-Sir-Archibald -Geikie-Gen-524-3-60&view=basic.

40.   "Marriages," *Gentleman's Magazine and Historical Review*, September 1858, 305.

41.   *Longworth or Yelverton v. Yelverton*, 90.

42.   Ibid., 86.

43.   Arvel B. Erickson and Fr. John R. McCarthy, "The Yelverton Case: Civil Legislation and Marriage," *Victorian Studies* 14 (March 1971): 277.

44.   Barbara Leigh Smith Bodichon, *A Brief Summary in Plain Language of the Most Important Laws Concerning Women, Together with a Few Observations Thereon* (London: J. Chapman, 1854), 13.

45.   Olive Anderson, "State, Civil Society and Separation in Victorian Marriage," *Past and Present* 163 (May 1999): 163.

46.   Francis Power Cobbe, "Criminals, Idiots, Women and Minors: Is the Clas-
       sification Sound?" (1869), in *The Disempowered: Women and the Law,* ed.
       Marie Mulvey and Tamae Mizuta (London: Routledge, 1993), 18–19.

47.   William Blackstone, *Commentaries on the Laws of England, Book I* (Oxford:
       Clarendon Press, 1765–69), 430, http://avalon.law.yale.edu/subject_menus/
       blackstone.asp.

48.   Erickson and McCarthy, "The Yelverton Case," 278.

49.   *Thelwall v. Yelverton*, 68.

50.   Ibid., 76–77.

51.   Ibid., 85.

52.   Ibid.

53.   Sally Mitchell, *Daily Life in Victorian England* (London: Greenwood Press,
       1996), 96.

54.   Anderson, "State, Civil Society and Separation in Victorian Marriage," 173.

Chapter Four: The Dublin Trial

1.   *The Yelverton Marriage Case, Thelwall v. Yelverton Unabridged Copyright
       Edition* (London: George Vickers, 1861), viii. Henceforth referred to as
       Yelverton Marriage Case.

2.   Erickson and McCarthy, "The Yelverton Case," 278.

3.   *Thelwall v. Yelverton*, 1.

4.   Quoted in Jonathan H. Grossman, *The Art of Alibi* (Baltimore: Johns Hop-
       kins University Press, 2002), 12.

5.   Quoted in Ibid., 32.

6.   *Thelwall v. Yelverton*, 15.

7.   Charles Dickens, *Oliver Twist* (1837; Oxford: Oxford World Classics, 1999), 157.

8.   *Thelwall v. Yelverton*, v.

9.   *Yelverton Marriage Case*, iii.

10.   Coventry Patmore, *The Angel in the House* (London: Macmillan, 1866), 36.

11.   Isaac Taylor, *Self-Cultivation Recommended: Or, Hints to a Youth Leaving
       School* (London: Rest Fenner, 1817), 7.

12.   *Yelverton Marriage Case*, iii.

13.   Jan Schramm, "Victorian Fiction" (lecture, University of Cambridge, Cam-
       bridge, UK, October 17, 2007).

14.   Wilkie Collins, *The Woman in White* (1860; New York: Penguin Classics,
       1999), 9.

15.   John Morely, *The Life of William Ewart Gladstone* (New York: Macmillan,
       1903), 2:283.

16.   C. L. Falkiner, "Sullivan, Sir Edward, first baronet (1822–1885)," rev. Na-
       than Wells, in *Oxford Dictionary of National Biography*, ed. H. C. G. Matthew

and Brian Harrison (Oxford: Oxford University Press, 2004), http://www
.oxforddnb.com/view/article/26774.

17.   *Thelwall v. Yelverton*, 10.

18.   Bracebridge Hemyng, "Prostitution in London," 487. (See above, chapter
      1, note 18.)

19.   *Thelwall v. Yelverton*, 10.

20.   *A Complete History of the Yelverton Family Since the Reign of Edward II to
      Which Is Added Some Account of the Longworth Family* (Manchester: Abel
      Heywood; London: George Vickers, n.d.), 15.

21.   *Thelwall v. Yelverton*, 9, 10, 11.

22.   Ibid., 14.

23.   Ibid., 9.

24.   Ibid., 11.

25.   Ibid. Shakespeare's actual wording is as follows: "Such an act / That blurs the
      grace and blush of modesty, / Calls virtue hypocrite, takes off the rose/ From
      the fair forehead of an innocent love / And sets a blister there, makes marriage-
      vows / As false as dicer's oaths; O such a deed / As from the body of contrac-
      tion plucks / The very soul, and sweet religion makes / A rhapsody of words."

26.   *Thelwall v. Yelverton*, 14

27.   Ibid., 15.

28.   Ibid.

29.   Ibid., 16.

30.   Quoted in James Wills and Freeman Wills, *The Irish Nation: Its History and
      Its Biography* (Edinburgh: A. Fullarton, 1876), 127.

31.   "Obituary: Right Hon. Abraham Brewster," *Irish Law Times and Solicitors'
      Journal* 8 (1874): 423.

32.   *Thelwall v. Yelverton*, 22.

33.   Ibid., 27.

34.   Ibid.

35.   Ibid., 17.

36.   Ibid., 31.

37.   Ibid., 17.

38.   Ibid.

39.   Ibid., 31.

40.   Ibid.

41.   Ibid., 32.

42.   Ibid., 34.

43.   Ibid., 36.

44.   Ibid., 37.

45.   Ibid., 38.

46.   Ibid.
47.   Ibid.
48.   Ibid., 39.
49.   Ibid., 42.
50.   Ibid., 38.
51.   Ibid., 39.
52.   Ibid., 40.
53.   Ibid., 42.
54.   Ibid., 43.
55.   Ibid., 44.
56.   Ibid., 43.
57.   Ibid., 42.
58.   Ibid., 40.
59.   Ibid.
60.   Ibid., 39.
61.   Ibid., 46.

Chapter Five: Vindication
1.   *Thelwall v. Yelverton*, 48.
2.   Ibid.
3.   Ibid.
4.   Ibid., 42.
5.   *Yelverton Marriage Case*, 165.
6.   *Thelwall vs. Yelverton*, 49.
7.   Quoted in Richard Altick, *Victorian Studies in Scarlet* (New York: Norton, 1970), 42.
8.   *Daily Express*, July 11, 1857, quoted in Hartman, *Victorian Murderesses*, 94. (See above, chap. 2, note 11.)
9.   *The Works of the Famous Philosopher Aristotle, Containing His Complete Master-Piece and Family Physician, His Experienced Midwife, His Book of Problems and Remarks on Physiognomy. To the Original Work Is Added, Essay on Marriage; Its Duties and Enjoyments.* Quoted in Roy Porter and Lesley Hall, *The Facts of Life: The Creation of Sexual Knowledge in Britain, 1650–1950* (New Haven, CT: Yale University Press, 1995), 129.
10. *Thelwall v. Yelverton*, 46.
11. Ibid., 62.
12. Ibid., 58.
13. Ibid., 55.
14. Ibid., 56.
15. Ibid., 57.

16. Ibid., 70.

17. Ibid.

18. Ibid., 73.

19. Ibid., 50

20. Ibid., 51.

21. Charles Kingsley, "The Three Fishers," in *Poems* (London: Macmillan, 1907), 255.

22. *Thelwall v. Yelverton*, 75.

23. Ibid., 79.

24. Ibid., 80.

25. Ibid., 82.

26. Ibid., 83.

27. Ibid., 93.

28. Ibid., 88.

29. Ibid., 96, 89.

30. Ibid., 97.

31. Ibid., 89.

32. Ibid., 93.

33. Ibid., 89.

34. Ibid., 96.

35. Ibid., 99.

36. Ibid., 104.

37. Ibid., 102.

38. Ibid., 106.

39. Ibid., 101.

40. Ibid., 115.

41. Ibid., 116.

42. Ibid.

43. Ibid., 121.

44. Ibid., 130.

45. The number of supporters may be exaggerated. See *Crowds in Ireland, c. 1720–1920*, ed. Peter Jupp and Eoin Magennis (New York: St. Martin's Press, 2000), 31–33.

46. *Thelwall v. Yelverton*, 130.

47. "Grand Triumph of Mrs. Yelverton," in *Poetical Broadsides, Etc.*, 93–183, British Library Manuscript Collection, London.

48. *Thelwall v. Yelverton*, 120.

49. Quoted in Peter Cominos, "Innocent Femina Sensualis in Unconscious Conflict," in *Suffer and Be Still: Women in the Victorian Age*, ed. Martha Vicinus (Bloomington: Indiana University Press, 1972), 167.

Chapter Six: Appeal

1. Eliza Lynn Linton, "The Girl of the Period," *Saturday Review* 25 (March 14, 1868): 339–40.

2. *Martyrs*, 1:68.

3. Ibid., 2:160.

4. Ibid., 2:256–57.

5. Ibid., 2:329.

6. Ibid., 2:101–2.

7. Ibid., 1:53.

8. "Martyrs to Circumstance," *Athenaeum* 1770 (September 28, 1861): 402–3. Ellen Miller Casey, "Weekly Reviews of Fiction: The 'Athenaeum' vs. the 'Spectator' and the 'Saturday Review,'" *Victorian Periodicals Review* 23, no. 1 (Spring 1990): 8.

9. George Henry Lewes, "Review of *Shirley*," *Edinburgh Review* (1850), in *Versatile Victorian: Selected Writings of George Henry Lewes*, ed. Rosemary Ashton (London: Bristol Classical Press, 1992), 18–19.

10. "Woman and Womankind, VI," *Tait's Edinburgh Magazine* 25 (June 1858): 348.

11. [H. L. Mansel], "Sensation Novels," *Quarterly Review* 11, no. 3 (April 1863): 483.

12. "Mrs. Yelverton's Novel," *Saturday Review* 11 (June 29, 1861): 671.

13. "Literary Gossip," *London Review* 9 (August 1864): 163.

14. Anthony Trollope, *An Autobiography* (London: William Blackwood and Sons, 1883), 2:29–30.

15. Linton, "The Girl of the Period," 340.

16. "Martyrs to Circumstance," *Athenaeum*, 402–3.

17. Quoted in Erickson and McCarthy, "The Yelverton Case: Civil Legislation and Marriage," 278. (See above, chap. 3, note 43.)

18. Erickson and McCarthy, "The Yelverton Case," 282.

19. *Longworth or Yelverton v. Yelverton*, 114.

20. Ibid., 96.

21. Ibid., 101.

22. Ibid., 109.

23. Ibid., 111.

24. Ibid., 116.

25. M. G. Williamson, *Edinburgh: A Historical and Topographical Account of the City* (London: Methuen, 1906), 193.

26. James Grant, *Old and New Edinburgh: Its History, Its People, and Its Places* (London: Cassel, Peter, Galpin, 1880), 158.

27. *Longworth or Yelverton v. Yelverton*, 178.

28. Ibid., 173.

29. Ibid., 174.

30. Ibid., 178.

31. Ibid., 205.

32. Ibid., 206.

33. The Guardian Index, 1842–1928 (Marlborough, England: Adam Matthew Publications, 1994), microfiche, reel 4.

34. "The Yelverton Case Has Once More Cropped up . . . ," *Times*, December 22, 1862.

35. "Registering the People: 150 Years of Civil Registration," http://www .groireland.ie/history.htm., paragraph 12.

36. Theresa Yelverton to A. H. Layard, May 6, 1863, British Library Manuscript Collection, London.

37. Ibid.

38. Theresa Yelverton to A. H. Layard, August 2, 1863, British Library Manuscript Collection, London.

39. Theresa Yelverton to unknown recipient, May 21, 1863, British Library Manuscript Collection, London.

40. "Yelverton Trial," letter to the editor, *Times*, June 14, 1864.

41. James Somerville, "The Yelverton Scotch Marriage Case," letter to the editor, *Times*, July, 12 1862.

42. *Correspondence*, vii.

43. Ibid.

44. Ibid., v.

45. Erickson and McCarthy, "The Yelverton Case," 282.

46. *Longworth or Yelverton v. Yelverton*, 228.

47. Ibid., 233.

48. Ibid., 257.

49. Ibid., 273.

50. Ibid., 276.

51. Erickson and McCarthy, "The Yelverton Case," 283.

52. *Longworth or Yelverton v. Yelverton*, 243.

53. "Foreign Criminal News," *National Police Gazette*, July 20, 1867, 4.

54. "A Matrimonial Dilemma," *Freeman's Journal and Daily Commercial Advertiser*, November 5, 1870.

55. "Gleanings in the Probate and Divorce Courts of the United Kingdom," *Albany Law Journal: A Weekly Record of the Law and the Lawyers*, October 22, 1870, 301.

56. "The Man with Two Wives," *New York Times*, November 26, 1870.

57. Theresa Yelverton, "British Marriage Law and Practice," *Galaxy: A Magazine of Entertaining Reading* 5 (February 1868): 197.

58.   Ibid.
59.   Ibid.
60.   Ibid.

Chapter Seven: The Lady Traveler

1.   Quoted in Shirley Foster, *Across New Worlds: Nineteenth-Century Women Travellers and Their Writings* (New York: Harvester Wheatsheaf, 1990), 6.

2.   "To the Royal Geographic Society," *Punch*, (June 10, 1893), 269.

3.   Quoted in Dea Birkett, *Spinsters Abroad: Victorian Lady Explorers* (Oxford: Basil Blackwell, 1989), 115.

4.   "Notes on the United States of America," *Blackwood's Edinburgh Magazine* 24, no. 145 (November 1828): 621.

5.   Frances Trollope, *Domestic Manners of the Americans* (1832; New York: Penguin Classics, 1997), 104.

6.   Ibid., 22.

7.   Harriet Martineau, *Retrospect of Western Travel* (1838; London: M. E. Sharpe, 2000), xi.

8.   Isabella L. Bird, *A Lady's Life in the Rocky Mountains* (1879; Norman: University of Oklahoma Press, 1960), 104.

9.   Thérèse Yelverton (Viscountess Avonmore), *Teresina in America* (London: Richard Bentley and Son, 1875), 2:81. Henceforth referred to as *Teresina in America*.

10.   "Passengers Arrived," *New York Times*, September 15, 1867.

11.   *Teresina in America*, 1:vi.

12.   Ibid., 1:10.

13.   Ibid., 1:3.

14.   Ibid., 1:6.

15.   Ibid., 2:240.

16.   Ibid., 2:264.

17.   Ibid., 1:18.

18.   Ibid., 2:269.

19.   "Minor Topics," *New York Times*, July 23, 1867.

20.   "Readings By Mrs. Yelverton," *Albion, a Journal of News, Politics and Literature*, March 31, 1866, 153.

21.   "A Highly Sentimental Letter from the Hon. Mrs. Yelverton," *Chicago Tribune*, October 25, 1867.

22.   "Mrs. Yelverton," *Round Table: A Saturday Review of Politics, Finance, Literature, Society and Art*, November 9, 1867, 146.

23.   "Amusements," *New York Times*, November 6, 1867.

24.   "Mrs. Yelverton in New York," *National Police Gazette*, November 16, 1867, 8.

25.   "Mrs. Yelverton," *Round Table*, 146.

26.   "Miscellaneous New Items," *Brooklyn Eagle*, October 30, 1868.

27.   *Teresina in America*, 1:113.

28.   Ibid., 1:44.

29.   Ibid., 1:49.

30.   Ibid., 1:60.

31.   Ibid., 1:70.

32.   Ibid., 1:66.

33.   Trollope, *Domestic Manners*, 140.

34.   Frederick Marryat, *Diary in America: With Remarks on Its Institutions* (London: Longman, Orme, Brown, Green, and Longmans, 1839), 1:293.

35.   Harriet Martineau, *Society in America* (New York: Saunders and Otley, 1837), 1:201.

36.   Showalter, *A Jury of Her Peers*, 158. (See above, chap. 1, note 16.)

37.   *Teresina in America*, 2:176.

38.   Trollope, *Domestic Manners*, 199.

39.   *Teresina in America*, 2:179.

40.   Ibid., 2:182.

41.   Ibid., 2:197.

42.   Ibid., 2:134.

43.   Ibid., 2:138.

44.   Ibid., 2:141.

45.   Ibid., 2:138–139.

46.   Ibid., 2:189.

47.   Ibid., 2:190.

48.   Ibid., 2:189.

49.   Ibid., 2:192.

50.   Ibid., 2:24.

51.   Sydney E. Ahlstrom, *A Religious History of the American People* (New Haven, CT: Yale University Press, 1972), 506.

52.   Mark Twain, *Roughing It* (Hartford, CT: American Publishing Company, 1872), 108, 119.

53.   Charles Dickens, "Bound for the Great Salt Lake," in *The Uncommercial Traveller* (1860; Dublin: Nonsuch, 2007), 235.

54.   Richard Francis Burton, *The City of the Saints and Across the Rocky Mountains to California* (London: Longman, 1861), 199.

55.   M. Hamlin Cannon, "The English Mormons in America," *American Historical Review* 57 (1952): 893.

56.   *Teresina in America*, 2:194, 386.

57.   Ibid., 2:37.

58.   Blanche Beechwood, "Why? Ah! Why?" *Latter Day Saints' Millennial Star*, November 17, 1874.

59.   *Teresina in America*, 2:41.

60.   Ibid., 2:35.

61.   Ibid.

62.   Ibid., 2:48.

63.   Ibid., 2:44.

64.   Ibid., 2:47.

65.   Ibid., 2:40.

66.   *Martyrs*, 2:53.

67.   *Teresina in America*, 2:41.

68.   Ibid., 2:45.

69.   Ibid.

70.   Jane Louis Mesick, *The English Traveller in America, 1785–1835* (New York: Columbia University Press, 1922), 229.

71.   Charles Dickens, *American Notes* (1842; New York: Penguin, 2000), 98–99.

72.   *Teresina in America*, 2:253.

73.   Ibid., 2:365.

74.   Ibid., 2:370.

Chapter Eight: California

1.   John S. Hittell, *A History of the City of San Francisco* (San Francisco: A. L. Bancroft, 1878), 382–83.

2.   Ralph Waldo Emerson, "The Young American," in *Emerson's Complete Works: Nature, Addresses and Lectures* (Boston: Houghton Mifflin, 1887), 344.

3.   Hittell, *A History of the City of San Francisco*, 381, 383.

4.   Quoted in Roger W. Lotchin, *San Francisco, 1846–1856: From Hamlet to City* (New York: Oxford University Press, 1974), 291.

5.   *Teresina in America*, 2:13.

6.   Ibid., 2:22.

7.   Hittell, *A History of the City of San Francisco*, 461.

8.   Richard F. Burton, *The City of the Saints and Across the Rocky Mountains to California* (London: Longman, 1861), 185.

9.   Bret Harte, *Bret Harte's California: Letters to the "Springfield Republican" and "Christian Register," 1866–67*, ed. Gary Scharnhorst (Albuquerque: University of New Mexico Press, 1990), 26–27.

10.   Quoted in Raymond L. Wilson, "Painters of California's Silver Era," *American Art Journal* 16, no. 4 (1984): 71.

11.   Franklin Walker, *San Francisco's Literary Frontier* (New York: Alfred A. Knopf, 1939), 258–59.

12.   John Muir, *John Muir Summering in the Sierra*, ed. Robert Engberg (Madison: University of Wisconsin Press, 1984), 14.

13.   Emerson, "The Young American," 349.

14.   Anna E. Dickinson, *A Ragged Register (of People Places and Opinions)* (New York: Harper and Brothers, 1879), 205–6.

15.   Quoted in Roger Austen, *Genteel Pagan: The Double Life of Charles Warren Stoddard*, ed. John W. Crowley (Amherst: University of Massachusetts Press, 1991), 42–43.

16.   Charles Warren Stoddard, *In the Footprints of the Padres* (San Francisco: A. M. Robertson, 1902), 196.

17.   Ibid., 197.

18.   Ibid., 203.

19.   Ibid., 203.

20.   Ibid., 204.

21.   Ibid., 242.

22.   Ibid., 206.

23.   Ibid., 207.

24.   Ibid., 247.

25.   Ibid., 252–53.

26.   Simon Schama, *Landscape and Memory* (New York: Knopf, 1995), 191.

27.   John Muir, *John of the Mountains: The Unpublished Journals of John Muir*, ed. Linnie Marsh Wolfe (Madison: University of Wisconsin Press, 1979), 99.

28.   *Teresina in America*, 2:66.

29.   Ibid., 2:68.

30.   Ibid., 2:75.

31.   Isabella L. Bird, *A Lady's Life in the Rocky Mountains* (1879; Norman: University of Oklahoma Press, 1960), 83. (See above, chap. 7, note 8.)

32.   *Teresina in America*, 2:70.

33.   James Mason Hutchings, "Miners' Ten Commandments," http://www.sfmuseum.org/hist7/tencom.html.

34.   James Mason Hutchings, *In the Heart of the Sierras: The Yo-Semite Valley, Both Historical and Descriptive* (Oakland: Pacific Press, 1888), 16.

35.   Mary Viola Lawrence, "Summer with a Countess," *Overland Monthly* 7 (November 1871): 474.

36.   Ibid., 475.

37.   *Teresina in America*, 2:87.

38.   The Englishmen who supposedly left Theresa insisted that there had been no arrangements to meet up once they had separated. "Lady Avonmore's Yosemite Adventure—A Statement by the English Noblemen Who Deserted Her," *New York Times*, December 5, 1870.

39. Lawrence, "Summer with a Countess," 478.

40. *Teresina in America*, 2:17.

41. Muir, *John Muir Summering in the Sierra*, 5.

42. Muir, *John of the Mountains*, 79.

43. John Muir, *The Writings of John Muir*, ed. William Frederic Badè (Boston: Houghton Mifflin, 1916–24), 9:208.

44. Thérèse Yelverton, *Zanita: A Tale of the Yo-semite* (New York: Hurd and Houghton, 1872) 7, 8. Henceforth referred to as *Zanita*.

45. John Muir to Jeanne Carr, in *The Writings of John Muir*, 9:272–73.

46. *Correspondence*, 109.

47. Muir, *John of the Mountains*, 77.

48. Ibid., 43–44.

49. Theresa Yelverton to John Muir, October 1870, *The John Muir Papers, 1858–1957*, microform, Library of Congress, Washington, DC.

50. Frederick Turner, *John Muir: Rediscovering America* (Cambridge: Perseus, 1985), 200–8.

51. John Muir to Jeanne Carr, December 22, 1870, *The John Muir Papers*.

52. Theresa Yelverton to John Muir, January 22, 1872, *The John Muir Papers*.

53. Ibid.

54. *Zanita*, 92.

55. Ibid., 40.

56. Ibid., 77.

57. *Teresina in America*, 1:263.

58. Quoted in Stoddard, *In the Footprints of the Padres*, 270.

59. Ibid.

60. Quoted in ibid., 248.

61. "Miscellaneous Study," *Reformed Church Messenger*, February 1, 1871, 7.

62. "Article 10," *Atlanta Constitution*, March 21, 1871.

63. "Here and There," *Journal of Choice Reading*, April 8, 1871.

64. "With the Soeurs at the Golden Horn," *Overland Monthly* 7 (July 1871): 9–21; "The Maison-Mère of the Soeurs," *Overland Monthly* 7 (September 1871): 249–58.

65. Quoted in Stoddard, *In the Footprints of the Padres*, 272.

66. "Notable Autographs," *Californian* 1 (April 1880): 353; also quoted, with slight variation, in Stoddard, *In the Footprints of the Padres*, 275.

Chapter Nine: The World

1. Thérèse Yelverton, "Barbaric Pageants," *Overland Monthly and Out West Magazine* 3 (April 1884): 357.

2. Ibid., 358.

3. Ibid., 360.

4. Ibid., 364.

5. *Teresina Peregrina*, 2:29–30.

6. Ibid., 2:31.

7. Ibid., 2:218.

8. Ibid., 1:151.

9. Ibid., 1:150.

10. Ibid., 1:151.

11. Thérèse Yelverton, "Chinese Interiors," *Overland Monthly* 8 (May 1872): 425.

12. *Teresina Peregrina*, 2:286.

13. Ibid., 2:287.

14. Ibid., 2:290–91.

15. Ibid., 2:296.

16. Ibid., 2:297.

17. John Ferguson McLennan, *Primitive Marriage: An Inquiry into the Form of Capture in Marriage Ceremonies* (Edinburgh: Adam and Charles Black, 1865), 208.

18. John Lubbock, *The Origin of Civilization and the Primitive Condition of Man*, ed. Peter Rivière (1870; Chicago: University of Chicago Press, 1978), 50.

19. George Stocking, *Victorian Anthropology* (New York: Free Press, 1987), 156.

20. Yelverton, "Barbaric Pageants," 358.

21. *Teresina Peregrina*, 2:219.

22. Ibid., 1:351.

23. Ibid., 2:66.

24. Ibid., 2:118.

25. Ibid., 2:107.

26. Ibid., 2: 322–23.

27. Ibid., 2:323.

28. Ibid., 2:344.

29. Ibid., 2:329.

30. Ibid., 2:351.

31. "Theresa Longworth," *Freeman's Journal*, September 29,1874, 2.

32. *Teresina Peregrina*, 2:325.

33. "A Lady's Rambles Round the World," *Chamber's Journal of Popular Literature, Science and Arts* 540 (May 1874): 285.

34. Ibid.

35. "Yelverton's (Thérèse) Teresina Peregrina," *Academy* 5 (January–June 1874): 481.

36. Gillian Beer, "*The Academy*: Europe in England," in *Science Serialized: Representations of the Sciences in Nineteenth-Century Periodicals*, ed. Geoffrey

Cantor and Sally Shuttleworth (Cambridge: Massachusetts Institute of Technology Press, 2004), 184.

37.   "Yelverton's (Thérèse) Teresina Peregrina," 481.

38.   "Teresina Peregrina," *Pall Mall Gazette*, March 26, 1874, 11.

39.   Ibid., 12.

40.   "Our Library Table," *Athenaeum*, March 7, 1874.

Chapter Ten: Sunset

1.   Robert Ross, *A Concise History of South Africa* (Cambridge: Cambridge University Press, 1999), 59.

2.   John Barrow, *An Account of Travels in the Interior of South Africa, in the Years 1797 and 1798* (London: A. Strahan, 1801), 77–78.

3.   Quoted in Michael Streak, *Victoria's Stepchildren: Public Opinion and the South African Problem, 1795–1899* (New York: University Press of America, 1998), 92.

4.   Quoted in ibid., 83.

5.   Quoted in ibid., 101.

6.   Jeff Guy, *The Destruction of the Zulu Kingdom: The Civil War in Zululand* (London: Longman, 1979), xxi.

7.   Quoted in David Duff, *Eugénie and Napoleon III* (New York: William Morrow, 1978), 199.

8.   Quoted in Jasper Ridley, *Napoleon III and Eugénie* (New York: Viking Press, 1980), 598.

9.   Comte Fleury, *Memoirs of the Empress Eugénie* (New York: D. Appleton, 1920), 1:165.

10.   Ibid., 160.

11.   Harold Kurz, *The Empress Eugénie, 1826–1920* (Boston: Houghton Mifflin, 1964), 305.

12.   Quoted in ibid., 299.

13.   Quoted in ibid., 302.

14.   Quoted in Duff, *Eugénie and Napoleon III*, 262.

15.   Ian Knight, *With His Face to the Foe: The Life and Death of Louis Napoleon, The Prince Imperial, Zululand, 1879* (Staplehurst: Spellmount, 2001), 245.

16.   Quoted in Kurtz, *The Empress Eugénie*, 315.

17.   Ridley, *Napoleon III and Eugénie*, 609.

18.   Brian Roberts, *Ladies in the Veld* (London: John Murray, 1965), 5.

19.   Evelyn Wood, *From Midshipman to Field Marshall* (London: Methuen, 1906), 100.

20.   Roberts, *Ladies in the Veld*, 15.

21.   Duff, *Eugénie and Napoleon III*, 75.

22.   Wood, *From Midshipman to Field Marshall*, 100.

23.   Arthur Bigge to Queen Victoria, May 27, 1880, quoted in Knight, *With His Face to the Foe*, 32.

24.   Arthur Bigge to Queen Victoria, June 7, 1880, quoted in ibid., 36.

25.   "Proposed Inscription for a Proposed Monument," *Punch*, August 2, 1879.

26.   "Pen and Ink Sketches," *Natal Witness*, January 29, 1881.

27.   Ibid., January 15, 1881.

28.   Ibid., January 22, 1881.

29.   Ibid., June 18, 1881.

30.   Ibid., March 26, 1881.

31.   Ibid., July 23, 1881.

32.   Ibid., June 11, 1881.

33.   Ibid., March 26, 1881.

34.   "Response to Kate the Critic," *Natal Witness*, January 25, 1881.

35.   "Pen and Ink Sketches," *Natal Witness*, February 19, 1881.

36.   Roberts, *Ladies in the Veld*, 73.

37.   *Teresina Peregrina*, 1:95.

38.   Transcription of Death Notice for Therese Yelverton (Lady Avonmore), September 30, 1881, Pietermaritzburg Archives Repository, Archives Group MSCE 5/262.

39.   "London Gossip," *Manchester Times*, September 17, 1881.

40.   "The Late House of Miss Longworth," *Liverpool Mercury*, November 25, 1881.

41.   "Of Foreigners Who Are Dead," *New York Times*, November 11, 1881.

42.   Stoddard, *In the Footprints of the Padres*, 277.

43.   "Of Foreigners Who Are Dead."

44.   "The Yelverton Scandal—Viscount Avonmore's Death Revives a Famous Episode in High Life," *Chicago Daily Tribune*, April 12, 1883. "End of a Noble Rake," *Daily Evening Bulletin*, May 4, 1883.

45.   "End of a Noble Rake."

46.   Pine, *The New Extinct Peerage* 20. (See above, chap. 1, note 22.)

Epilogue

1.   Marvin S. Robinson, *A Popular Treatise on the Law of Marriage and Divorce: Giving the Laws of the Various States of the United States, England and the Continent* (Chicago: Donohue and Henneberry, 1884), 8.

2.   *The Works of the Famous Philosopher Aristotle*, quoted in Porter and Hall, *The Facts of Life*, 320 note 22. (See above, chap. 5, note 8.)

3.   Smith, *The Marriage Laws of England, Scotland and Ireland*, 8. (See above, chap. 2, note 41.)

4.   Ibid.

5.   John Ferguson McLennan, "Marriage and Divorce—The Laws of England and Scotland," *North British Review* 35 (August 1861): 199.

6.   J. R. O'Flanagan, *Gentle Blood; or, The Secret Marriage* (Dublin: Moore and Murphy, 1861), vi.

7.   Richard Altick, *Deadly Encounters: Two Victorian Sensations* (Philadelphia: University of Pennsylvania Press, 1986), 141.

8.   Cyrus Redding, *A Wife and Not a Wife* (London: Sunders, Otley, 1867), 2.

9.   Ibid., iv.

10.   Norman Page, introduction to *Man and Wife* by Wilkie Collins (1890; New York: Oxford University Press, 1995), xi.

11.   Wilkie Collins, *No Name* (1862; New York: Penguin Books, 1994), 103.

12.   Ibid., 104.

13.   Caroline Sheridan Norton, *Lost and Saved* (London: Hurst and Blackett, 1863), 2.

14.   Ibid.

15.   Wilkie Collins, *Man and Wife* (London: F. S. Ellis, 1870), 1:xii; Jeanne Fahnestock, "Bigamy: The Rise and Fall of a Convention," *Nineteenth Century Fiction* 36, no. 1 (June 1981): 47.

16.   Collins, *Man and Wife*, 2:11.

17.   Ibid., 3:186.

18.   Arthur Rackham Cleveland, *Woman under the English Law, from the Landing of the Saxons to the Present Time* (London: Hurst and Blackett, 1896), 301–2.

19.   Sarah Grand, "The New Aspect of the Woman Question," *North American Review* 158 (March 1894): 272.

20.   Virginia Woolf, "Professions for Women," in *The Death of the Moth and Other Essays* (Orlando, FL: Harcourt and Brace, 1942), 238.

21.   William Thackeray, *The History of Pendennis: His Fortunes and Misfortunes, His Friends and His Greatest Enemy* (Boston: James R. Osgood, 1875), 210.

22.   *Correspondence*, 40.

23.   Ibid., 63.

24.   Ibid., 77.

25.   Ibid., 46.

26.   Ibid., 43.

IMAGE CREDITS

Frontispiece
Theresa Longworth Yelverton
The Yelverton Correspondence (Edinburgh: Thomas Laurie, 1863), p. 12

William Charles Yelverton
*The Yelver*ton *Correspondence* (Edinburgh: Thomas Laurie, 1863), p. 13

Chapter One:
Portrait of a *vivandière*, 1885
Library of Congress, Prints & Photographs Division

Charles Alexandre Fay, Théâtre des opérations, 1867 (Map of the Black Sea region)
Library of Congress, Prints & Photographs Division

Galata Tower
Library of Congress, Prints & Photographs Division

Istanbul, as seen from Galata
Library of Congress, Prints & Photographs Division

Chapter Two:
Map of Edinburgh, 1844
David Rumsey Map Collection

James Ross and John Thompson, Edinburgh from the Castle, c. 1850
National Galleries of Scotland

William Donaldson Clark; The Cowgate Arch of George IV Bridge, Edinburgh;
c. 1860
National Galleries of Scotland

The Quays at Waterford, Ireland
Library of Congress, Prints & Photographs Division

Chapter Three:
A Highland landscape
Library of Congress, Prints & Photographs Division

Edouard Manet, *The Port of Bordeaux*, 1871
The Yorck Project: *10.000 Meisterwerke der Malerei*. DIRECTMEDIA Publishing
GmbH, 2002.

Chapter Four:
The Four Courts, Dublin.
Public domain

Interior of the Four Courts
Irish Architectural Archive

The *Newgate Calendar*
Andrew Knapp and William Lee Baldwin, *The Newgate Calendar* (London: J.
Robins, 1828), p.1

Chapter Six:
Cover of *Martyrs to Circumstance*
Theresa Longworth Yelverton, *Martyrs to Circumstance* (London: Richard Bent-
ley, New Burlington Street, 1861).

Court of Sessions, Edinburgh
James Grant, *Old and New Edinburgh*, volume 1, p. 164

John Harrington; House of Lords; photographic print, 1869
British Library

Chapter Seven:
Tourists Viewing Niagara Falls
Library of Congress, Prints & Photographs Division

Pierre Havens; Bonaventure, Savannah, Georgia; stereograph, 1869
The Smithsonian Institution

A Mormon Town, "Stores in Main Street"
Richard F. Burton's *The City of the Saints and Across the Rocky Mountains to California*
(London: Longman, 1861), p. 217

Chapter Eight:
James Ford; *San Francisco, Corner of California and Montgomery Streets*; c. 1857
The Smithsonian Institution

Image on the Title Page of the *Overland Monthly*
Public domain

Ina Coolbrith
The Bancroft Library, University of California, Berkeley

C.E. Watkins, *Charles Warren Stoddard*
The Bancroft Library, University of California, Berkeley

Bret Harte
The Bancroft Library, University of California, Berkeley

Carleton Watkins, *Yosemite Falls 1600 ft*, c. 1870
New York Public Library

Carleton Watkins, *Piwac, Vernal Falls, 300 feet, Yosemite*, 1860
New York Public Library

George Fiske, *The Big-Tree Room at the Barnard Hotel*, 1884
The Bancroft Library, University of California, Berkeley

Theresa Yelverton in Yosemite
Public domain

Bradley and Rulofson, John Muir, c. 1872
Library of the Pacific

Chapter Nine:
Kandyan Chief and Family, c. 1880
Public domain

View of Queens Road, Hong Kong, from the clock tower
Wellcome Trust

Anamese river huts, Annam, Cochin China [Vietnam]
Wellcome Trust

Manchu Bride, Beijing
Wellcome Trust

Praya or Des Voeux Road, Hong Kong
Wellcome Trust

Reception room in a mandarin's house
Wellcome Trust

Chapter Ten:
Map of South Africa, 1885
Public domain

Image of Zulu Warriors with Shield and Assegai
In Lands Afar: a Second Series of Mission Stories of Many Lands ed. Elnathan Ellsworth Strong (Boston: Congregational House, 1897), p. 44

Empress Eugenie
LIFE

Louis Napoleon, Prince Imperial
LIFE

INDEX

A NOTE ON THE AUTHOR

Chloë Schama has written for the *New Republic*, the *New York Sun*, the *Financial Times*, the *San Francisco Chronicle*, and the *Guardian*. She lives in Washington, D.C. This is her first book.